ECONOMIC AND SOCIAL COMMISSION
FOR ASIA AND THE PACIFIC
Bangkok, Thailand

ENERGY, ENVIRONMENT AND SUSTAINABLE DEVELOPMENT II

ENERGY RESOURCES DEVELOPMENT SERIES NO. 35

UNITED NATIONS
New York, 1995

ST/ESCAP/1623

UNITED NATIONS PUBLICATION
Sales No.: E.96.II.F.25
Copyright © United Nations 1996
ISBN 92-1-119714-7
ISSN 0252-4368

CONTENTS

Page

i

PREFACE

The *Energy Resources Development Series* is a biennial publication of the Economic and Social Commission for Asia and the Pacific (ESCAP) which addresses a selected theme of current interest to analysts, policy-makers and planners in the energy sector.

This publication, No. 35 in the series, takes up the theme of Energy, Environment and Sustainable Development for the second consecutive time. It is largely based on material presented at the Senior Expert Group Meeting on Energy Resiliency and the Integration of Environment into Energy Policy and Planning, held in Bangkok from 4 to 6 October 1995.

Most of the operational activities of ESCAP in the area of energy development and management rely on extrabudgetary sources of funding, from multilateral agencies such as the United Nations Development Programme and from bilateral sources such as the Governments of Australia, China, France, Japan and the Netherlands. However, this publication and the senior expert group meeting which was the source of the material for it were part of the ESCAP regular programme of work for 1994-1995. It is the hope of the ESCAP secretariat that the publication will find a receptive and appreciative audience among its readers.

FOREWORD

The term "Sustainable Development" has become the catchword within as well as outside the United Nations system ever since the Brundtland report was published in 1987. No self-respecting politician or diplomat would avoid the term in his or her speech. However, aside from the general meaning as set forth in the Brundtland report, that is "development that does not compromise the needs of future generations", the rhetoric is still vague. The search for an operational concept of the term continues.

The launching of Agenda 21 at the Earth Summit in Rio de Janeiro in June 1992 at least provided guidelines for all countries to follow. Regardless of the disappointing follow-up action taken since then – or, should one say, action which has not been taken – Agenda 21 reminded the world that the globe was pursuing an unsustainable development path, that the main factors of unsustainability were unsustainable consumption patterns which had to be radically changed, inexorable population growth which should be brought under control and rampant poverty which needed to be eradicated. An important message of Agenda 21 was also the fact that the globe, as a consequence of the pursuit of its unsustainable path of development, was also pursuing unsustainable energy development, causing environmental degradation, polluting the atmosphere and possibly heading towards sea-level rise.

The complexities and uncertainties of future long-term global developments are such that one can only suggest hypotheses about long-term sustainable development. First, there must be a limit to sustainability commensurate with a certain global, stable population level enjoying a certain level of standard of living, consistent with the carrying capacity of the world (which at any time would depend on the scientific and technological capability of mankind). Second, at this point one is unaware what that penultimate level of standard of living will be but one is hopeful that it will still be higher than present-day standards. Third, it would be prudent to proceed henceforth on a more deliberate course of development, by incorporating as much as possible the "green" paradigm, such as no regrets, recycling and reusing, conservation and efficiency. One could qualitatively debate and argue about these hypotheses and concepts, and one may even come to the conclusion that much research remains to be done on these ideas of sustainable development. Perhaps the more important and relevant matter is the question how the transition is to be achieved from the vestiges of the unsustainable growth paradigm towards the long-term truly sustainable development path.

It may just be possible that "energy" could be used as a surrogate for "natural resources". Then one may investigate if conclusions reached in energy could be applicable to natural resources.

The common wisdom in energy is that sustainable energy development means, first and foremost, the integration of environment into energy policy and planning. Second, it is generally accepted that, ultimately, mankind will have only two sources of energy to rely upon: nuclear and solar energy. Third, given the requirements of both the industrialized and the developing countries in the near-term and the medium-term future, the depletion of hydrocarbons will occur within the next 50 years or so, and of coal within the subsequent 100 years or so. Fourth, the transitory paths already present themselves: increase in efficiency (which would prolong the fossil-fuel depletion date) and fuel switching to nuclear energy and renewables.

Thus, the energy transition will be the primary global concern in the use of energy in the first half of the twenty-first century. In view of the numerous alternatives and options of energy types and technologies, and of the uncertainties in supplies and prices, it may be useful to adopt the idea of energy resiliency of a national economy. This is simply the ability of an economy to withstand shocks, whether internal or external. Towards the end of the twentieth century then, it was thought that it would be fruitful to discuss both this idea of energy resiliency and the prerequisite for sustainable development: the integration of environment into energy policy and planning.

This publication begins in chapter I with the report of the Senior Expert Group Meeting on Energy Resiliency and the Integration of Environment into Energy Policy and Planning. Chapter II presents a report by the ESCAP secretariat, which was distributed at a conference organized by the United Nations Development Programme in Kuala Lumpur from 27 to 29 March 1995, which is intended to set the backdrop for overall regional development. Chapters III to VI present the papers which the secretariat prepared or commissioned: Chapter III sets the background for discussion on energy developments and trends, Chapter IV on the integration of environment into energy policy and planning, Chapter V on energy resiliency and Chapter VI on regional energy cooperation. Finally, Chapter VII contains a selection of reports presented by the participating experts, a brief overview of energy developments in their respective countries.

ABBREVIATIONS

ADB	Asian Development Bank
AIDS	acquired immune deficiency syndrome
ASEAN	Association of South East Asian Nations
BOE	barrels of oil equivalent
FAO	Food and Agriculture Organization of the United Nations
FDI	foreign direct investment
GDP	gross domestic product
GEF	Global Environment Facility
HIV	human immunodeficiency virus
NGO	non-governmental organization
NIE	newly industrialized economy
OECD	Organisation for Economic Cooperation and Development
OPEC	Organization for Petroleum Exporting Countries
PACE-E	Programme for Asian Cooperation on Energy and the Environment
REDP	Regional Energy Development Programme
TCDC	technical cooperation among developing countries
TOE	tons of oil equivalent
UNDP	United Nations Development Programme
UNIDO	United Nations Industrial Development Organization

I. REPORT OF THE SENIOR EXPERT GROUP MEETING ON ENERGY RESILIENCY AND THE INTEGRATION OF ENVIRONMENT INTO ENERGY POLICY

A. ORGANIZATION OF THE MEETING

1. Attendance

1.   The Senior Expert Group Meeting on Energy Resiliency and the Integration of Environment into Energy Policy and Planning was held at Bangkok from 4 to 6 October 1995. It was attended by experts from Cambodia, China, Indonesia, the Islamic Republic of Iran, Nepal, Pakistan, the Philippines, Sri Lanka, Thailand, Viet Nam and a consultant from the United Kingdom. The Asian Institute of Technology and the Australian Bureau of Agricultural and Resource Economics were represented.

2. Opening of the Meeting

2.   In his opening statement, the Executive Secretary noted that profound changes were taking place in the world and the energy sector was certainly one of those being significantly affected. When the Brundtland report was issued in 1987, the United Nations system was galvanized into a series of meetings, preparations and debates on the many issues raised, culminating in the so-called Earth Summit of 1992. ESCAP also organized ministerial-level conferences, including the Ministerial level Conference on Environment and Development in Asia and the Pacific in 1990. Another Ministerial Conference as a follow-up to the Earth Summit would be held in Bangkok from 22 to 28 November 1995. He also stated that, within the United Nations system, the development paradigm had been changing following the Earth Summit and its related follow-up agreements, declarations, conventions and meetings. One which was closely related to the energy sector was the United Nations Framework Convention on Climate Change.

3.   The Executive Secretary further stated that it was timely to discuss the concept of energy resiliency which was taken to mean "the ability of a country's economy to overcome problems associated with external or internal shocks such as, for instance, price shocks". He would welcome other definitions offered by the experts. It was also appropriate to discuss the integration of environment in energy policy and planning, a sine qua non in the pursuit of sustainable development.

3. Election of officers

4.   The Meeting unanimously elected Mr P. L. Coutrier (Indonesia) Chairperson, Mr Qu Shiyuan (China) and

Dr Shankar Prasad Sharma (Nepal) Vice-Chairpersons, and Mr Shavindranath Fernando (Sri Lanka) Rapporteur.

5.   The Meeting adopted the following agenda:

1.   Opening of the Meeting.

2.   Election of officers.

3.   Adoption of the agenda.

4.   Global and regional energy secene and trends.

5.   Integration of environment into energy policy and planning: regional developments.

6.   Energy resiliency: regional prospects.

7.   Regional cooperation in energy.

8.   Other matters.

9.   Adoption of the report.

B. PROCEEDINGS OF THE MEETING

1. Global and regional energy scene and trends
(Item 4 of the agenda)

6.   The ESCAP secretariat presented document ENR/SEG/EPP/2, entitled "Asian and Pacific energy scene and trends". The purpose of the paper was to provide an overview of the regional energy and environment situation. It also raised several issues, including energy resiliency and environmental aspects, to stimulate discussion on the subject. In reviewing the energy scene and trends in the Asian and Pacific region, the paper examined the current and prospective policy in energy development and the integration of environmental aspects of energy development and management in energy policy and planning in the region. In the regional energy scene review, the past and future trends in energy demand were analysed and compared with resources in the region. The paper highlighted the salient issues and suggested feasible ways, including regional cooperation, to address them. It put forward some aspects of energy policies and issues in the area of energy planning, development and management. It also discussed energy resiliency in terms of self-reliance, possible supply disruptions, security of supply and pricing policy. Regional cooperation was stressed in developing energy strategies and policies that could collectively address energy issues based on an environmentally sustainable pattern of use.

7. In the discussion that followed, several points were raised for clarification or further elaboration. Members of the secretariat, as well as a number of experts, shared their views on those points. Some of the major areas of discussion are noted below.

8. Energy issues raised in the secretariat's paper included "infrastructure" as a separate issue. The question was whether it could be included in other issues such as energy supply. The secretariat clarified that, in the Commission's deliberations in recent years, the lack of infrastructure had been identified as a major impediment in development and the power sector had also been included as infrastructure. Therefore, infrastructure was shown separately to focus on the issues. However, it was agreed that infrastructure was more a financing or investment issue than a supply issue. It included both the physical infrastructure and the institutional (soft) infrastructure. It was also noted that private sector participation was seen as a new source of investment in energy infrastructure. On project financing, a suggestion was made to identify and rank national projects for financing by private and public sectors.

9. Environmental issues were discussed at great length. While it was recognized that the cost of externalities should be internalized as much as possible, too much regulation should not impede development. Some examples were cited whereby, despite favourable environmental impact assessment reports, some projects were rejected for no apparent good reason. A suggestion was made that experts should be engaged to carry out those reports in a more transparent and professional manner to meet the concerns of environmental lobbyists. It was agreed that natural resources should be used on a long-term sustainability basis for the benefit of people. Environment and development should be complementary rather than adversarial.

10. As an explanation of the scenario S3 (energy conservation with investment and fuel switching) in the ESCAP projection, the secretariat reported that the scenario was based on the assumption that extra investments in terms of energy efficiency equipment and for fuel switching would take place to induce mitigation of greenhouse gas emissions, while in scenario S2 only those efficiency investments would be undertaken which were economic in their own right (without including greenhouse mitigation benefits) while S1 was the "business as usual" scenario with no emphasis on efficiency gains.

11. A question was raised on what could or should be done to encourage increased utilization of natural gas in the long run. Among the constraints recognized was lack of infrastructure (gas pipelines, liquified natural gas facilities) for gas trade in the region. That infrastructure was normally large-scale (for example, in liquified natural gas plants) and capital-intensive. Nevertheless, the utilization of domestic gas was on the rise, including the use of compressed natural gas in the transport sector of some countries, such as

Indonesia and Thailand. In that context, the secretariat informed the Meeting that a symposium was being organized by ESCAP in Beijing in November 1995 to discuss natural gas issues and future activities. An ESCAP publication on the subject was offered to interested participants.

12. The Meeting recognized that coal would remain a dominant fuel not only in the producing countries but in other countries as well, through increased use of imported coal. As a consequence, the environmental problem would also increase likewise. Therefore, wider application of clean coal technology was seen as a possible measure to contain pollution. It was, however, noted that, although local pollution was largely controllable, nothing much could be done to limit CO_2 (a major greenhouse gas) emissions. A related issue that came out in the discussion time and again was the issue of technology transfer. Although clean coal technology was well developed, the transfer was constrained by the cost and funding issue in developing economies. Regarding a mechanism for technology transfer, a reference was made to provisions in the United Nations Framework Convention on Climate Change; the signatories from developing economies expected assistance from developed nations in clean and efficient technologies. "Joint implementation" was suggested as one appropriate modality. Private sector participation in power generation was also seen as a way to bring in technology to developing countries, but in some countries the use of indigenous local low-grade coal posed some problems with imported technologies not being suitable for local coal. On some of the latest technologies, such as the integrated gasification combined cycle, the Meeting was informed that the technology could not yet compete with modern high efficiency conventional technologies in countries such as Australia. However, in countries where less efficient conventional technologies were in use, it might be a better option.

13. The experts from Cambodia, China, Indonesia, the Islamic Republic of Iran, Nepal, Pakistan, the Philippines, Sri Lanka, Thailand and Viet Nam provided information on the energy situation in their countries, followed by some discussion and clarification.

2. Integration of environment into energy policy and planning: regional developments
(Item 5 of the agenda)

14. Professor Lefevre, of the Energy Planning Central Consultant Team at the Asian Institute of Technology introduced a document entitled "Progress report on case studies on energy-environmental planning". The Asian Institute of Technology was currently implementing programme element "energy environment planning" within the framework of the Programme for Asian Cooperation on Energy and the Environment (PACE-E) funded by the United Nations Development Programme and the Government of France. The presentation highlighted three main areas: (a) introduction to the general framework of energy

environment planning; (b) the energy-environment situation in Asia with an emphasis on the energy sector's impacts and stressing the role that energy planning should play in the context of sustainable development; and (c) the framework for the in-country studies that energy environment planning would bring to further strengthen national capabilities in assessing the energy-environment situation. Some case studies on integrating environmental concerns into energy planning policies conducted in China, India and Thailand, as well as some regional projects, were also reported during the presentation. Some of the key elements to obtain meaningful studies were:

(a) To ensure that key decision-making personnel were involved in order to secure the acceptance of such studies;

(b) To identify and address the most important issues and to be realistic and practical in scope. It was mentioned that it was not feasible to conduct too "comprehensive" a study without losing the overall view. Furthermore, it was mentioned that economic instruments addressing technological solutions must be incorporated into the underlying scenarios;

(c) To ensure, among other things, the availability of reliable relevant data, which was always a limiting factor.

15. Many experts agreed that energy choices were part of economic development strategies and that optimal balance of energy supply should be decided by respective governments. Therefore, countries which were to be involved in the in-depth in-country studies (proposed by the programme element energy environment planning within the framework of PACE-E) should first identify particular problems and constraints that they would like to address, whether it be air quality (emissions), utilization of land resources with political, geographical, technological, and socio-economic constraints, or others. The question was not only to select one model but to ascertain the flexibility of any model to address particular problems set out by the countries based on country specific needs. He re-emphasized the importance of the involvement of decision-makers at an early stage in the process to ensure acceptance and transparency.

3. Energy resiliency: regional prospects
(Item 6 of the agenda)

16. Mr Michael Clegg, consultant to ESCAP, introduced document ENR/SEG/EPP/1 entitled "Resilient strategic planning under conditions of energy and environmental uncertainty". In his presentation, the consultant suggested a definition for resiliency in energy planning according to which a resilient strategic plan for energy was a plan that provided a high level of security for energy supplies, and their economic and environmental costs, in order to protect both the economic well-being and the planned improvement

thereof, of the nation and the commercial or industrial organizations concerned, recognizing the uncertainties and unpredictable nature of the future global energy demand and supply, and its economic structure. In his presentation, Mr Clegg explained the main differences between conventional models formulated for forecasting of economic developments, energy requirements, consumption and energy-related emissions. Unlike conventional models, the concept of scenario-building sought to provide a tool to clarify risks. Scenarios provided a framework for reflections on explicit and implicit model assumptions. He introduced different types of scenarios (for example, "archetype scenarios", "exploratory scenarios", "phantom scenarios", and "first and second generation scenarios") and outlined the various prerequisites and objectives of scenario planning, involving an iterative learning process with top-level decision-makers.

17. The Meeting then discussed the various national and regional aspects of energy resiliency. The participants reflected on the role of scenario planning and analysis for long-term policy and investment decisions. The participants felt that forecasting models and scenario analysis were complementary to a considerable degree. However, participants agreed that both approaches could only offer useful planning tools if the respective decision-makers were actively involved in the model or scenario-building exercises, as emphasized by the consultant. As regards the regional perspectives on energy resiliency, it was noted that energy demand would continue to increase and that environmental concerns and regulations would also need to be given greater attention in the future. Management of energy demand would therefore remain essential to increase national and regional energy resiliency.

18. In that connection, the need to cover possibilities outside a "consensus" view were emphasized, so as to render the exercise useful to the decision-makers, since too narrow a focus would defeat resiliency (contingency planning) objectives.

19. For the additional information of participants, the Regional Adviser on Energy at ESCAP presented a selection of slides which provided a summary comparative and historical overview of international carbon dioxide emissions from fossil fuel use, of comparison of energy intensities by using gross domestic product (GDP) in current dollars and in terms of purchasing power parity, as possible "building blocks" for any scenarios contemplated by the participants.

4. Regional cooperation in energy
(Item 7 of the agenda)

20. The secretariat presented document ENR/SEG/EPP/3 on regional cooperation in energy, highlighting the extrabudgetary activities of ESCAP with a strong component of regional cooperation, particularly in the activities under the coordination of the various regional working groups in

each of the programme elements of PACE-E and in the fields of new and renewable sources of energy. In the field of new and renewable source of energy, regional working groups on wind and geothermal energy development and utilization had been established by ESCAP. The secretariat paper also emphasized the importance and benefits of private sector participation in the activities of ESCAP.

21. The meeting supported the approach of ESCAP in energy studies, which was in line with government policies while also leading to market opportunities for the private sector. It was suggested that the approach should concentrate on critical issues. Environmental issues were considered crucial in the execution of energy projects, particularly in large hydro projects. It was suggested that environmental considerations should be included in the feasibility studies of energy projects, including considerations of decommissioning issues at the end of projects.

5. Conclusions and recommendations

22. The meeting made the following conclusions and recommendations:

(a) Environmental considerations were being incorporated into energy policies and planning in countries of the Asian and Pacific region in varying degrees. Most countries already had in place the necessary legislation and regulations concerning emissions of pollutants by power plants, and the market penetration of unleaded gasoline was steadily increasing in large cities. However, there were still some constraints in environmental monitoring and enforcements, and there were difficulties in raising the price of oil products or electricity tariffs to more economically viable levels.

(b) It was important for a country to aim for a higher energy resiliency, by ensuring better security of supply and by having a more balanced energy supply mix. However, the country's economy must itself also be more resilient, for instance by being more export-oriented. In that regard, the Philippines in the recent past had achieved a limited success in increasing its exports while at the same time overcoming the problem of power shortage and outages. But it was also recognized that it was not easy to shift to other fuels and to choose from technology options. Coal-fired plants were generating power cheaper than gas-fired plants, except when natural gas reserves were readily available close to the consumption centre. But clean premium coal should be used, unless clean coal technology could be developed and utilized.

(c) In view of the complexity of a country's energy system, studies concerning future scenarios, developments and forecasting, which were not mutually exclusive, needed to be continually updated. The use of computer models was of great assistance in that respect. But it was noted that the involvement of decision-makers was crucial for developing and generating the scenarios. The formulation and implementation of a national energy plan would be greatly facilitated if the country also pursued a long-term development plan through a series of five-year plans.

(d) The promotion of energy efficiency was important as part of a "no-regrets" policy, since energy saved could be used by new customers or for new developments.

6. Adoption of the report

23. The Meeting adopted its report on 6 October 1995.

II. DEVELOPMENT ISSUES AND CHALLENGES OF COMMON CONCERN TO COUNTRIES OF THE ASIAN AND PACIFIC REGION*

A. INTRODUCTION

1.   It is being increasingly recognized that development is an integrated, multidimensional concept which incorporates mutually interactive economic, social and environmental dimensions so as to ensure sustainable progress for humankind. The United Nations system has played a leading role in articulating this comprehensive view of development. The international consensus on a holistic approach to development is embodied in the Secretary-General's Agenda for Development 1995, the International Development Strategy for the Fourth United Nations Development Decade, the Copenhagen Declaration on Social Development and Programme of Action of the World Summit for Social Development, and Agenda 21.

2.   It should also be emphasized that it is not feasible for countries to develop in isolation from each other. The world is fast becoming a global village, spurred by progress in the technologies for information flows, transport and trade. Very uneven patterns of development in any of its dimensions with some countries or regions lagging far behind create large negative spillover effects on the development of others. Enhancing the development of each country is thus beneficial to all.

3.   In the light of the conceptual background delineated above, this chapter addresses the major development issues and challenges of the Asian and Pacific region. For analytical convenience these are grouped under four categories: mainstreaming the lagging economies, coping with exposure to the global economy, facing the challenges to sustainable development and improving the support structures of human resources, infrastructure and public administration. However it is emphasized that these are not independent elements, rather the synergy between them requires that progress be made on all fronts simultaneously.

B. MAINSTREAMING THE LAGGING ECONOMIES

4.   The Asian and Pacific region is vast, stretching from the Central Asian republics to the many small Pacific island economies. In between are several of the world's most populous countries: Bangladesh, China, India and Indonesia. It is therefore only natural that economic performance and social conditions of individual countries in the region vary

widely. The developing countries of the region have gained the reputation of the fastest growing group of countries in the world, with an average growth rate in GDP of 7 per cent during the period 1991-1994 compared with the world economic growth of 1.1 per cent during the same period. This rate is much higher than the average rate for all developing countries (4.5 per cent). Within the region, the newly industrialized economies (NIEs), the countries of the Association of South East Asian Nations (ASEAN) and China have experienced comparatively high rates of economic growth of between 7 and 12 per cent, and those in South Asia more moderate but encouraging rates of around 5 per cent. While growth appears to be picking up in the least developed countries, growth in many Pacific island countries remains at around 2 per cent and in the disadvantaged economies in transition it has been consistently negative in recent years. Also, the share of the region's developing countries in global trade has increased to 15.6 per cent in the period 1991-1994 from around 7 per cent in the early 1980s, with manufactured products accounting for a substantial and expanding proportion of exports. However, again, a large proportion of this trade is accounted for by a handful of countries.

5.   Available projections indicate that the overall picture will remain largely unchanged in the immediate future. The increasingly affluent and open markets of the region, including the big emerging markets of China, India and Indonesia, are arousing the interest of the international business community as the markets of the future for trade and investment. Hence, the region is likely to be a major epicentre of world economic growth in the coming years; it is projected that Asian countries will account for almost half of the increase in global output through the year 2000. Yet, there are many countries in the region that remain on the margin of this bright scenario.

6.   The growth experience of developing Asian and Pacific countries, particularly that of the economies of East and South-East Asia, has become the subject of intensive research by development economists in recent years. It is being increasingly appreciated that countries in the region are not a homogeneous group and that, even among countries which achieved similar results in terms of economic growth, there have been considerable differences in terms of policy regimes, experiences with structural adjustment measures, approaches to integrating social development with economic growth and the role accorded to the private sector in both the economic and social fields. Nevertheless, there is a perceptible growing convergence in macroeconomic policies being pursued by countries in the region towards an outward-

*   Prepared by the ESCAP secretariat for the Regional Development Dialogue and Regional Development Cooperation Meeting of the United Nations Development Programme, held at Kuala Lumpur in March 1995.

oriented and market-driven economic development strategy, with the private sector being the principal agents of production and trade of goods and services and the public sector providing a conducive, enabling environment and infrastructure for its activities. There is also a growing consensus on the need to pursue economic and social goals in tandem. In this situtation, there is considerable interest in the region to undertake efforts to mainstream the lagging economies.

C. COPING WITH EXPOSURE TO THE GLOBAL ECONOMY

7. The Asian and Pacific region maintained a high growth rate during 1991-1993 when the world economy as a whole suffered from a marked recession. The region, even with its large degree of external openness, demonstrated a remarkable resilience in the face of constrained external demand for its output. Most of the high performing economies of the region, which together account for a considerable proportion of regional GDP and trade flows, have acquired the skill and expertise to take advantage of the opportunities offered by changing global economic conditions. Based on past acumen in seizing trading opportunities, the Asian and Pacific region will be singularly poised to benefit from the economic recovery forecast for the industrialized countries. Furthermore, the implementation of the recently concluded Uruguay Round of multilateral trade negotiations is expectd to create a more congenial external trading environment. No other group of developing countries is likely to be as able to avail itself of the opportunities thus created as the economies of the Asian and Pacific region.

8. However, this optimistic picture needs to be tempered by several important considerations. The positive experience to date is confined to only a handful of countries in the region, with many others including the Pacific island economies and the disadvantaged economies in transition being much more vulnerable to changes in external demand. This is particularly so as their export sectors are quite highly concentrated on a few, usually primary products and textiles, their expertise in penetrating and maintaining markets is much weaker and they are significantly reliant on food imports to feed their populations. The impact of the Uruguay Round, especially the agreements on agriculture, tropical product and textiles, for these more fragile economies may be to make their economies even more vulnerable as the agreements introduce greater competitiveness for all countries by shifting towards reciprocity and away from preferential treatment. This will inevitably put increased strain on countries in the region with weaker trade sectors and increase the need for their mainstreaming within the region.

9. In addition, as economies in the region adopt policies towards greater participation in the global economy for trade and investment, they are also increasingly integrated into the global financial system. This system itself has undergone major liberalization in recent years and fluctuations in financial markets and exchange rates have become increasingly frequent. Many countries of the region, particularly the larger ones, are already experiencing strains in coping with some negative effects of this instability, often originating from outside the region, on their efforts to sustain economic growth and social development. Such effects are clearly visible in the recent volatility in stock markets and exchange rates in the region as a result of the Mexican crisis. Mechanisms need to be devised urgently to cope with the implications of financial liberalization at both the country and the regional level.

10. Countries of the region have thus to tackle the implications of their policies of market orientation, deregulation, liberalization and privatization for the conduct of trade, pricing systems, monetary and fiscal regimes, the stimulation of savings and investment, as well as for social development and protection of the environment. Three important elements of a strategy of being able to cope with the consequences of global economic events are stimulating domestic demand to reduce overexposure to external events, attracting foreign direct investment to build more robust and competitive domestic production structures and promoting intraregional trade and investment.

1. Stimulating domestic demand

11. Growing domestic demand has been very important in sustaining the growth momentum of the Asian and Pacific region. Fast growth in per capita income, together with large populations, have created sizeable markets. This has been reinforced by the growing middle class in the region in both absolute and relative terms. As the number of households with substantial real income increases, so does the demand for sophisticated goods and services. This, in turn, is expected to enhance the market size within individual economies, to create a greater degree of inter-industry linkages and to encourage technological upgrading and investment in higher value-added industries. Further movement towards more robust domestic markets will be an important component in sustaining growth impulses in the region and be an antidote to fluctuations which result from liberalization and increased exposure to global fluctuations.

2. Attracting foreign direct investment

12. The pace of growth in the Asian and Pacific region has, to an important extent, been sustained by an acceleration of foreign direct investment (FDI) inflows. Such inflows amounted to $US 53 billion in 1994, an increase of 5 per cent over the previous year. The region succeeded in increasing its share of FDI inflows of developing countries from an average of 38 per cent during the period 1981-1985 to 68 per cent in 1994. However, almost three-quarters of

these inflows went to a very limited number of countries in the region. Prospects for high growth rates, the large and increasingly affluent domestic markets, low production costs in a number of countires and continued liberalization of economies involving privatization, deregulation and provision of greater incentives for exports are likely to sustain the momentum of FDI inflows in the region. Another important aspect is that, in addition to Japan, a number of the region's developing countries or territories, including the NIEs, China, Malaysia and Thailand, are building up a network of investment in manufactured goods within the region. However, there is increasing global competition for FDI, including the countries of Eastern Europe. For many countries, especially the lagging economies of the region, attracting FDI will become increasingly difficult and will be predicated on their adopting conducive investment regimes backed by credible regulatory frameworks of property rights, tax laws and financial flows.

3. Promoting intraregional trade

13.   A major positive factor in the growth performance of the Asian and Pacific region was their ability to participate in the international division of labour, particularly by way of sustained increases in their exports. While the destination of such exports traditionally has been the major developed market economies, the share of intraregional exports in the total exports of the region increased from 33 per cent in 1975 to over 45 per cent in 1992. Nearly 70 per cent of the developing countries' trade in primary commodities takes place within the region, with Japan the predominant destination. In contrast, intraregional trade absorbs only 40 per cent of their manufactured exports, most of which is among the developing countries themselves. Varying natural resource endowments, differences in economic performance and vast differentials among countries of the region in capital accumulation and technological capabilities have created complementarities to sustain growing volumes of intraregional trade, but attention needs to be devoted to ensuring that its composition is of a self-sustaining nature.

14.   Almost all developing Asian and Pacific economies are eager to enjoy the benefits of expanding intraregional trade and to take greater advantage of their emerging complementarities. While many have implemented or are implementing trade reforms to reduce controls on imports and exports and make foreign exchange systems more market-driven, more emphasis has been put on expanding exports than on lowering barriers to imports, particularly non-tariff barriers. This is largely on account of inadequate recognition of the fact that the benefits of an outward-oriented development strategy come from the consumption of goods which are available more cheaply, of better quality and in far greater diversity through imports than in any one single domestic market. Thus, more needs to be done among countries in the region, including as a consequence of the Uruguay Round agreements, to reduce their barriers to trade, especially non-tariff barriers, as well as barriers to flows of

labour and capital. The potential and opportunities offered by border trade should be fully exploited to maximize the positive impulses of intraregional trade for economic development.

D. CHALLENGES FOR SUSTAINABLE DEVELOPMENT

15.   While the above-mentioned concerns are crucial for sustaining the pace of economic growth in the Asian and Pacific region, the region faces a number of other challenges to which urgent attention must be paid if economic growth is to lead to sustainable development. These are as follows.

1. Alleviating poverty

16.   Despite the rapid economic growth achieved by many countries of Asia and the Pacific, poverty and other critical socio-economic problems have persisted and continue to pose a major challenge to the region's planners. A broad-based pattern of social progress throughout much of the region has come about directly as a result of high economic growth rates and indirectly through strengthened government intervention which tends to accompany increased sensitivity to social concerns in the presence of sustained economic growth. Increased per capita incomes have enhanced access to goods and services and to a better quality of life for large numbers of people. With greater public revenue, Governments, increasingly in collaboration with the private sector and non-governmental organizations, have improved the provision of social services in these countries. Consequently, life expectancy, literacy and primary education and access to basic health care services have increased, while average infant mortality has been reduced in most countries of the region.

17.   However, an estimated 800 million people, or nearly three-quarters of the world's absolute poor, live in the region, particularly but not only in South Asia. The significant reductions observed in the percentage of populations below the poverty line do not translate into similar decreases in total numbers of absolute poor. A large number of these people and other disadvantaged and vulnerable groups such as slum dwellers, rural women, people with disabilities, the elderly and minority groups continue to face problems such as poor nutrition and health, lack of education and training, chronic unemployment and underemployment, lack of access to land and capital, inadequate shelter, environmental degradation of their surroundings, natural disasters, crime, lack of social protection, lack of social cohesion and disintegration of families and communities. Furthermore, the Asian and Pacific region is witnessing a rise in numbers of drug abusers, especially among the urban young, accompanied by an escalation in the spread of HIV/AIDS.

18.   The challenges in poverty alleviation include the increasingly urgent need to redress the situation of the millions of people in the region who continue to endure the

hardships of economic and social deprivation, as well as differential access to various economic and social activities between the rich and the poor, men and women, and the rural and urban sectors. Thus, a combination of overall growth promoting policies and target-oriented programmes which embody recognition of the importance of developmental as well as welfare aspects of poverty alleviation will need to be pursued. Beneficiaries of poverty alleviation programmes and projects need to participate more in the design and implementation of these activities. The poor and other disadvantaged and vulnerable social groups need to be targeted, not just as beneficiaries of economic and social progress, but also as useful participants in productive activities. The core issue of poverty alleviation is thus the expansion of productive employment, the enhancement of social integration and the empowerment of the poor.

2. Containing population growth and coping with migration

19. Closely related to poverty alleviation is the issue of reduction in population growth. The Asian and Pacific region currently contains around 60 per cent of the world's population. The Governments in the region recognized the problems resulting from rapid population growth as early as in the 1960s, adopted anti-natal population policies and set up national family planning programmes to lower birth rates. These programmes, aided by substantial economic and social progress, have succeeded in bringing about a notable sustained decline in the total fertility rate and the population growth rate. The success has been more remarkable in East and South-East Asia relative to South Asia, and stemming population growth rates will remain a major policy concern for South Asian countries for some time to come. With a faster spread of education, particularly among women in rural areas, and improved family planning services to which practically all South Asian countries are committed, one can expect a further significant reduction in the population growth rate in these countries.

20. One visible result of the disparity among economic as well as population growth rates of countries in the region, and between parts of larger countries, as well as of political circumstances, is the enormous flux of migrants and refugees in the Asian and Pacific region, many of whom have moved without any legal status. Coping with rural-to-urban migration, with illegal migrants and temporary migrant workers who wish to be considered permanent migrants, as well as with refugee populations, creates economic and social strains in and between countries and has become an issue of major concern in the last several years. While economic growth will alleviate some of this problem through increased employment opportunities, there is an urgent need for countries to reconsider their policies and devise cooperative action in the migration field, including the development of more systematic, formal arrangements for contract labour migration between the labour-exporting and labour-importing countries in the region.

3. Protecting the environment

21. Economic growth in the Asian and Pacific region has been accompanied by a substantial environmental cost. The incidence of urban congestion and pollution, industrial pollution, deforestation, depletion of mineral and marine resources, contamination of water resources, and degradation of land and soil has become widespread. The causes of environmental problems include both underdevelopment as well as unsustainable, inefficient patterns of development involving rising energy requirements, excessive pressure on natural resources and rapid industrialization and urbanization without sufficient attention to the conditions of air and water and treatment of wastes. Promoting people's awareness and participation, the formulation and implementation of appropriate technology policies and cooperation at all administrative levels are important support measures for achieving sustainable development.

22. Fortunately, consciousness with respect to the need to address environmental problems has increased notably. Most countries have set up institutional arrangements for the design, formulation and implementation of environmental policies, headed in many cases by Cabinet ministers. The institutional arrangements are being supported by formulation of environmental laws and regulations, including both market-based and regulatory instruments designed to arrest environmental deterioration and to promote conservation and efficiency in resource use. However, in many cases implementation and enforcement remains weak, with countries lacking the ability to monitor compliance, to extract penalties and to arbitrate or negotiate investment agreements which include enforceable environment protection clauses with entities, both public and private, foreign and domestic, carrying out production activities. Also, policies have tended to be sector-specific in nature. The integration of environmental considerations in the formulation of development projects and programmes is still inadequate. The interface between macroeconomic policies and microlevel environmental implications is not fully understood or absorbed. These deficiencies need to be corrected urgently if the region is to start reversing its deteriorating environmental situation.

23. It is a fact that the increasing populations of the Asian and Pacific region will need more food in coming years. It is also true that, with very few exceptions, all cultivable land is already in agricultural production, with a consequent increased reliance being placed on agricultural inputs. To help to alleviate the environmental problems associated with overuse and misuse of agro-chemicals and fertilizers, more exchanges of experience and information, as well as development of national capacities, is required. Asian and Pacific populations will also need increased energy and water supplies. Much needs to be done to promote energy and water conservation and efficiency, including rationalizing pricing systems and removing subsidies so that there is less waste and a more economic use of energy and

water, as well as to expand supply capacities. The conundrum of encouraging exploitation of forest, mineral and fish resources for economic gain while preserving nature and the environment leads to a need for exchange of experience and common understanding among groups of countries on approaches to defining the responsibilities of commercial partners and enforcing them. Climate change, the potential rise in sea level and the greenhouse effect threaten to increase natural disasters in the Asian and Pacific region for which enhanced efforts are needed at the country and regional levels to mitigate property damage and human suffering. The treatment of the above concerns could benefit greatly from increased accessibility by developing countries in the region to environmentally sound technologies, including applications of space technology.

E. DEVELOPING SUPPORT STRUCTURES

24.   The above scenario of continued growth in GDP and trade, of sustainable development through eradicating poverty and protecting the environment and of enabling policies for these endeavours will not occur without adequate simultaneous attention to the basic support structures of the development of technological and human resources, the provision of infrastructure in all its dimensions and the endogenization of the role of public administration as an impartial agent for the monitoring and enforcement of agreed regulatory frameworks. These three areas are primarily the responsibility of Governments because of the externalities involved in investment in them, as well as the recognition of the problem of unequal access to them by groups within a country.

1. Developing technological and human resources

25.   To date, much of the region's economic growth can be attributed to expanded use of natural resources and relatively cheap, unskilled labour coupled with the greater availability of capital from domestic savings and investment inflows. There are, however, natural limits to this scenario. As natural resources of all sorts become increasingly scarce, as the growth of the labour force slows as a result of slower population growth and as competition for use of investment funds increases, further growth will increasingly depend on increasing productivity, improving the skill level of labour and management, enhancing the ability to develop, absorb and utilize more sophisticated technologies, and increasing the flexibility of labour to move between jobs. While FDI has made and will continue to make a significant contribution to the economic growth of the region, particularly through the promotion of manufactured exports, it has not always brought about major improvements in indigenous technological capabilities. As wages rise in response to higher living standards brought about by fast economic growth as well as in response to slower growth in the size of the labour force as a result of declining population growth and increased ageing, many countries of the region will tend to lose comparative advantage in the export of labour-intensive goods. They will then be obliged to compete in the export markets of sophisticated technology and skill-intensive products.

26.   In order to increase their competitiveness in the markets for such products, more focused attention will have to be paid to enhancing domestic technological capacities through research and development, and to improving human capital formation and increasing labour force flexibility. Countries of the region are showing greater awareness of the emerging problems connected to training its workforce, and are tackling them with a combination of government provision of facilities, private sector and NGO involvement and family commitments. There is an increasing emphasis on making secondary level and technical education available to the population at large. Growing attention is being paid to developing indigenous research and development capacities and trying to cope with the needs for technology which is simultaneously efficient and environmentally friendly. However much remains to be done if the level of human resource development is to keep pace with that of the economy.

2. Relieving strains on infrastructure

27.   Another major challenge facing the Asian and Pacific region is to relieve the increasing strain on infrastructure resulting from high rates of economic growth. A recent estimate by ESCAP shows that the region would require within the period 1990-2000 approximately $US 1.4 trillion of investment in infrastructure, including power supplies, water supply and waste treatment, telecommunications, railways, roads, urban transport systems, airports and seaports. Mobilizing financial resources of this magnitude is a formidable task; it will require a combination of accelerated external financial assistance, improved domestic resources mobilization and increased involvement of the private sector in financing infrastructure investment. Several countries of the region have already adopted policies to encourage the involvement of the private sector. Measures are also being taken to improve the public administration of infrastructure, including its planning, as well as supervision and regulation of public and private partners, to increase utilization of existing capacities through better operating efficiency and repair and maintenance, and to implement more realistic pricing in the furtherance of cost recovery. These measures deserve international support as there is a real risk that neglect of an overall growth-promoting policy measure such as improving infrastructure will render target-oriented programmes rapidly unsustainable.

3. Adapting public administration

28.   The role of government in a liberalized, deregulated, private sector-oriented economy is still very important, though substantially different from that in a more regulated,

planned one where the government either owns production and marketing activities or actively intervenes in the pricing system. The strains on government officials of pursuing market-oriented policies coupled with sustainable development and environment and poverty concerns is leading to a very visible need to rethink the content and conduct of public administration. Civil service cadres are having to learn about modalities for monitoring and enforcing the myriad rules and regulations within which a market-oriented system functions efficiently and does not degenerate into a free-for-all in favour of those with economic and political power. They must cope with new types of regulatory and enforcement frameworks involving fines and court cases, with increased reliance on measures which induce the behaviour desired rather than legislate it and on the setting-up of a conducive regulatory framework and competition policy rather than devising micro-production or marketing-level interventions. They have to develop modalities for private sector or government partnerships for progress in many fields, economic ventures as well as ones providing social services such as education, health and infrastructure. Yet the assistance available to them for learning how to operate their new system is very haphazard and weak. There is an urgent need to foster exchange of experience on policy implementation modalities and to revitalize and reformulate the training available to public administration officials. Helping countries to cope with the changing role of public sector officials is a very positive way of supporting their further development.

F. FOSTERING REGIONAL DEVELOPMENT COOPERATION

29.   All of the development challenges discussed above lend themselves to the use of regional and subregional cooperation as an important means of finding solutions. In fact, regional and subregional organizations, both governmental and non-governmental in nature, are viewed by countries of the region as an essential component of their expressed strategy for enhancing existing regional cooperation. The forms of subregional and regional cooperation include exchanging experience, learning lessons from the experience of others, undertaking joint activities and agreeing on common strategies, as well as reducing barriers to flows of goods, services, capital, labour and information among countries.

30.   In the economic field, regional cooperation can help to mainstream the lagging economies by fostering subregional intraregional trade and investment. There have been several moves in this direction through the establishment, strengthening and enlargement of subregional economic groupings. Notable among these are ASEAN and the ASEAN Free Trade Area, the Economic Cooperation Organization, the South Asian Association for Regional Cooperation, the South Asian Preferential Trading Arrangement, the South Pacific Forum and the South Pacific

Commission. These institutional arrangements are complementing regional integration brought about by production activities of transnational corporations from both within and outside the region. Another interesting effort towards enhanced regional cooperation is embodied in the various "growth triangles" designed to exploit complementarities arising from different endowments of labour, capital and natural resources in geographically contiguous areas of different countries with a view to stimulating local economies and using them as a more convenient base of operation for export industries. A feature that characterizes the triangles is the close collaboration between the private and public sectors. The private sector has been the main provider of commercial investment and the public sector has assisted through infrastructure development, provision of incentives, and the streamlining of administrative procedures and regulations to facilitate private investment. A third initiative has been increased regional interaction in the private sector organized through Chambers of Commerce. This involves stimulating flows of information on investment opportunities, export promotion and exchanges of personnel.

31.   There has been growing regional cooperation in social fields, including human resource development. The region has several centres of excellence, including secondary schools, technical institutes and universities which are increasingly being used for training, education and research for personnel outside of the country of location. There are several specialized research institutes which are joint ventures among countries for undertaking research and development for a particular sector or product. There are environment protection groupings such as the South Pacific Regional Environment Programme which are used for tackling environmental problems which are not contained within one country's borders. The increasing involvement of the private sector in the health and education fields is also leading to multicountry ventures and cooperation.

32.   There is still much scope for regional subgroupings to learn from each other's experience and explore further opportunities in neighbouring subregions. Operating within a framework of subregional cooperation has proved helpful to many of the region's developing countries in deriving benefits from their complementarities. A regional economic cooperation strategy will be needed to sustain the tempo of outward-oriented trade-led growth that the region's developing countries are pursuing. Regional strategies for fostering social development and for coping with environment protection are also required. In this context, regional development cooperation strategies will need to involve the designing of adequate responses at subregional and regional levels to the changes taking place in the global economy in order to meet the challenges and take advantage of the opportunities. There is also an increasing need for dialogue among the regional and subregional entities to ensure harmony of responses initiated at different levels.

33.   ESCAP has been playing a catalytic role in trying to widen the cooperation among the subregional groupings through its recently instituted annual meetings of heads of subregional organizations. The issues discussed and actions initiated through these meetings cover a widening gamut of areas in the economic and social fields. However, much remains to be done if the aspirations of the poeople of the Asian and Pacific region are to be met.

III. GLOBAL AND REGIONAL ENERGY SCENE AND TRENDS*

A. INTRODUCTION

1.   The purpose of this chapter is to provide an overview of the regional energy and environment situation. It also attempts to raise several issues, which are not exhaustive, including energy resiliency and environmental aspects, to stimulate discussion on the subject.

2.   In reviewing the energy scene and trends in the Asian and Pacific region, this chapter examines the current and prospective policy in energy development and the integration of environmental aspects of energy development and management in energy policy and planning in the region. In the regional energy scene review, the past and future trends in energy demand are analysed and compared with resources in the region. On the basis of the analysis, the chapter highlights the salient issues and suggests feasible alternative ways, including regional cooperation, to address them. It puts forward some aspects of energy policies and issues in the area of energy planning, development and management. It also discusses energy resiliency in terms of self-reliance, possible supply disruptions, security of supply and pricing policy. Regional cooperation is stressed in developing energy strategies and policies that collectively address energy issues based on an environmentally sustainable pattern of use. The analyses are based on research, utilizing the latest data available from the United Nations Statistics Division, *BP Statistical Review of World Energy, Energy Indicators of Developing Member Countries of Asian Development Book* and other publications and reports.

3.   The analysis contains information of the present trends and future perspectives for energy in countries of the ESCAP region, excluding the Central Asian republics; energy data for this group of countries are available only for 1992.

4.   Energy is essential for economic and social development and improved quality of life and has been at the top of the international agenda, particularly since the first oil shock in the early 1970s. The situation in developing economies, particularly in the ESCAP region, is such that adequate supply of energy to sustain the high economic growth is the top priority of Governments. As a matter of fact, adequate and guaranteed supply of energy has always been a concern for all countries and remains a critical concern despite the apparent abundance of oil on the market and its unexpected sustained low price since the late 1980s. The

centre of concern, however, has shifted from the fear of resource depletion to that of the environmental impacts of energy production and use. However, uncertainties still persist regarding a host of other issues concerning energy supply, including possible energy shocks in the future and demand management. Lessons learnt from the previous shocks have influenced countries to enhance their self-reliance on energy to a certain extent but the threat of surprises still remains. This is particularly true for oil supply and demand. The reserves are concentrated in a few countries or subregions, whereas the demand is scattered around the world and is growing at a high rate, particularly in developing economies. Countries, particularly the oil-importing economies, are becoming increasingly more dependent on a few sources of supply, making them more vulnerable to possible supply disruptions and price escalation.

5.   There is a need to have a trade-off between development and preservation of the environment. Countries with fossil fuels such as poor quality coal and lignite or with resources like hydro or geothermal, are not always able to exploit this potential owing to their negative environmental consequences. However, in many cases, with proper planning and the right choice of technology, most of the negative impacts can be minimized to an acceptable limit. Integration of environmental costs in energy pricing should be the ultimate objective to be achieved over a period of time and according to the situation in individual countries. In Agenda 21, energy has been highlighted in several chapters because of both its importance and its negative impacts on the environment resulting from the way it is being produced and consumed.

6.   Why does energy figure so prominently in discussions about the environment? Energy is perceived as a major and important player in the ever-increasing environmental concerns of the world community. Its impact is felt not only through global concerns such as climate change and ozone layer depletion, but also through its effects on the local, subregional and regional environment through air and water pollution, land degradation and ecological damage. It is well recognized that the industrialized countries have been largely responsible for most of the greenhouse gas emissions. However, the situation will worsen further as more and more energy will be needed to sustain economic growth, particularly in developing economies, which is the immediate priority. It may be useful to keep in mind that the environmental impact of energy is indirect: the actual services required by consumers are not energy per se but heating, cooling, lighting, moving and transport, and so the demand for energy is a derived demand. It is the process chosen to produce the services that produces the environmental

---

* Prepared by the ESCAP secretariat for the Senior Expert Group Meeting on Energy Resiliency and to Integration of Environment its Energy Policy and Planning, Bangkok, 4 to 6 October 1995.

impacts. It is well recognized that all the negative impacts cannot be eliminated totally. What can be done, however, is to minimize the impacts or in some cases reduce them through planned and systematic responses and/or remedial measures, as has been advocated in Agenda 21. There are several ways to minimize the overall negative impacts of energy.

7.   Over the past few years, thanks to the United Nations Conference on Environment and Development, held in Rio de Janeiro in June 1992, major environmental issues have been better recognized that before. What is next? Where do we or should we go from here, and how? It appears that there is no easy answer to these questions. Although some initiatives have been taken in a few developing countries, in general a comprehensive plan of action has yet to be made in most developing countries. The total integration of environmental aspects in energy and economic policy planning is far from being realized. Inadequate capacity, a lack of resources, both financial and human, and a lack of technology are some of the reasons for slow or no progress in the developing countries in general, although some good work has been done in some relatively better-off developing countries.

B. ANALYSIS OF ENERGY RESOURCES

8.   As of the end of 1993 (see table 1), in terms of world reserve/production ratios, coal reserves continued to be the highest (236 years), followed by natural gas reserves (64.9 years) and oil (43.1 years). The situation is similar in Asia and Australasia, although oil reserves are substantially lower in Australasia. The trend of continuous increase in the overall reserves and production of oil has almost halted since 1991.

Even reserves and production of natural gas, which rose by about 10 per cent in 1992 over the 1991 figure, did not show any further increase in 1993. Compared with previous estimates made as of the end of 1992, the world coal reserves/production ratio at the end of 1993 showed a modest increase of about 1.7 per cent, while that of oil remained the same. In the Australasia subregion, the reserves/production ratio of natural gas and oil remained at about the same level but the coal reserves/production ratio fell by about 4.5 per cent.

9.   In the ESCAP region, only China, India, Japan, Pakistan, the Republic of Korea and Taiwan Province of China use nuclear energy to generate part of their electricity. Hydropower resources, though abundant in the region, remained grossly unexploited for various reasons, including environmental objections.

C. ENERGY SUPPLIES

1. Commercial primary energy

10.   Commercial primary energy includes solids, liquids, gas and electricity. Solids comprise hard coal, lignite, peat and oil shale; liquids comprise crude petroleum and natural gas liquids; gas comprises natural gas; and electricity comprises primary electricity generated from hydropower, nuclear and geothermal sources.

11.   Table 2 shows the production of commercial primary energy in the ESCAP region, excluding the Central Asian republics. The 1992 data for the Central Asian republics are shown in the footnote of the table. The production of all forms of commercial energy registered yet another

Table 1. World's proven reserves of fossil fuels, end 1993

	Oil		Natural gas		Coal	
	Amount (billions of tons)	Reserves/ production ratio (years)	Amount (trillions of cubic feet)	Reserves/ production ratio (years)	Amount (billions of tons)	Reserves/ production ratio (years)
World	136.7	43.1	5 016.12	64.9	1 039.2	236
OECD	7.3	9.5	474.8	14.9	438.0	262
OPEC	104.9	79.6	2 020.4	>100	..	..
Asia and Australasia (including China, but excluding the Middle East)	6.0	17.6	354.5	53.0	303.9	171
China	3.2	21.9	59.0	>100	114.5	..
Middle East	89.6	95.1	1 581.0	>100		
Islamic Republic of Iran	12.7	92.9	730.0	>100	..	..

Source: *BP Statistical Review of World Energy,* June 1994.

Notes: Proven reserves are generally taken to be those quantities which geological and engineering information indicate with reasonable certainty can be recovered in the future from known reservoirs under existing economic and operating conditions. Reserves tabulated under various groups of economies are not mutually exclusive as there are overlaps among some groups.

Reserves/production ratio: if the reserves remaining at the end of any year are divided by the production in that year, the result is the length of time that those remaining reserves would last if production were to continue at the then current level.

Two dots (..) indicate that data are not available or are not separately reported.

Table 2. Production of commercial primary energy in the ESCAP region, excluding Central Asian republics
(Million tons of oil equivalent)

	1970	1973	1975	1980	1985	1990	1991	1992	Average annual growth rates (percentage)			
									1980/ 1970	1990/ 1980	1990/ 1970	1992/ 1991
Solids	302.0 (48.3)	337.4 (39.6)	372.1 (41.5)	460.4 (52.6)	664.3 (54.6)	847.8 (53.2)	875.3 (52.7)	908.0 (53.1)	4.3	6.3	5.3	3.7
Liquids	283.5 (45.3)	457.7 (53.7)	452.2 (49.8)	318.1 (36.3)	395.8 (32.6)	482.1 (30.2)	499.9 (30.1)	503.5 (29.5)	1.2	4.3	2.7	0.7
Gas	23.8 (3.8)	39.2 (4.6)	50.2 (5.6)	65.3 (7.5)	109.9 (9.0)	151.2 (9.5)	166.5 (10.0)	177.9 (10.4)	10.6	8.8	9.7	6.8
Electricity	16.3 (2.6)	17.7 (2.1)	22.4 (2.5)	31.9 (3.6)	45.8 (3.8)	113.1 (7.1)	118.3 (7.1)	119.5 (7.0)	6.9	13.5	10.2	1.0
Total	625.7 (100)	852.1 (100)	896.9 (100)	875.6 (100)	1 215.8 (100)	1 594.2 (100)	1 660.0 (100)	1 708.9 (100)	3.4	6.2	4.8	3.0

Source: United Nations, *Energy Statistics Yearbook,* various issues.

Note: The figures in parentheses show the share as the percentage of the total.

Central Asian republics figures in 1992: total 239,685; solids 81,271; liquids 45,573; gas 110,894; and electricity 1,947 thousand TOE.

Table 3. Shares of traditional energy in aggregated national energy demand in selected countries of Asia and the Pacific
(Million tons of oil equivalent and percentages)

Country	Year	Aggregate national demand (rural and urban)		
		Commercial energy	Traditional energy	Total energy demand
Bangladesh	1989	4.84 (32.95)	9.85 (67.05)	14.69 (100.00)
China	1987	462.40 (63.60)	264.60 (36.40)	727.00 (100.00)
Fiji	1986	0.21 (44.68)	0.26 (55.32)	0.47 (100.00)
India	1983	81.29 (34.10)	157.10 (65.90)	238.39 (100.00)
Indonesia	1990	40.56 (<57.86)	> 29.54 (>42.14)	> 70.1 (100.00)
Malaysia	1990	13.23 (83.00)	2.71 (17.00)	15.94 (100.00)
Myanmar	1989	1.93 (16.32)	9.90 (83.68)	11.83 (100.00)
Nepal	1989	0.36 (4.48)	7.68 (95.52)	8.04 (100.00)
Pakistan	1989	21.49 (68.24)	10.00 (31.76)	31.49 (100.00)
Philippines	1989	10.71 (68.00)	5.04 (32.00)	15.75 (100.00)
Sri Lanka	1989	1.31 (22.13)	4.61 (77.87)	5.92 (100.00)
Thailand	1990	28.86 (80.03)	7.20 (19.97)	36.06 (100.00)
Tuvalu	1986	0.03 (37.50)	0.05 (62.50)	0.08 (100.00)
Viet Nam	1990	4.83 (48.84)	5.06 (51.16)	9.89 (100.00)

Source: Based on *Rural Energy Systems in the Asia-Pacific: A Survey of their Status, Planning and Management,* edited by K. V. Ramani, M. N. Islam and A. K. N. Reddy (Asian and Pacific Development Centre, Kuala Lumpur, 1993).

increase in 1992. Thus, at the end of the review period (1992), the total primary energy production in the region reached 1,709 million tons of oil equivalent (mtoe) from 1,660 in 1991. Though the production grew slowly (an average annual growth of 3.4 per cent) during the 1970s, the period during which two major oil price shocks occurred, growth picked up quite strongly thereafter, achieving a steady average annual rate of over 6 per cent during the 1980s. Growth at the beginning of the 1990s (1991 and 1992) appeared to slow down again to 4.1 and 3 per cent respectively. The growth rates of liquid fuels and primary electricity have fallen drastically to 0.7 and 1 per cent respectively in 1992 from an annual rate of 4.3 and 13.5 per cent during the 1980s. Although it is possible that, in 1992, the oil production did not really grow much or the primary electricity production also was lower than expected, this looks like more an exception than a new trend, which may possibly be due to an anomaly in the data, as many data for later years are provisional and are often revised when more accurate information is available. On the other hand, a steady growth of almost 7 per cent in the production of gas is clearly following the previous trend.

2. Non-commercial energy

12. Certain types of traditional sources of energy, such as fuelwood, agricultural residues and other biomass, are considered non-commercial energy, although some trading in fuelwood does occur. Renewable sources in general, except hydropower and geothermal, fall under this category.

13. Non-commercial energy plays an important role in the energy supply, particularly in rural areas, in developing countries of the ESCAP region. In a number of countries in Asia and the Pacific, the share of non-commercial energy in the total energy supply is over 60 per cent. Table 3 shows

the dependency on the traditional energy sources in selected economies of the region.

D. ENERGY DEMAND TRENDS

1. Regional aggregated commercial energy consumption trends

14. Commercial energy is consumed in the form of solids, liquids, gases and electricity. The consumption of solids refers to the use of primary forms of solid fuels, net imports and changes in stocks of secondary fuels; the consumption of liquids refers to the use of petroleum products (including feedstocks), natural gasoline, condensate and refinery gas and to inputs of crude petroleum to thermal power plants; the consumption of gases refers to the use of natural gas and coke-oven gas, net imports and changes in stocks at gas works; and the consumption of electricity refers to the use of primary electricity and net imports of electricity.

15. Table 4 shows the historical trend of consumption of all forms of commercial primary energy in the ESCAP region and aggregate world trends. The latest revised data indicate that the regional primary energy consumption increased at an average annual rate of 5.1 per cent over the period 1970-1990, a significant growth rate compared with the world average of 2.7 per cent. Primary electricity consumption refers only to electricity generated from hydropower, nuclear, geothermal and other new and renewable sources of energy, and thus does not include the consumption of secondary electricity generated from the conversion of fossil fuels. The regional total commercial energy consumption reached 1,847.6 mtoe, up from 1,768.9 mtoe in 1991, registering yet another increase of 4.5 per cent. This consistent high growth over a long period was achieved as a result of the impressive

Table 4. Consumption of commercial primary energy in the ESCAP region
(excluding Central Asian republics) and the world
(Million tons of oil equivalent and kilogrammes of oil equivalent per capita)

| | 1970 | 1973 | 1975 | 1980 | 1985 | 1990 | 1991 | 1992 | Average annual growth rates (percentage) | | | |
									1980/ 1970	1990/ 1980	1990/ 1970	1992/ 1991
World	4 433.5 (1 212)	5 115.6 (1 322)	5 121.7 (1 267)	5 891.5 (1 339)	4 275.6 (1 326)	7 594.3 (1 403)	7 634.9 (1 415)	7 654.4 (1 395)	2.9	2.6	2.7	0.3
ESCAP region	624.7 (330)	794.0 (372)	849.4 (377)	1 039.4 (424)	1 299.6 (477)	1 698.0 (569)	1 768.9 (589)	1 847.6 (605)	5.2	5.0	5.1	4.5
Developed economies of the ESCAP region	265.3 (2 543)	334.5 (2 675)	329.9 (2 569)	363.2 (2 700)	405.1 (2 897)	496.8 (3 450)	511.8 (3 535)	517.8 (3 557)	3.2	3.2	3.2	1.2
Developing economies of the ESCAP region	359.4 (190)	459.5 (228)	519.5 (245)	676.2 (292)	894.5 (346)	1 201.2 (423)	1 257.1 (439)	1 329.8 (457)	6.5	5.9	6.2	5.8

Source: United Nations, *Energy Statistics Yearbook*, various issues.

Note: The figures in parentheses show the per capita energy consumption. Central Asian republics = 129,949 thousand TOE and 3,221 KOE.

Figure I. Commercial energy consumption in industrialized and developing economies of the ESCAP region

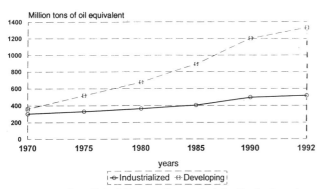

Source: Based on United Nations, *Energy Statistics Yearbook,* various issues.

Figure II. Commercial energy production and consumption in countries of the ESCAP region, 1970-1992

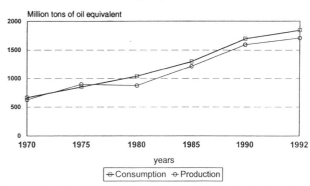

Source: Based on United Nations, *Energy Statistics Yearbook,* various issues.

growth in the developing economies of the region. The consumption in those economies has been rising continuously despite several energy crises during the 1970s. Figure I shows the evolution of energy consumption in the developing and industrialized economies of the ESCAP region. Whereas the consumption in the industrialized economies from 1970 to 1992 increased by only 95 per cent, that of the developing economies increased more than three and a half times. During the 1980s, the average annual growth rate was 5.9 per cent in the developing economies of the region, compared with 3.2 per cent in the developed economies of the region. The higher growth in the developing economies has been attributed to their low energy consumption level but their higher than world average economic growth rate, high population growth, rapid urbanization, high energy intensity owing to the stage of economic development, and less efficient energy use than state-of-the-art technology would allow. Because of the lack of time series data, total consumption in 1992 for the Central Asian republics is shown in the footnote of the table.

16.   As expected, in 1992 the region remained a net importer of energy, a status it acquired in the late 1970s. In 1992 it produced 1,708.9 mtoe while it consumed 1,847.6 mtoe. Even if the production and consumption figures of the Central Asian republics of 1992 are included in the analysis, the region still remains a net importer. Figure II shows the energy production and consumption trends in the region.

17.   The 1992 average per capita commercial energy consumption in the developing economies of the ESCAP region was only 457 kilograms of oil equivalent (kgoe); the per capita consumption of the Central Asian republics as a group was 3,221 kgoe, close to 3,557 kgoe consumption by the developed economies of the ESCAP region. The regional average, excluding the Central Asian republics, was 605 kgoe compared with the world average of 1,395 kgoe in 1992. The situation in individual countries varies over a wide range. As noted earlier, many developing economies depend on non-commercial forms of energy to meet the

bulk of their energy demand. Nevertheless, the overall energy consumption in the developing economies of the ESCAP region is low.

18.   The consumption pattern in terms of energy mixes of commercial primary energy in the ESCAP region is shown in table 5. Historically, solid fuels have had the largest share of consumption in the region; except in a few years of the 1970s they maintained a share of around 50 per cent in total commercial energy consumption. The share of liquid fuels declined significantly, from a high of 48.5 per cent in 1973 to 32.8 per cent in 1988. Since then, the growth in the liquid fuels share has been showing a clear sign of regaining a part of its lost share; it increased gradually to about 34 per cent in 1991 and further to 34.4 per cent in 1992. Gaseous fuel has established a strong presence in the regional energy mix by steadily increasing its share from only 3.4 per cent in 1970 to 9.2 per cent in 1992. Its growth rate has been particularly impressive (9-12 per cent) during the last two decades. The share of primary electricity increased slightly, from 2.5 per cent in 1970 to 3.5 per cent in 1985, but during the late 1980s it jumped to over 6 per cent primarily because of an increase of its share in Japan. As noted above, this share does not truly reflect the share of electricity in final energy consumption because fossil-fuel-generated electricity is not included in this category and there are no "conversion factors" to give it a comparable "weight" to fossil fuels.

19.   Tables 6 and 7 show the commercial energy consumption patterns in the developed and developing economies of the ESCAP region. China, as both the largest producer and the largest consumer of energy among the developing economies, influences the consumption pattern of these economies. Table 8 highlights this phenomenon for 1992 in respect of the consumption pattern of commercial primary energy in the developing economies of the ESCAP region with and without the two largest economies of the region, China and India.

20.   Figure III shows how the structure of energy consumption has changed over time in the ESCAP region.

**Table 5. Consumption pattern of commercial primary energy in the ESCAP region,
excluding Central Asian republics**
(Million tons of oil equivalent)

	1970	1973	1975	1980	1985	1990	1991	1992	Average annual growth rates (percentage)			
									1980/ 1970	1990/ 1980	1990/ 1970	1992/ 1991
Solids	319.0 (51.1)	360.1 (45.4)	392.0 (46.2)	487.9 (46.9)	690.4 (53.1)	860.1 (50.7)	897.1 (50.7)	922.6 (49.9)	4.3	5.8	5.1	2.9
Liquids	268.7 (43.0)	385.4 (48.5)	393.6 (46.3)	452.6 (43.5)	456.7 (35.1)	572.1 (33.7)	600.0 (33.9)	635.4 (34.4)	5.4	2.4	3.9	5.9
Gas	21.3 (3.4)	30.8 (3.9)	41.4 (4.9)	66.9 (6.4)	106.6 (8.2)	152.8 (9.0)	153.5 (8.7)	170.5 (9.2)	12.0	8.8	10.3	11.1
Electricity	15.7 (2.5)	17.8 (2.2)	22.4 (2.6)	31.9 (3.1)	45.8 (3.5)	113.0 (6.7)	118.2 (6.7)	119.0 (6.4)	7.4	13.5	10.4	0.7
Total	624.7 (100)	794.0 (100)	849.4 (100)	1 039.4 (100)	1 299.6 (100)	1 698.0 (100)	1 768.9 (100)	1 847.6 (100)	5.2	5.0	5.1	4.5

Source: United Nations, *Energy Statistics Yearbook,* various issues.

Note: The figures in parentheses show the share as the percentage of the total.

Central Asian republics figures in 1992: total 129,949; solids 55,170; liquids 8,994; gas 64,028; and electricity 1,757 thousand TOE.

Table 6. Consumption pattern of commercial primary energy in developed countries of the ESCAP region
(Million tons of oil equivalent)

	1970	1973	1975	1980	1985	1990	1991	1992	Average annual growth rates (percentage)			
									1980/ 1970	1990/ 1980	1990/ 1970	1992/ 1991
Solids	81.9 (27.0)	74.2 (22.2)	75.1 (22.8)	83.5 (23.0)	109.1 (26.9)	119.5 (24.1)	124.1 (24.2)	124.8 (24.1)	0.5	3.7	2.7	0.6
Liquids	207.5 (68.4)	242.7 (72.5)	230.1 (69.7)	230.2 (63.4)	216.2 (53.4)	241.4 (48.6)	244.6 (47.8)	247.2 (47.2)	2.9	0.5	1.7	1.1
Gas	4.5 (1.5)	8.4 (2.5)	12.5 (3.8)	31.7 (8.7)	55.4 (13.7)	68.8 (13.9)	71.8 (14.0)	73.4 (14.2)	20.6	8.1	14.2	2.3
Electricity	9.5 (3.1)	9.2 (2.8)	12.2 (3.7)	17.8 (4.9)	24.4 (6.0)	67.1 (13.5)	71.4 (13.9)	72.4 (14.0)	7.0	14.2	10.6	1.4
Total	303.4 (100)	334.5 (100)	329.9 (100)	363.2 (100)	405.1 (100)	496.8 (100)	511.8 (100)	517.8 (100)	3.2	3.2	3.2	1.2

Source: United Nations, *Energy Statistics Yearbook,* various issues.

Note: The figures in parentheses show the share as the percentage of the total.

Table 7. Consumption pattern of commercial primary energy in developing countries
of the ESCAP region, excluding Central Asian republics
(Million tons of oil equivalent)

| | 1970 | 1973 | 1975 | 1980 | 1985 | 1990 | 1991 | 1992 | Average annual growth rates (percentage) | | | |
									1980/ 1970	1990/ 1980	1990/ 1970	1992/ 1991
Solids	239.9 (66.6)	285.9 (62.2)	316.9 (61.0)	404.4 (59.8)	581.3 (65.0)	740.6 (61.2)	773.0 (61.5)	797.8 (60.0)	5.4	6.2	5.8	3.2
Liquids	96.3 (26.7)	142.7 (31.1)	163.5 (31.5)	222.4 (32.9)	240.5 (26.9)	330.7 (27.5)	355.4 (28.3)	388.1 (29.2)	8.7	4.1	6.4	9.2
Gas	17.4 (4.8)	22.4 (4.9)	28.9 (5.6)	35.2 (5.2)	51.2 (5.7)	84.0 (7.0)	81.8 (6.5)	97.1 (7.3)	7.6	9.4	8.5	18.8
Electricity	6.8 (1.9)	8.5 (1.9)	10.1 (2.0)	14.1 (2.1)	21.4 (2.4)	46.0 (3.8)	46.9 (3.7)	46.7 (3.5)	7.8	12.6	10.2	(0.4)
Total	360.5 (100)	459.5 (100)	519.5 (100)	676.2 (100)	894.5 (100)	1 201.2 (100)	1 257.1 (100)	1 329.8 (100)	6.5	5.9	6.2	5.8

Source: United Nations, *Energy Statistics Yearbook,* various issues.

Note: The figures in parentheses show the share as the percentage of the total.

Central Asian republics figures in 1992: total 129,949; solids 55,170; liquids 8,994; gas 64,028; and electricity 1,757 thousand TOE.

Table 8. Consumption pattern of commercial primary energy in developing economies, 1992
(with and without Central Asian republics, India and China)
(Thousand tons of oil equivalent)

	China	India	Central Asian republics	ESCAP developing countries total	ESCAP developing countries total excluding CARs	Developing economies of the ESCAP region, excluding China, India and the Central Asian repubics
Solids	544 535 (80.0)	143 931 (69.7)	55 170 (42.5)	852 975	797 805 (60.0)	109 339 (24.7)
Liquids	109 826 (16.1)	52 755 (25.6)	8 994 (6.9)	397 134	388 140 (29.2)	225 559 (51.0)
Gas	14 682 (2.2)	1 886 (0.9)	64 028 (49.3)	161 177	97 149 (7.3)	80 581 (18.2)
Electricity	11 819 (1.7)	7 886 (3.8)	1 757 (1.4)	48 425	46 668 (3.5)	26 963 (6.1)
Total	680 862 (100.0)	206 458 (100.0)	129 949 (100.0)	1 459 711	1 329 762 (100.0)	442 442 (100.0)

Source: United Nations, *Energy Statistics Yearbook*, 1992.

Note: The figures in parentheses show the share as the percentage of total.

Figure III. Energy consumption structure by type of fuels in the ESCAP region

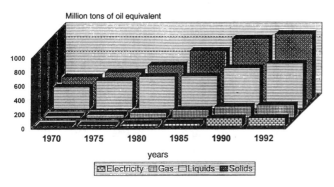

Source: Based on United Nations, *Energy Statistics Yearbook,* various issues.

Figure IV. Energy consumption by type of fuels in industrialized countries of the ESCAP region

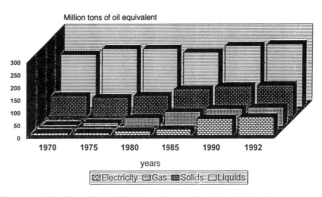

Source: Based on United Nations, *Energy Statistics Yearbook,* various issues.

Figure V. Energy consumption by type of fuels in developing countries of the ESCAP region

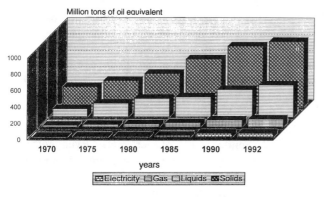

Source: Based on United Nations, *Energy Statistics Yearbook,* various issues.

Figure VI. Energy consumption by type of fuels in developing economies of the ESCAP region, excluding China and India

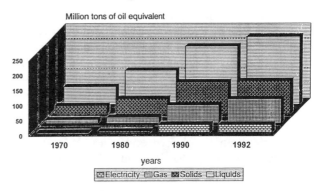

Source: Based on United Nations, *Energy Statistics Yearbook,* various issues.

21.   As of 1992, although solids appear to be the dominant fuel (60 per cent) for the developing economies, when China is excluded the share of solids drops to 39 per cent and the share of liquids jumps to 42.9 per cent from 29.2 per cent. If India is also excluded from the other developing economies, the share of solids drops further to 24.7 per cent and that of liquids rises to almost 51 per cent.

22.   Figures IV, V and VI highlight the consumption patterns in the industrialized, developing economies and developing economies without China and India.

2. Dominance of fossil fuels

23.   A further analysis of consumption patterns reveals that commercial energy consumption in the world, including the ESCAP region, is dominated by fossil fuels. This situation is particularly significant in relation to environmental degradation. Table 5 and figure III show that, although in the ESCAP region the share of fossil fuels use has declined slightly from 97.5 per cent in 1970 to 93.6 per cent in 1992 because of the increased use of primary

electricity (nuclear, hydropower and geothermal), it remains dominant and this trend will not change much in the foreseeable future. This is also because of a statistical bias in reporting the weight of primary electricity in consumption. However, the share of electricity (both primary and secondary) in the final commercial energy consumption of Asian developing economies is quite significant; in 1990, the share ranged from 27.4 to 39.8 per cent in various subregions of Asia.[1]

3. Energy intensity

24.   Intensity is a measure to show how much energy is used in overall economic development for example, tons of oil equivalent per US$ 1,000 of GDP. Figure VII shows the evolution of energy intensity in various groups of economies in the world. The world's aggregate energy intensity in all groups, except developing economies, has been decreasing steadily over the last few decades and is expected to decrease

---

[1]   Asian Development Bank, *Energy Indicators of Developing Member Counries of Asian Development Bank*, July 1992.

Figure VII. Energy Intensity

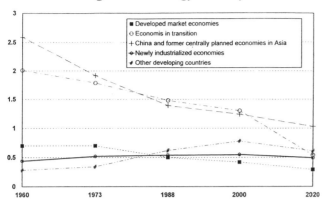

Source: "Energy and sustainable development: issues concerning overall energy development with particular emphasis on developing countries" (E/C.13/1994/2), p. 11 table 3.

Notes: Energy intensity is measured in metric tons of coal equivalent per thousand United States dollars of GDP, in 1980 United States dollars and at 1980 exchange rates, historical and projected under high growth scenario, by region.

further in the coming decades. However, the situation in developing countries (other than China and other centrally planned economies in Asia) is understandably different as they need increasing amounts of energy to fuel the growth of their developing economies. Although there are some elements of inefficiency in energy use in these economies, structural changes from being low-energy-intensive to being high-energy-intensive economies is the main reason for their (except the centrally planned economies in Asia) energy intensity rising until perhaps beyond 2000, when it is likely to level off. The newly industrializing economies are exhibiting a similar pattern, but at a much lower level of intensity.

4. Future perspective

25. As observed in the historical trend of energy consumption, the continuing dominance of fossil fuels in the commercial energy mix is here to stay. It is widely expected that the historical trend observed during the 1980s will continue in the future, though it is likely that the Asian and Pacific economies will diversify their energy mix and thereby become less dependent on oil. However, given recent relatively low oil prices, this interfuel change may slow down, or even reverse, in the short term. This is already apparent from the increasing liquid fuels share in the energy mix following the oil price crash in 1986. Although this brings short-term benefits to importing countries, in the long run, when oil price rises sharply, there may be a greater risk of an adverse impact on the economy.

26. Natural gas will be a major component of the energy mix owing, probably, to its recognition as an environmentally friendly fuel, and more so owing to its occurrence in many Asian and Pacific economies. It is also expected that, despite its poor image as a polluting fuel, coal will remain a dominant

fuel in the regional energy mix, in particular in the power sector and other energy-intensive industries such as steel mills and cement plants. Technological advances such as integrated gasification combined cycle and fluidized bed combustion will mitigate some of the harmful environmental impacts of coal development and utilization. Other conventional technologies are also undergoing changes towards pollution control.

27. Two projections, which were made sometime ago but which appear to be representative of the current situation, are analysed here to examine future energy perspectives: a recent report of the Secretary-General[2], which contains the likely fossil fuel energy consumption levels in the years 2000 and 2020; and a forecast by the ESCAP secretariat for the Asian and Pacific region.

(a)   Report of the Secretary-General

28. Table 9 shows the level of fossil fuel consumption for different years for various regions of the world under an optimistic (high economic growth with improvements in energy efficiency) scenario. By 2020, the fossil fuel consumption in developing countries will surpass by almost 40 per cent that of the developed market economies. According to the projection, by 2020, world fossil fuel consumption will rise to 13,754 mtoe, representing an annual average growth rate of 2.23 per cent. The corresponding figures for developing countries are 6,562.7 mtoe and 4.21 per cent respectively, while those of developed countries are 4,742.2 mtoe and 1.04 per cent. Even with this phenomenal growth in energy consumption in developing economies, the per capita consumption will increase only slightly from 974.4 to 1,002.8 kgoe. This is less than a third of the 1990 level of per capita consumption of 3,786.6 kgoe in developed countries.

(b)   ESCAP energy scenarios

29. Table 10 is the result of ESCAP work on the projection of the likely energy demand of the members and associate members of the ESCAP region.

30. In the business-as-usual scenario, the annual growth rate of regional commercial energy consumption is projected to be 4.4 per cent for the period 1990-2000 and 4.3 per cent for the period 2000-2010. In the energy efficiency scenario, the annual growth rate is 4 per cent for the period 1990-2000 and 4.1 per cent for the period 2000-2010; a slightly lower (3.9 per cent) growth is projected for the conservation with higher investment and fuel-switching scenario.

31. When compared with the historical annual growth rate of 6.2 per cent in commercial energy consumption by

---

[2]   "Energy and sustainable development: issues concerning overall energy development, with particular emphasis on developing countries" (E/C.13/ 1994/2).

Table 9. Estimates of GDP and fossil fuel consumption, 1990 and 2020

| | 1990 | | | | 2020 | | | | Growth rate in fossil fuel consumption 1990-2020 (percentage) |
| | GDP | | Fossil fuel consumption | | GDP | | Fossil fuel consumption | | |
	Total	Per capita	Total	Per capita	Total	Per capita	Total	Per capita	
World	22 325.6	4 230.2	6 893.5	1 306.1	56 812.9	7 046.4	13 754.1	1 705.9	2.23
Developed market economies	16 626.8	18 295.4	3 440.6	3 786.0	38 536.1	36 771.1	4 742.2	4 524.9	1.04
Economies in transition	1 835.8	4 538.4	1 670.6	4 129.9	3 786.7	8 051.7	2 449.2	5 207.8	1.23
Developing countries	3 862.9	974.4	1 782.3	449.5	14 490.2	2 214.1	6 562.7	1 002.8	4.21
Newly industrializing countries	1 550.8	2 526.1	430.9	702.0	6 244.3	6 832.5	1 484.1	1 623.9	4.00
Other developing countries	1 958.7	894.5	663.0	302.8	6 566.8	1 590.7	2 475.7	599.7	4.26
Centrally planned Asia	353.4	304.5	688.4	593.0	1 679.1	1 117.1	2 602.9	1 732.6	4.30

Source: "Energy and sustainable development: issues concerning overall energy development with particular emphasis on developing countries" (E/C. 13/1994/2), p. 12, table 4.

Notes: GDP in billions of constant 1990 United States dollars.

GDP per capita in constant 1990 United States dollars.

Energy in million tons of oil equivalent.

Energy per capita in kilograms of oil equivalent.

Table 10. Primary commercial energy consumption and scenarios S1, S2 and S3 to the year 2010
(Thousand tons of oil equivalent and percentages)

| Subregions of Asia and the Pacific | Consumption | | Projections | | | | | Average annual growth rate (percentage) | | | | |
	1980	1990	2000:S2	2000:S1	2010:S3	2010:S2	2010:S1	1990-00:S2	1990-00:S1	2000-10:S3	2000-10:S2	2000-10:S1
East and North-East Asia	489 858	830 003	1 283 760	1 321 440	1 968 920	2 003 850	2 098 520	4.5	4.8	4.4	4.6	4.7
South-East Asia	70 383	126 651	227 810	237 320	395 340	406 900	433 980	6.0	6.5	5.7	6.0	6.2
South and West Asia	143 149	286 325	498 250	521 800	820 030	847 000	916 770	5.7	6.2	5.1	5.4	5.8
Central Asia		95 196	118 100	130 200	139 700	146 700	178 300	2.2	3.2	1.7	2.2	3.2
Pacific	2 704	3 432	4 200	4 400	5 100	5 400	5 900	2.0	2.5	2.0	2.5	3.0
Total Asia and the Pacific												
Developing economies	706 094	1 341 607	2 132 120	2 215 160	3 329 090	3 409 850	3 633 470	4.7	5.1	4.6	4.8	5.1
Industrialized economies	424 900	530 400	644 400	655 000	724 300	731 400	750 900	2.0	2.1	1.2	1.3	1.4
Grand total, Asia and the Pacific	1 130 994	1 872 007	2 776 520	2 870 160	4 053 390	4 141 250	4 384 370	4.0	4.4	3.9	4.1	4.3

Source: ESCAP secretariat, based on United Nations, *Energy Statisitcs Yearbook,* World Tables of the World and other sources.

Notes: Central Asian energy consumption is for 1990; if represents only oil and gas consumption for five countries (excluding Azerbaijan).

Scenarios: S1: Business as usual scenario assuming past trends continue.

S2: Conservation scenario without significant investment.

S3: Conservation with higher level of investment and fuel switching.

developing economies of the ESCAP region during the 1980s, the projected growth rates of commercial energy of 4.6 to 5.1 per cent for these economies are considered somewhat conservative. However, lower economic growth rates and expected energy conservation efforts in developing countries may justify lower energy demand growth over the next two decades. Although these growth rates are somewhat higher than the global fossil fuel energy projections of 4.2 per cent for the period 1990-2020 (see table 10) for developing countries, these appear reasonable given the fact that the Asian and Pacific region is the most dynamic growth region of the world. The recently concluded Uruguay Round of multilateral trade negotiations and the new World Trade Organization will also favour higher energy use in Asia.

32. As discussed earlier in the report, similar or even higher growth is expected in electricity demand. In fact, the current electricity supply situation in some countries (Indonesia, especially Java, the Philippines and Thailand) is vulnerable to interruptions because of the lack of reserve capacity.

33. Figure VIII shows the likely energy mix of developing economies of ESCAP in 2010 based on the above projection.

Figure VIII. ESCAP energy projection, 2010: scenarios S1, S2 and S3

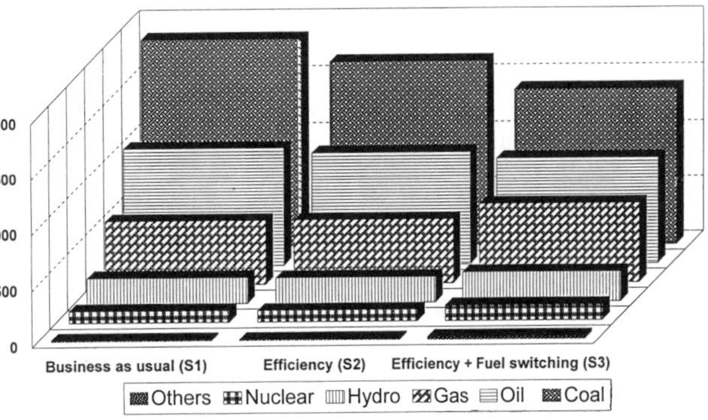

Source: Based on United Nations, *Energy Statistics Yearbook*, various issues.

E. ENERGY ISSUES AND POLICIES

34. How to meet high energy demand growth in the region, particularly in developing economies, is the core issue of energy development and management. Among other issues centred around that core issue is the concern over the environmental degradation caused by energy development and use, which is creating tremendous pressure on the environment. This added constraint has also aggravated the economics of energy owing to additional costs. The issue is not only how to meet the aggregate demand but also how to do it with minimum adverse impact on the environment. Financing energy infrastructure remains a related major issue. Energy pricing is a sensitive and crucial area which also needs to be addressed in the proper context to reflect "true energy costs", whatever they are. All these issues affect the resiliency of an economy in one way or another, particularly when there are sudden changes in one or more of the variables or uncertainties. In the following paragraphs these issues are analysed in more detail, together with relevant policy aspects.

1. Environmental costs

35. Owing to rapid growth in energy consumption in developing economies, the environmental impacts associated with energy have been rising and will almost certainly rise further in the future. From the current low level of pollutant emissions in absolute terms, the pollution levels in developing economies are forecast to increase several times in the coming decades. A projection (see table 11) of air emissions indicates that the emissions of carbon, sulphur oxides and nitrogen in developing countries will surpass those of developed countries by 50 to over 100 per cent, though on a per capita basis the figure will still remain at a lower level (see table 12). Although there are some doubts about these figures and their inherent assumptions about the pattern of energy consumption, there is no doubt that there will be a substantial increase in pollution levels and most of the future incremental emissions will be generated in developing economies. Thus, it is prudent for developing countries to pay greater attention to environmental issues so that they may follow a development path that is more sustainable.

36. Sound energy policy and planning should take into account the cost of health and environmental damage as components of the full social costs of energy supply. The cost of environmental damage to humans, which may be borne immediately or at some point in the future, is manifested principally in losses in health, productivity and amenity.[3] All health and other environmental impacts affect the society. It is, therefore, essential to make an assessment of the associated costs as far as practicable and try to internalize them within the energy costs. When these costs are not internalized, the society as a whole has to bear them in the future, if not today, in other ways.

37. In some developing countries, with the introduction and enforcement of environmental standards, a part of the environmental cost is now internalized in the utilities (mainly in the electric power sector) cost, but it is difficult to say whether these costs are passed on to the consumers as the price is generally controlled by the Government.

38. On global and regional emission issues, such as CO_2 and acid rain, a number of initiatives have been undertaken to make in-depth study of the issues together with their appropriate policy responses in Asia. These projects include:

---

[3] World Bank, *World Development Report 1992, Development and the Environment* (New York, Oxford University Press, 1992).

Table 11. Air emissions, 1990 and 2020

	1990			2020		
	Carbon[a]	Sulphur oxides[b]	Nitrogen[c]	Carbon[a]	Sulphur oxides[b]	Nitrogen[c]
Developed market economies	2 790	45	35	3 800	45	43
Economies in transition and Commonwealth of Independent States	1 320	45	21	1 900	37	29
Developing countries	1 530	37	22	5 550	99	83
World	5 640	127	78	11 250	181	154

Source: "Energy and sustainable development: issues concerning overall energy development with particular emphasis on developing countries" (E/C. 13/1994/2).

[a] Carbon from fossil fuels (millions of metric tons).

[b] Sulphur oxides (millions of metric tons of sulphur dioxide equivalent).

[c] Millions of metric tons of nitrogen dioxide equivalent.

Table 12. Per capita air emissions, 1990 and 2020

	1990			2020		
	Carbon[a]	Sulphur oxides[b]	Nitrogen[c]	Carbon[a]	Sulphur oxides[b]	Nitrogen[c]
Developed market economies	3.07	0.05	0.04	3.63	0.04	0.04
Economies in transition and Commonwealth of Independent States	3.26	0.11	0.05	4.04	0.08	0.06
Developing countries	0.39	0.01	0.01	0.85	0.02	0.01
World	1.07	0.02	0.01	1.4	0.02	0.02

Source: "Energy and sustainable development: issues concerning overall energy development with particular emphasis on developing countries" (E/C. 13/1994/2).

Note: Calculations based on table 11.

[a] Carbon from fossil fuels (tons per capita).

[b] Sulphur oxides (tons of sulphur dioxide equivalent per capita).

[c] Tons of nitrogen dioxide equivalent per capita.

(a) the GEF/UNDP Asia Least-Cost Greenhouse Gas Abatement Strategy, a part of which (the country study for the Democratic People's Republic of Korea) is being implemented by ESCAP in collaboration with the Asian Development Bank; (b) the North-East Asian Regional Environment Programme; and (c) Acid Rain and Emissions Reduction in Asia (World Bank/ADB).

39.   Integrated least-cost planning approaches that include both supply and demand (conservation and efficiency) side options should be used as the basis for policy formulation and decision-making. A useful principle commonly recommended is the user-pays-principle.

2. Energy demand and supply balance

(a)   Demand management

40.   As discussed earlier in the chapter, the primary concern of the developing economies is how to balance the ever-growing energy demand with supply to fuel their high economic growth. Under a normal scenario, there are only two broad ways: either to increase the supply and adjust or reduce the demand through other means. The demand/supply balance is greatly disturbed under the surprise scenario, such as supply disruption or price shock. The question is how best an economy is prepared to cope with that kind of a situation. Crises in the past have shown that many economies suffered a setback in economic growth to varying degrees. Figure IX, drawn from energy consumption before and after the two oil shocks of the 1970s, shows how the demand pattern behaved over the period, particularly as a result of the oil shocks. It is interesting to observe that, although the immediate impact on energy consumption was noticeable in industrialized economies, the impact on developing economies was less prominent and delayed. Although this appears somewhat surprising, it makes sense when viewed from a different angle. Although the impact has been felt elsewhere, such as, in shocking import bills with rising balance of payments, developing countries had very little choice but to cut back immediately on their energy consumption, which in most cases were already at a very

Figure IX. Energy demand pattern including the period of oil shocks

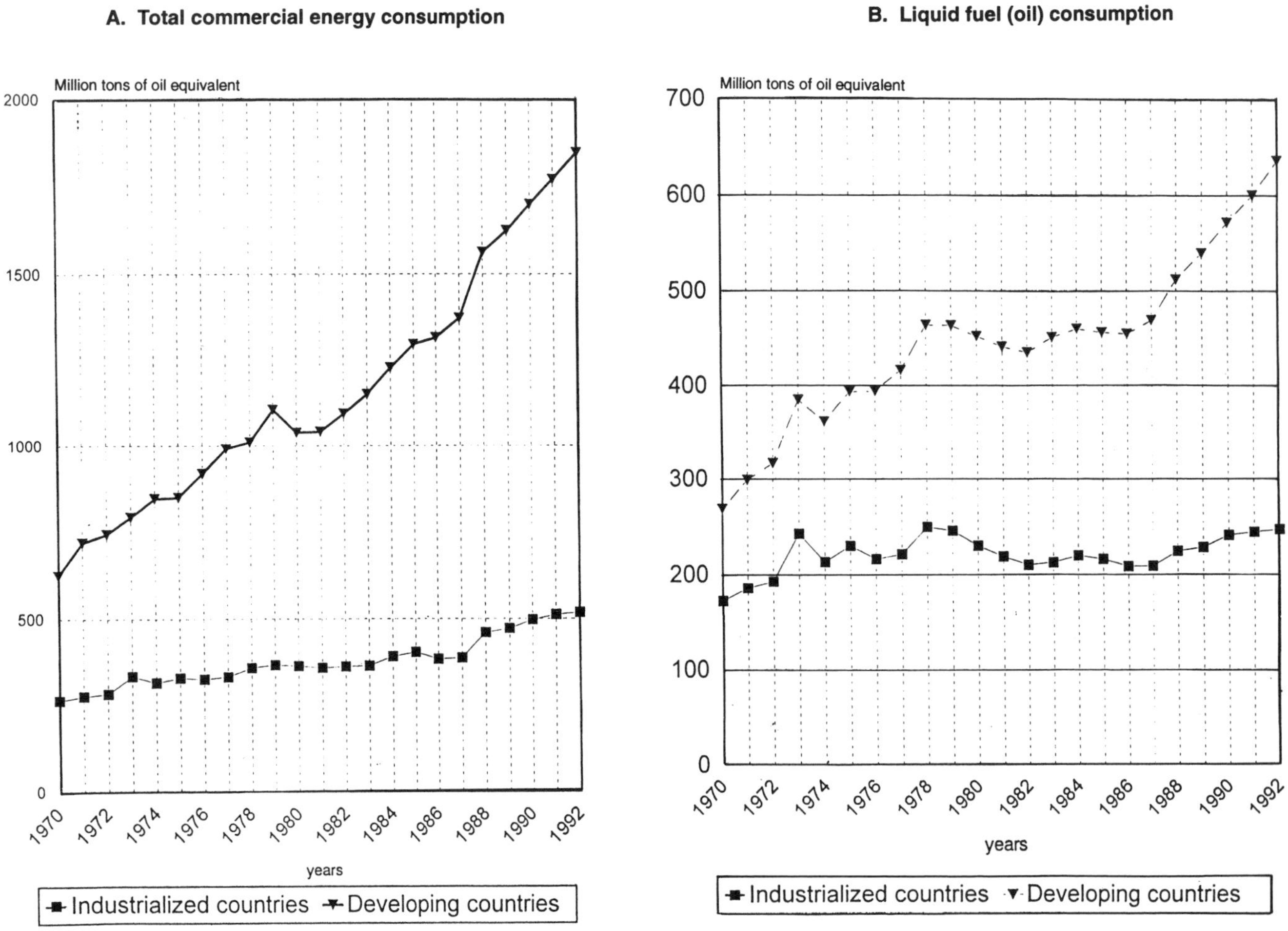

A. Total commercial energy consumption

B. Liquid fuel (oil) consumption

Source: Based on United Nations, *Energy Statistics Yearbook*, various issues.

Source: Based on United Nations, *Energy Statistics Yearbook*, various issues.

low level. Whereas in industrialized countries, energy conservation could immediately be realized.

41. Demand side management is gradually being recognized as a resource in developing countries. Managing demand is a complex process whereby success is highly dependent on the consumers' acceptance. Given the relatively low energy prices, many enterprises in which energy represents only a small fraction of total output costs are reluctant to make any changes in their consumption pattern. However, the energy conservation and efficiency improvement potential is quite large in most cases. This is also an area which can play a major role in reducing environmental pollution, including greenhouse gas emissions.

42. While in the medium term the developing economies are likely to continue to increase their energy intensity (see figure VII), as the structure of their economy changes, they may achieve their development objectives with lesser amounts of energy per unit output than the developed economies used during the initial stages of their development. This "leap-frogging" is possible as a result of technological advances that have led to better energy efficiency in both

end-use equipment and energy production processes, as well as characteristics of the emerging "information society".

43. In respect of policy, it is advisable to use both pricing and non-pricing tools in influencing consumers to accept demand management as a means to conserve energy. Pricing policy that reflects the true cost of energy is critical as it gives the right signals to consumers to adapt to market forces. Many countries have not yet succeeded in establishing an appropriate pricing level. On the other hand, non-pricing measures such as regulations and standards can supplement pricing measures, particularly in cases where responses to prices are inelastic.

(b)   Supply options

44. With increasing environmental concerns, choices of energy resources to provide useful energy have become a complex issue. Although, in most cases, the decision still lies with the Government, enhancing environmental awareness is playing an increasing role in influencing the Government's decision. For example, public opinion against nuclear power, hydropower, coal power plants or even

geothermal power development often forces decision makers to delay or even cancel some projects. Whereas a large part of the decisions is based on the availability of resources within national boundaries, many countries are now opting to obtain their energy supplies from across their borders. This trend is not necessarily detrimental; if managed properly, it could lead to the optimization of the uses of resources in a greater regional or subregional context with higher overall efficiency. However, the resiliency of an economy depends on the availability of indigenous energy resources. Resource-poor countries may diversify the sourcing of supplies and perhaps get into an emergency sharing arrangement or stock piling as adopted by the countries of the Organisation for Economic Cooperation and Development.

45. Natural gas, a less polluting fuel than other fossil fuels, is becoming more popular in countries where there are enough reserves. Although trade takes place, either through gas pipelines or as liquified natural gas, international trade in gas is still limited owing to high infrastructure costs and sometimes low gas prices. Regional and subregional cooperation in this aspect is quite possible. There are some indications of interest in pipeline projects in South-East Asia, South-West Asia, East Asia and Central Asia.

46. Another significant potential for cooperation exists in the area of electricity trade and exchange. Neighbouring countries in some of the above-mentioned regions are in a unique situation to develop resources in a subregional context for their common benefit. Examples are hydropower, oil and gas exploitation, coal with "mine-mouth power generation" and integrating electricity grids for trading and sharing electrical energy. With the changing political and economic atmosphere, this option appears to be closer to reality in the region or subregions than at any time before.

47. Energy supply to rural areas is a big issue in itself. Some of the developing economies in the region depend heavily on traditional forms of energy for meeting as much as 70-90 per cent of their total energy requirement. Biomass accounts for the largest part of the total rural energy requirement. Increasing demand for this kind of fuel owing to high population pressure and to the clearing of wood lots for agriculture has created a critical situation in rural areas in terms of both energy shortage and environmental degradation (desertification). An appropriate rural energy policy for rural areas needs special attention by the policy makers.

3. Energy conservation and efficiency

48. Although over the last few years energy supply and international energy prices have remained favourable, energy conservation and efficiency are still important and attractive options for managing energy demand. There are at least two good reasons for this: (a) these options meets the environmental objective from all angles and (b) they could,

in most cases, be cost-effective and more attractive than investing in energy supply. Moreover, they benefit both the energy supply industry and the consumers. One should not, however, overlook their limitations, particularly when energy demand growth is phenomenal.

4. Infrastructure

49. Lack of adequate infrastructure in the energy sector is a big concern of developing economies. In many instances, even if energy resources are available in a country, owing to inadequate infrastructure in the upstream as well as downstream energy production-supply process, energy demand often cannot be met. This, in most cases, results in unreliable energy supply in the country.

50. A recent study by ESCAP[4] looked at, among other infrastructure, the electric power sector of developing economies of the Asian and Pacific region. It estimated that, during the period 1990-2000, the required power-generating capacity would be in the range of 679-735 gigawatts (GW) to meet an estimated energy demand of 2,580-2,800 TWh. Given no other constraints, (such as the capability to build and manage the mega projects and absorption capacity), the financing needed would be about US$ 576-674 billion for the supply of electric power infrastructure in the developing economies of the ESCAP region between 1990 and 2000, which is a considerable burden for Governments.

51. One of the recent trends observed in infrastructure development is the opening of many public sectors, including the power supply industry of developing countries, to private sector participation. One of the main reasons for this is to be able to mobilize additional financial resources. Private sector investors have their own objectives, including the financial objective of an adequate rate of return on their investment. As with investment in any other business, private sector investors will assess the risk of the investment and compare it with the opportunity costs of their capital. If the investment is riskier than other alternatives, a higher return, including a risk premium, will be expected. Thus, it appears that only utilities with a good operating record and financial health will be able to attract private sector participation. Moreover, the private sector is expected to become involved gradually and will not be able to meet the huge financing demand. Nevertheless, private sector participation can become a significant supplementary source of funding. The participation of the private sector can be expected in such projects as: (a) cogeneration; (b) captive generation; (c) build-operate-transfer and build-own-operate; (d) privatization of existing utilities; and (e) other arrangements. Investment in environment-related technologies may facilitate both technology transfer and capital flow.

---

4   ESCAP, *Infrastructure Development as Key to Economic Growth and Regional Cooperation* (ST/ESCAP/1364), 1994.

5. Pricing and financing

52.   In discussing energy pricing, reference is made to international as well as domestic energy prices, which are closely related.   Moreover, prices of energy are largely influenced by international oil prices. Following the two energy crises of 1973/74 and 1979/80, there were massive and sudden increases in energy prices, which remained high until the oil price collapse in 1986. Since then, oil prices have stabilized in the range of US$ 15-18 per barrel.

53.   Why is oil price an issue? Apart from its shocking effects for a prolonged period in the past which had a tremendous economic and financial impact on the oil-importing countries, market volatility also affects both energy producers and consumers. While experience in forecasting oil prices with accuracy has not been good in the past, the concern now is about the stability of the maket rather than the higher price. When the maket stability is disturbed, the economic development suffers, although the degree of impact would depend on the resiliency level of an individual economy. Past experience shows that, in many developing economies, energy consumption did not come down to the extent expected with high energy prices as there may not be any room for any significant reduction in consumption.

54.   The next question that arises is whether international oil prices affect the domestic energy market proportionately. They do not necessarily do so, and therein lies the problem which needs careful attention by policy makers. More often than not, the domestic market price is distorted by taxes and other interventions both across the market and among fuels in the form of subsidies and cross-subsidies. This, in turn, affects the tariff policy and consequently the financial health of the utility and the Government. The World Bank, in its *World Development Report 1992*, estimated that subsidies for energy, for example, cost the Governments of developing countries (including the former Soviet Union and Eastern Europe) more than US$ 230 billion a year, more than four times the total volume of official development assistance. The Report further noted that the removal of all energy subsidies, including those on coal in industrialized countries, would not only produce large gains in efficiency and fiscal balances but also would sharply reduce local pollution and cut worldwide carbon emissions from energy use by 10 per cent (with some possible welfare losses to the poor).

55.   The next issue concerns financing energy infrastructure.   In the Asian and Pacific developing economies, in the power sector alone, US$ 576-674 billion is needed over the period 1990-2000 for infrastructure development; this estimate does not include the cost of mitigating environmental impacts. The problem is to find a source of this huge amount of money.

56.   A World Bank estimate[5] indicates that the developing countries' additional environmental abatement costs could be in the range of US$ 7 billion in 2000 for coal-fired power stations alone; as a percentage of generation costs this could range from less than 1 per cent to as high as 50 per cent of generation costs,[6] depending on the technology chosen and the degree of abatement required. As policies to mitigate the effects on the environment of energy production and consumption, the same World Bank report suggested taking two complementary approaches: (a) using economic instruments and institutional reforms to encourage more efficient use of energy and (b) either developing technologies that reduce the polluting effects of conventional fuels or using fewer polluting substitutes.

F. ENVIRONMENTAL POLICY AND CONSTRAINTS IN ENERGY POLICY, PLANNING AND MANAGEMENT

57.   To address environmental problems holistically, a fundamental change is necessary in development policy and planning. The environment should not be treated as an external isolated problem, but instead must be integrated and factored into the decision-making processes. All economic activities, including energy development and use, involve environmental degradation through resource depletion, transformation or utilization. One pressing problem is associated with resources such as air and water which are regenerative but undervalued and therefore misused, leading to future scarcity. Although these resources are renewable; they have a finite capacity to assimilate emissions and wastes generated from economic activities. Therefore, a trade-off is necessary to ensure development that lasts. Since energy is at the core of development, as a large industry in itself and as a producer of services required for economic development, its adequate and sustained supply is critical. Therefore, to minimize the unavoidable negative effects of energy on the environment, proper policy and planning are needed.

1. The energy-environment interface

58.   Energy as a natural resource is closely intertwined with the environment. There are a number of areas where the effects of energy on the environment are strong and visible. Environmental impacts are generally grouped in three categories, local, regional and global. These impacts range from localized air pollution to transboundary or global air pollution, water and land pollution and degradation, waste disposal, and hazardous and radioactive pollutants. The strong cause and effect relationship between energy and the environment makes the energy sector more likely to be perceived as a polluter than any other development sector contributing to environmental degradation. The situation is likely to worsen as energy consumption rises further, particularly in developing economies. By 2020, the share of pollution from developing economies will surpass that of

---

5   World Bank, op. cit., p. 174, table 9.1.

6   Ibid., p. 119, box table 6.1.

developed economies, and although increasingly environmental issues are taken more seriously by both the developed and the developing economies, there is a clear difference in perception and priorities. Whereas local pollution, such as oxides of sulphur and nitrogen, smog, particulates emission, waste disposal, water pollution, deforestation and land degradation, are of immediate concern to developing countries, global issues such as greenhouse gas emissions and ozone layer depletion seem to be the priority in developed economies.

59. Pearson[7], in his analysis, has discussed three types of policy responses: (a) the reactive approach (adapt only when the impact arises); (b) proactive measures (adapt before full impacts materialize); and (c) preventive measures. The key question is to what extent some of these measures should be implemented. The situation will be different in different countries. Therefore, each country should study carefully the implications of the energy chain on its own environment and take appropriate steps to meet an achievable standard, based on its situation. Towards this objective good knowledge of the overall energy system supported by a reliable database is critical. Capacity-building through human resources development to undertake this task over a long period is needed.

60. Under the United Nations Framework Convention on Climate Change, all Parties are required to "develop, periodically update, publish and make available to the Conference of the Parties, in accordance with Article 12, national inventories of anthropogenic emissions by sources and removals by sinks of all greenhouse gases not controlled by the Montreal Protocol". According to the first Conference of the Parties, held from 28 March to 7 April 1995, 15 communications were received in the first reporting from the Parties and most developed countries are required to submit their second national communications by 15 April 1997. The report of the above Convention, States that 116 countries and the European Union were the Parties. Developing countries who are signatories of the Convention are also expected to make an effort to prepare their reports voluntarily by the above deadline.

61. Options to reduce environmental impacts related to energy can be categorized broadly into three main groups: (a) supply options, including fuel switching; (b) energy conservation and efficiency options; and (c) technology options. To make energy development sustainable, all options as appropriate are to be included in the energy-environment policy and planning process.

---

7 P.J.G. Pearson, "Environmental impacts of electricity generated by developing countries: issues, priorities and carbon dioxide emissions", in *IEE Proceedings-A*, vol. 140, No. 1, January 1993.

2. Options to mitigate environmental impacts

(a) Supply options

62. Supply options included the optimization of the use of existing supplies and switching to sources of energy that produce less pollution per unit of useful energy delivered. Subject to the availability or access to alternative sources of energy, environmental considerations do induce fuel substitution in favour of less polluting fuels, particularly for new energy projects. For example, in several countries, higher priority is given to more environmentally benign fuels such as natural gas than to coal and oil. In some cases, with proper environmental protection measures, hydropower has prospects for further development, although there is strong public opposition in many countries. Small hydropower, on the other hand, has little negative impacts but its potential as a major contributor to the energy mix is rather limited, as is the potential of other new and renewable forms of energy such as solar and wind, to penetrate the energy market in the near future. In the very long-term perspective, however, with technological breakthroughs that could reduce energy production costs drastically, some of these resources may become significant options. Because of its perceived potential environmental risk and high front-end costs, nuclear energy, though an otherwise environmentally benign fuel, is not likely to play a major role, particularly in developing countries that do not have nuclear fuel.

63. Although fuel switching from high carbon intensive to low carbon intensive fuels is a general policy in a number of countries for economic and environmental reasons, coal, which contains a high amount of pollutants, is likely to remain a major source of energy in the commercial energy mix. Therefore, abating environmental pollution through clean fuel technology and efficiency improvement is indispensable.

(b) Energy conservation and efficiency options

64. Energy conservation and efficiency improvements in energy production and in end use are increasingly recognized as viable options for both economic reasons and environmental benefits. In a number of cases, together with clean energy technology measures, they are the only options currently available for effectively reducing certain types of pollutants, such as energy-related greenhouse gas emissions (CO_2), and for reducing many other pollutants simultaneously.

(c) Technology options

65. Environmentally sound technology plays a big role in abating the effects of many environmental pollutants. With further research and development, its role as a major player in the energy-environment area would certainly be enhanced. Unfortunately, most of the latest technology has a high cost and is controlled by private companies in

developed countries, thus limiting initial penetration unless it is subsidized, an increasingly difficult task. The costs of pollution abatement will depend on the environmental standard chosen as a target, the time-frame in which to achieve targets and the instruments applied. However, the main constraint to wider application of the technology is the access to, and transfer, of technology; cost is an important associated issue.

66. In chapter 34 of Agenda 21, it is said that the availability of scientific and technological information and access to and transfer of environmentally sound technology are essential requirements for sustainable development. It also recognizes that there is a need for favourable access to and the transfer of environmentally sound technologies, in particular to developing countries, through supportive measures that promote technology cooperation and that should enable the transfer of necessary technological know-how, as well as the building up of economic, technical and managerial capabilities for the efficient use and further development of transferred technology. There is no easy way to meet this need. Both the recipients and the suppliers of the technology will have to cooperate with each other for their mutual interest. In this respect, Agenda 21 notes that technology cooperation entails an iterative process involving government, the private sector, and research and development facilities to ensure the best possible results from the transfer of technology.

67. As the energy sector is highly capital-intensive, it stands to benefit most from technological cooperation. It is heartening to note that developing countries are trying to adopt more advanced technologies, primarily for economic advantages (higher efficiency) with environmental advantages as an additional benefit. Their main concern is the high cost of some of these technologies and the overall investment need. In some areas, such as oil and gas exploration, joint ventures between Governments and multinational companies have already been playing a major role in technology transfer. In the power sector, a new trend towards private sector participation appears to be a positive step in technology transfer. In most cases, independent power producers are bringing in not only investment but also technology. However, the use of independent power producers has limitations and is not without problems. Conflicts of interest between the producers and public utilities are yet to be resolved. Pricing and power purchase agreements are some of the problem areas. The secretariat, within the framework of the UNDP-funded Programme for Asian Cooperation on Energy and the Environment, commissioned a study to look at the relevant issues of independent power producers in the region. The results of the study indicate that a positive impact is likely in the power sector, though the sector needs structural and regulatory adjustments or changes to benefit from the trend.

68. Another potential area for applying advanced technologies is energy efficiency in both production and end-use equipment. Examples are the improvement of efficiency in power generation, reduction of transmission and distribution losses, efficient end-use equipment for motive power, heating and lighting and reduction in energy intensity in industrial processes.

3. Regional cooperation

69. Collective efforts in addressing some of the issues concerning sustainable energy development and management may be more effective through the sharing of information and experience among the countries in the region. Regional cooperation may cover areas in both the development of resources and their optimum utilization through the sharing and trading of energy and electricity in the region and in formulating or adopting a regional strategy for sustainable development, including a possible environmental standard. In addition to technical and economic benefit, such cooperation may help in gaining higher resiliency against sudden changes in the energy supply/demand scene. An effort in initiating an emergency sharing arrangement may be initiated or enhanced at subregional levels.

70. Existing forums, such as regional working groups, established and operationalized within the framework of the UNDP/ESCAP intercountry energy programmes, the Regional Energy Development Programme (1982-1991) and continuing with the Programme for Asian Cooperation on Energy and the Environment (1993-1997), should be used fully to initiate or strengthen cooperation. However, for long-term sustainability, a more regular forum at a higher level, perhaps at the ministerial level, could be considered.

G. CONCLUSIONS AND RECOMMENDATIONS

71. Managing high energy demand growth remains the main concern of developing economies of the Asian and Pacific region. Therefore, enhancing the resiliency against uncertainties, including possible supply disruptions and price escalation, should be given a priority in the formulation of energy policy.

72. Enhancing energy supplies through indigenous energy production will remain a major policy in energy self-reliance. In that context, the dominance of fossil fuels in the energy mix will continue for many more years. As a cleaner source than other fossil fuels, natural gas utilization will increase in the short and medium terms. However, coal will remain a dominant fuel in the region, particularly in power generation. Other alternative resources, such as renewable energy resources, may become a preferred option in the longer term in commercial energy use. Nevertheless, the role of these forms of energy is well recognized in rural energy supplies.

73. A constraint in energy policy and planning that cannot be ignored and which is a growing concern for policy makers

is the environment. The integration of environment into energy policy and planning is crucial for addressing pollution and other negative impacts of energy development and use. Local pollution, caused by energy development and use, is of immediate concern to developing countries, while global issues such as greenhouse gas emissions and ozone layer depletion are generally assigned a higher priority in developed economies.

74. The potential for energy efficiency improvements in the region, both in energy conversion and production and in end use, is large and is important both for economic reasons and for environmental benefits.

75. Gradual and systematic policies are needed by all economies to develop a sustainable energy path through steps including environmental impact assessment, adoption of emission standards achievable for each individual country, rules and regulations on environmental quality, and regional and subregional cooperation measures.

IV. INTEGRATION OF ENVIRONMENT INTO ENERGY POLICY AND PLANNING*

PART I: THE ENERGY-ENVIRONMENT PLANNING ELEMENT OF THE PROGRAMME FOR ASIAN COOPERATION ON ENERGY AND THE ENVIRONMENT (PACE-E)

1. Introduction

The major goal of the Energy Environmental Planning Element (EEP) is the enhancement of the environmental perspectives in energy planning and policy making in the developing countries of Asia. Three immediate objectives can be mentioned. In the first place the strengthening of energy-environment databases in Asia. Secondly, the development and application of innovative and effective energy impact assessment methodologies, which will amongst others facilitate the conceptually sound consideration of environmental concerns in energy cost analysis and pricing. The third objective will be the identification of suitable institutional structures which will amongst other things result in the more transparent treatment of energy-environment concerns in national energy plans and subsectoral (e.g. coal, natural gas) development strategies.

In the framework of this Programme Element I, four activities have been proposed: EEP1, EEP2, EEP3 and EEP4. However, only the first three will be discussed as they are under the direct supervision of the Economic and Social Commission for Asia and the Pacific (ESCAP) and the Asian Institute of Technology (AIT). All activities in the framework of EEP1 to 3, for which contributions will be provided to the Working Group on EEP (WG/EEP) by Asian Countries, the UNDP, the Government of France, and possibly from other international agencies will take place between October 1993 and December 1997.

EEP1's immediate objective is to strengthen the capacities in the methodologies of survey, sample design and the techniques of data processing. The strengthening of the sectoral energy demand analysis and scenario building through acquisition of comprehensive and reliable data will assist countries in formulating environmentally sound energy demand management and efficiency improvement policies.

EEP2's main objective is to assist in the application of methods and tools of sectoral energy demand analysis and scenario building to evaluate energy conservation and fuel switching potentials.

EEP3 will consist of the review and application of methodologies and procedures for integrating environmental considerations into energy planning and policy analysis.

The direct recipients of this programme will be policy makers, administrators and technicians from 20 Asian countries dealing with energy and environment planning and management. In addition, representatives from the private sector and the academia will be invited to participate in the training activities of the programme. In the framework of above mentioned sub-activities, In-Country Teams will be established and EEP Sub-focal points (Project Coordinators) will be selected by the Governments of participating countries to carry out In-Country Studies on above mentioned subjects; the Energy Planning Central Consultant Team (EPCCT/AIT) in addition to the transfer of methodologies and procedures through Regional Training Workshops, will guide the In-Country Teams through training and Technical and Advisory Missions (TASM) in order to implement the National Studies. The project is executed by ESCAP and implemented by EPCCT/AIT.

As of 30 June 1995, the three sub-activities are in progress; some activities have already been partly carried out (EEP1 and EEP3) and others are under intensive preparation (EEP1, EEP2 and EEP3). Detailed reports on all activities are being prepared and some of them have been available since the end of 1994 (synthesis and methodological reports, training materials as well as users and technical manuals on developed methodologies). The dissemination of all methodological developments prepared by EPCCT/AIT has been done through Training Workshops in September 1994 (EEP1) and in August 1995 (EEP3) or will be done in the framework of other Regional Training Workshops which should be organized in 1995 and 1996 in the framework of each of the EEP sub-activities: EEP2 in November 1995 and EEP1 (Second Workshop) in April 1996.

2. Project Organization

The Energy Environmental Planning Core Consultant Group is based mainly on the Energy Planning Central Consultant Team (EPCCT) of AIT with the main cooperation of French experts from the Institute of Energy Policy and Economics (IEPE – France) and ENERDATA s.a (France) and with the technical support of the Energy Resources Section of the Environment and Natural Resources Management Division (ERS/ENRMD) from ESCAP.

---

* Prepared by Thierry Lefevre, Asian Institute of Technology. This chapter is reproduced in the form in which it was received; only country names have been changed to conform to United Nations usage.

EPCCT is responsible for the implementation of the three sub-activities in consultation with ESCAP and with the In-Country Study Teams for the overall approach as well as for the methodologies and procedures to be used in the framework of the project; it ensures assistance on methodological and implementation aspects in each of the activities; it is in charge of the dissemination and follow-up of the methodologies and tools transferred to the In-Country Study Teams through Regional Training Workshops and also through on-the-job trainings and Technical and Advisory Missions all along the Project; EPCCT will prepare the synthesis reports of all activities which will be presented in the final Regional Workshops of each sub-activity together with the In-Country Studies prepared by the In-Country Teams; editing and publication of methodological developments, software users and technical manuals and final reports (synthesis reports) will be prepared by EPCCT; in addition EPCCT will cooperate with the In-Country Teams to edit and publish their National Reports.

The In-Country Study Teams participating in the various sub-activities are from the following countries: Cambodia, China, Democratic People's Republic of Korea, India, Indonesia, Islamic Republic of Iran, Lao People's Democratic Republic, Malaysia, Mongolia, Nepal, Pakistan, Philippines, Republic of Korea, Sri Lanka, Thailand, Viet Nam.

The In-Country Study Teams are composed of several energy/environment planners and researchers coming from governmental agencies and also from universities or research centres to ensure the sustainability of these activities and the continuity for future methodological developments and for In-Country training purposes; they will be coordinated by an In-Country Team Leader (or PACE-E/EEP Sub-focal Point).

The In-Country Teams are responsible for conducting the In-Country Studies in their respective countries, including data identification and collection, application of methodology and techniques, coordination of activities with PACE-E National Focal Points, with the Central Consultant (EPCCT), and with the WG on EEP, final delivery of study results and reports, and participation in dissemination activities. The teams will be represented by their most specialized team members at the occasion of the Training Workshops; the Team Leaders will participate in the Coordination Meetings and in the Regional Workshops to present the results of the Study. The In-Country Team Leaders or the EEP Sub-focal points report to the Central Consultant for overall technical and administrative support.

All project workshops and meetings are initiated and directed by the Central Consultant with the assistance of EPCCT, of ESCAP and of the WG on EEP. For dissemination activities, which are to be held all along the Project, the Central Consultant would coordinate with ESCAP, the PACE-E national EEP Sub-focal Points and concerned national agencies to identify the most qualified participants and to work out follow-up recommendations. The Central Consultant reports to ESCAP on all project-related matters.

3. Methodological Approach

3.1 Energy-Enviromnent Situation in Asia

An adequate supply of safe, affordable energy is a basic need. Without it, economic development and elimination of poverty is inconceivable. However, all forms of energy that are widely available at an acceptable cost impose environmental penalties. Thus, an important challenge for each country, and for the world as a whole, is to manage the trade-off between adequate and affordable energy supplies and environmental quality. This trade-off must be managed with consideration for future as well as current generations.

"Sustainable development", defined as a process which recognizes that current consumption cannot be financed for long by incurring economic debts that others must repay, is a crucial concept in effectively addressing the energy-environment interface. In the energy context, it means that natural resources must be used in ways that do not create ecological debts by over-exploiting the carrying and productive capacity of the earth. While recognizing that sustainable development is now widely embraced as a key societal goal, it is clear that the specification of sustainable policies for the energy sector is a complex task that poses serious dilemmas for many countries in Asia. In particular, the pressure to reconcile economic development imperatives with effective and efficient environmental management practices is likely to remain a source of potential tension in both domestic and international policy-making arenas for some time to come.

Throughout the developing countries of Asia, energy production and/or imports have strained to keep up with desired energy consumption. Because the countries are developing rapidly and energy production capacity must be added quickly, emphasis has been placed on minimizing capital costs, with relatively little concern for environmental consequences.

Most countries have to import some or all basic energy sources, crowding out other goods and services whose import is essential for development. Others have undeveloped energy export capacity that could potentially be used to finance pressing development needs. The oil price shocks of 1973-74, 1979-80 and 1990 reinforced the realization of vulnerability of oil-importing nations. They also increased the attractiveness of natural gas and coal as substitutes for petroleum. Thus, basic economics, the realization of vulnerability to foreign supply disruptions, and increased sophistication have modified the energy strategy from a preoccupation with capacity expansion and importation to planning more emphasis on efficiency of use and on development of domestic energy resources.

Compounding the problem of rapid consumption growth and volatile petroleum supply has increased global and local awareness of the environmental consequences of energy production and consumption. Addressing problems of sustainable growth concerned with energy-environmental problems in general have not been priorities with developing countries struggling to simply meet demand in a way that requires the least monetary outlay, particularly for foreign exchange. Increasingly however, countries are feeling pressure from multilateral lenders and donor countries to pay more attention to environment and sustainable development in their energy development programmes. Also, as many of these countries have become more prosperous, their citizens are becoming less willing to sacrifice environmental quality (including public health) for cheap energy. As a consequence, the developing countries of Asia are seeking technical and scientific information, as well as state-of-the-art methodologies and tools for energy-environmental analysis, to help them make informed decisions in the area of energy-environmental policy.

The present project, "Energy-Environmental Planning (EEP)", is a programme element of a larger UNDP-sponsored "Programme for Asian Cooperation on Energy and the Environment (PACE-E)", which finances a variety of interventions across the energy-environment sector. The project will finance the costs of twenty (20) country studies aimed at providing current data on energy demand and pricing, critical to the development of national policies on conservation and environmental protection. The country studies constitute the practical application of the skills imparted in the training seminars, and thus are critical, not only as the key output for policy developments, but as a means for institutionalizing a self-reliant, sustainable analytical capacity in the participating countries.

3.2 Programme Justification

a. Problem to be addressed

The UNDP-sponsored Regional Energy Development Prograrnme (REDP), in operation between 1981-91, had as its overall objective assisting the developing countries of the Asia-Pacific region to adapt to the volatility of the energy market, chiefly in petroleum. The combined interventions of this project, in which twenty (20) countries of the region participated, are considered to have largely met the development objective of increasing the overall supply of energy in the countries, as well as greatly strengthening (and, in some cases, creating) the energy planning capability within the countries.

However, a major area of unfinished business to be addressed by PACE-E, the successor to REDP, is the "environmental connection" to the whole problem of increasing the availability of energy. In this area, issues such as demand estimation, fuel conservation and substitution, and environmental impact analysis are of paramount concern, and place new and incremental demands upon a nation's analytical and planning capability. At present, the planning capabilities of the countries participating in PACE-E is unequal to the challenge of providing the kind of sophisticated analysis and scenario stimulation required to inform policy makers in the energy-scenario simulation required to inform policy makers in the energy-environment sector. Thus, nations of the regions, all of whom must contemplate major investments in energy-producing infrastructure over the next decade, do so with critical uncertainties and gaps in information, which may produce environmentally undesirable choices.

It should also be emphasized that the current planning capability of the countries (which, to some degree, mirrors their level of economic development), is highly uneven. Countries like China, the Republic of Korea and Thailand, for example, made tremendous progress in developing a planning capability under REDP and other UN programmes during the last ten years. Countries such as Lao People's Democratic Republic, by contrast, have begun to develop effective data bases for some energy subsectors (e.g. electricity), but have yet to produce reliable data for others (sectoral energy demand). This variability among the participating countries creates additional challenges to the implementors of the project, who must adapt their technology and training material accordingly. It also underscores the importance of the **In-country studies,** both as a planning instrument, and as an indication of which countries have truly grasped the methodologies involved in sophisticated energy planning, and which will require further training and technical assistance.

In this regard, one final point needs to be made regarding the importance of "enrolling" as many countries as possible in the overall regional initiative. Clearly, in energy-environment more than in any other sector, what counts is the sum of all the efforts at conservation and pollution reduction, and not isolated country initiatives.

b. Expected End of Programme Situation

By the end of the four-year project period, the analytical capability of at least ten (10) countries of the region will have been upgraded to take into account (a) sectoral energy use (demand side analysis) and scenario building to evaluate energy conservation an fuel switching potentials, and (b) environmental concerns when developing plans and policies for the energy sector (supply and demand side analysis). Specific skills and technologies transferred will include: (1) environmental impact analysis of increased demand for energy from industrial, transport, services, agricultural, household sectors, and also of the energy sectors, (2) evaluation of benefits and costs of different scenarios of energy conservation, and (3) improved energy environment data base to support other sub-activities.

The principal outputs of the project, the quality of which will serve as the primary indicator of the extent to which skills have been successfully transferred, will be the twenty (20) country studies. Ten (10) of these will focus on demand side management, efficiency and conservation issues, and ten (10) will deal with the integration of environmental considerations into energy policy and planning of the overall energy system.

c. *The Beneficiaries*

In as much as all segments of society use energy and are impacted by the environment, all individuals can be regarded as beneficiaries of the project's activities. However, the direct recipients of this programme are the policy makers, administrators and technicians, dealing with energy planning and environmental concerns. In addition, representatives from the private sector and the academia are included in the training activities of the programme to permit in the future a follow-up of the activities as well as to create the capacity to carry out trainings within the countries and to ensure the sustainability to the Project.

d. *Programme Strategy and Institutional Arrangements*

The ESCAP Secretariat, as the coordinator of the Working Group on EEP is the executing agency of this project, while the Asian Institute of Technology (AIT) is the implementing agency. Three Sub-activities are being developed within the framework of the programme. To ensure continuity with past interventions under REDP, the Project employs a team (the Energy Planning Central Consultant Team (EPCCT/AIT)) and methodological approach, relying upon experts from the School of Environment, Resources and Development at the Asian Institute of Technology (AIT) as well as from other international institutions to provide training and technical assistance to the countries.

In the first Sub-activity (EEP1), the Energy Planning Central Consultant Team at AIT prepared a Guide Book on Energy Surveys which has been disseminated to the Asian participating countries at the occasion of the Training Workshops; a synthesis of the actual status on energy surveys, energy statistics and sectoral energy data has also been prepared by EPCCT in the framework of this activity. In addition, specific sectoral energy surveys will be prepared with the participants at the occasion of the Second Training Workshop to be held in the framework of this activity.

In the second Sub-activity (EEP2), EPCCT is reviewing past applications of methodologies, models and existing data bases and eventually modifying them to render them suitable for the evaluation of energy saving (conservation) and fuel switching potentials under various scenarios. Scenarios under study will involve "Demand Side Management" (DSM) options, improved efficiency in end-use and fuel switching options resulting in lowered demand for energy and as a consequence in an improvement of the environmental situation. Results of this review will then be used to design the Regional Training Workshops

required for activities (country studies) to be implemented between 1996-97. In particular, the results obtained in the framework of the EEP4 sub-activities executed and implemented by APDC/APENPLAN will be an important input for this sub-activity.

As a follow-up to the Regional Training Workshop, the project will implement ten (10) In-Country Teams, to be established in the last quarter of 1995 via activities being undertaken under the aegis of PACE-E to undertake the In-Country Studies. The advisory missions would be fielded to assist each In-Country Team, i.e., at the beginning, middle and end of the In-Country studies. The report from the In-Country Studies would be synthesized by the Central Consultant's team and PACE-E secretariat in the second and third quarter of 1997 to obtain a regionally aggregated picture of likely conservation and fuel switching potentials and strategies as well as their expected impacts on the environment. The synthesis report will serve as the principal resource document for a regional workshop, scheduled in the first quarter of 1998. Publication of the findings, conclusions and recommendations of the workshop will also occur in the first quarter of 1998.

The same strategy will be employed in the third Sub-activity (EEP3): integration of environmental considerations into energy planning and policy analysis. In this case, AIT undertook a review of existing methodologies and procedures for incorporating environmental factors into energy planning. The emphasis was on identifying an appropriate energy analysis methodology and tool, capable of integrating scenarios covering the overall energy system, and determining the structure of the supply system, given various demand scenarios, and relating these to environmental impacts, and rendering it "user-friendly" in the context of the participating countries. Upon completion of the review (by the end of June 1995), AIT presented its findings and recommendations at a Regional Training Workshop, held in August 1995. During the same workshop, participants were trained on the application of the chosen "user-friendly" software, and an In-Country Study Framework was presented and discussed with the participants.

Following the workshop, AIT energy planning specialists, are organizing with the countries' participants, approximately ten (10) In-Country Studies on the energy impacts on the environment of the energy systems. AIT energy planning specialists, also conversant with the methodology, will assist the In-Country Teams in conducting three advisory missions to each country, to initiate, follow-up the progress, and evaluate the quality of the country reports. Finally, the consultants will prepare a synthesis report, aggregating the results contained in the In-Country Reports, and will present these at a regional seminar, attended by policy makers from the ten (10) participating countries.

A key aspect of the project strategy is the "bottom-up" approach in which technical and administrative officials encharged with formulating national energy sector plans and policies are made responsible for the execution of the project activities, e.g., the In-Country Studies. The participation of research and/or academic institutions of the participating countries is an important element to secure the follow up and technical support of the in-country teams.

3.3 Development Objective

The development objective of the larger Programme for Asian Cooperation on Energy and the Environment (PACE-E), of which the present study is one component, is to enable countries of Asia to make progress towards the achievement of balanced, sustainable economic growth based upon the environmentally responsible production and use of energy. As such, the proposed project should be seen as building upon and extending the development principles expounded in the Brundtland Commission Report and strongly endorsed at the Rio Conference.

The project also embodies a strong element of regionality. Its geographical scope extends over most of Asia. Its organizational structure is based upon the integration of inputs from approximately 20 countries of the region. It seeks to enhance regional capabilities in the various planning, management and technical fields that will enable individual nations to develop and utilize energy resources in a way that is compatible with the objective of sustainable development.

3.4 Expected Outputs

The expected outputs of this sub-activity are mainly:

(a) Training Workshops and published methodological guidelines, together with case study applications, which could be used as the basis for new training courses with a primary environmental focus;

(b) The organization of training programmes on energy cost analysis and pricing to share experiences on whether subsidized energy is achieving its objectives, what alternatives to energy subsidies might achieve the same goals, and how to analyze energy costs and set prices in such a way that resource depletion and environmental damage are accurately taken into account;

(c) A combination of training and review seminars for senior energy and environmental specialists from the governments of the region specifically directed towards identification of current institutional constraints and

shortcomings coupled with the design of model institutional structures through which energy-environment concerns may be more actively addressed. These model structures would be promoted in the form of guidelines for circulation to countries in the region;

(d) New training programmes in energy-environment data base development, supported by the preparation of appropriate training materials. In addition, it may be useful to consider the preparation of the technical guidelines for the development of energy-environment data bases within an agreed common framework for application within developing Asian countries;

(e) Publication of Methodological Training, Users and Technical Manuals as well as Guide Books covering all the aspects of the three (3) sub-activities EEPl, EEP2 and EEP3.

3.5 Inputs

(a) At the REDP Tripartite Review Conference of August 1991, many countries agreed to make resources available. Though these were indicated in the context of the REDP 1992-1996 cycle, they represent an *initial estimate* of level of contribution that may be made available to PACE-E. Note that the contribution by participating countries would be in local currencies and a large part of the contribution is in the form of services on in-country experts. The hosting of training programmes or policy seminars have also been included in the contributions pledged by the countries.

(b) UNDP: US$ 927,400.00 (for activities EEP1 to EEP3).

(c) EPCCT/AIT: Overall coordination, guidance and assistance, with the cooperation of ESCAP and the WG/EEP.

(d) Participating countries: TCDC contributions for specific WG activities from the WG/EEP countries.

(e) The Government of France: US$ 980,000.00 (for activities EEP2 and EEP3).

3.6 Overall Budget and Time Schedule

The overall budget and time schedule which have been modified on various occasions since August 1994, are at the present time as follows:

Project Number: RAS/92/071/A/01/53
Project title: Programme for Asian Co-operation on Energy and the Environment

Programme Budget Covering UNDP Contribution for AIT Execution of Sub Contract 21-01 Activity EEPI-III (AIT)

		Total	1993	1994	1995	1996	1997
21	Sub Contracts						
21-01	EEP I (AIT)						
	• 1994 Workshop No. 1		80,250.00				
	• 1995 Workshop No. 2					80,000.00	
	• Miscellaneous						
	Sub-total 1	160,250.00	80,250.00			80,000.00	
21-02	EEP II (AIT)						
	• Regional Training Workshop			26,650.00	[35,000.00]*		
	• Consultants (specialists)				14,000.00		
	• In-country studies					100,000.00	30,000.00
	• Consultant TASM mission and training material				5,000.00	25,000.00	20,000.00
	• Regional Workshop						
	• Publication of reports, Workshop Proceedings and training material				[15,000.00]*		25,000.00
	• Miscellaneous				2,500.00		
	Sub-total 2	298,150.00		26,650.00	71,500.00	125,000.00	75,000.00
21-03	EEP III (AIT)						
	• Regional Training Workshop			67,500.00			
	• Consultants (specialists)		20,000.00	52,250.00			
	• In-country studies					100,000.00	30,000.00
	• Consultant TASM missions and training material				10,000.00	25,000.00	20,000.00
	• Regional Workshop						80,000.00
	• Publication of reports, Workshop Proceedings and training material						25,000.00
	• Miscellaneous				2,500.00		
	Sub-total 3	364,750.00	20,000.00	52,250.00	12,500.00	125,000.00	155,000.00
21-05	EEP V (AIT)						
	• Shrot term Consultants					20,000.00	20,000.00
	• Group Training					40,000.00	40,000.00
	• Publications						50,000.00
	Sub-total 4	170,000.00				60,000.00	110,000.00
	TOTAL 1+2+3	993,150.00	100,250.00	78,900.00	84,000.00	390,000.00	340,000.00

[*] managed directly by ESCAP

As of 25 Septemeber 1995

Programme for Asian Cooperation on Energy and the Environment (PACE-E)
(RAS/92/071)
WORKPLAN OF THE PACE-E PROGRAMME ELEMENT 1: ENERGY-ENVIRONMENTAL PLANNING

Activity	Responsible Implementing Agency/Institution & Collaborating Agency (ies)/ Institution (s)	1993 IV	1994 I	1994 II	1994 III	1994 IV	1995 I	1995 II	1995 III	1995 IV	1996 I	1996 II	1996 III	1996 IV	1997 I	1997 II	1997 III	1997 IV	1998 I	1998 II
EEP-1 Training in methodologies of sample design and on techniques of data Processing for improvement of sectoral energy demand	AIT/ENERDATA/ CEREN/ESMAP SOFRES																			
• Training definition		Oct.–Dec.																		
• Recruit consultant			Jan.–Mar.																	
• Workshop. No.1					Sept. 94															
• Workshop No.2							Jan.–Mar.													
EEP-2 Application of sectoral energy use assessments and demand scenarios to evaluate the potential for energy conservation and fuel switching	AIT/IEPE/ ENERDATA																			
• Methodological review and developments		Oct. 93–Oct. 95																		
• Regional Training										Nov. 95										
• In-country studies definition										Dec.95–Mar.96										
• In-country studies										Dec. 95–Sept. 97										
• Consultant TASM missions											April 96–Sept. 97									
• National seminars																April–Sept. 97				
• Synthesis report																		Oct.–Dec.		
• Regional workshop																			Jan.–Mar.	
• Publication of reports and proceedings																				April–June
EEP-3 Review of methodologies and procedures for integrating environmental considerations into energy planning and policy analytic effectiveness of E.I.A. guidelines for the energy sector in Asian developing countries	AIT/IEPE/ ENERDATA																			
• Consultant recruitment					July–Sept.															
• Regional study review of methodologies and models developments						Oct. 94–June 95														
• Regional training									Aug. 95											
• In-country studies definition														July–Dec. 96						
• In-country studies									Oct. 95–Sept. 97											
• Consultant TASM missions										Jan. 96–Sept. 97										
• National Seminars																April–Sept. 97				
• Regional Training																		Oct.–Dec.		
• Synthesis Report																			Jan.–Mar.	
• Publication of reports																				April–June

Latest update: 14 September 1995

4. Concluding Remarks

The various issues addressed by EEP1, EEP2 and EEP3 activities are of huge importance in Asian Countries, particularly in the actual context of economic and energy development of these countries; it is important to provide the energy planners, working in governmental and official institutions, the knowledge and the tools which will help them to analyze their country's situation and to make wise decisions for the future, integrating economic growth, sound environmental concerns and efficient energy development.

As presented before, the main objective of EPCCT/AIT in the framework of these EEP Sub-activities is to give to the decision makers the information (data), the knowledge (methodological approach of the energy-environmental problems) and the tools (models) to help them in their day to day planning and policy activities. EPCCT/AIT and ESCAP have been working for the last ten (10) years in this direction, developing new methodological approaches to the energy/environmental problems, designing and developing new tools to carry out the planning activities and collecting, checking and organizing energy-environmental data to enable the Asian Countries to use more effective energy-environmental planning tools. During all these years, the ESCAP and EPCCT/AIT action have been focussed on assisting the Asian Countries to strengthen their capabilities in carrying out their own energy planning and policy activities: significant importance has been given to the In-Country Studies, once the methodologies and tools have been transferred and in addition, the training will be carried out on-the-job, i.e. officials and planners receive their professional training in short time periods as part of their professional activities and in the framework of the implementation of their In-Country Studies; the In-Country Energy Planners, with the support of the main Consultant Team, will try, by themselves, to develop an integral energy-environment planning activity, passing through all the phases of this process from data gathering to the production of a final report presenting the policy options to the decision makers. The final objective of this activity being the integration into the day to day planning activities of the knowledge and skills acquired during the project and which will represent in fact the long term effect sought with this activity. Another important facet of the project, is the incorporation since the beginning of the project of representatives from universities and research centers during the training activities as well as in the In-Country Study Teams. Their involvement is an important element in the Project because they will permit in the future the reproductibility of training activities needed at national level and they will also enable the methodological and software development in cooperation with the official National Planning Agencies, ensuring the long term sustainability sought by the project.

PART II: PROGRESS REPORT ON ENERGY-ENVIRONMENT STUDIES
IN ASIAN COUNTRIES

1. The Energy-Environment Situation
in the Asian Context

1.1 Causes of the Environment Problem in Asia

Overall situation of the environment has become a worrying issue for all Asian developing countries. Problems such as urban environmental degradation, industrial pollution, atmospheric emission, soil erosion, land and water degradation, deforestation are not only a threat but an acute reality that Asian developing countries are facing now on their way toward civilization. Asian current demographic and socio-economic conditions underscore the root causes responsible for its environmental problems. First of all, Asia continent has large and fast growing population, which is projected to rise from 2.8 billion today to 4.3 billion in 2025 – over 50 per cent of the world total. This strain is exacerbated by the 700 million people currently living in absolute poverty. Second, industrialization and urbanization processes in many Asian developing countries at the end of twentieth century seem to gain remarkable momentum imposing complex demand on assimilative capacity of the environment especially urban environment. Third, probably the most important is the fundamental market failure regarding rational use of natural resources and environment. It is further aggravated by the lack (or the weakness) of government policy to ensure environmental protection, institutional enforcement, economic incentives, environmental standards and regulations, that are very common in many Asian countries. Lastly, for most of Asian countries the implementation of environmental protection measures is limited by financial constraints even if the public and the government are aware of the necessity of such measures.

1.2 Main Characteristics of the Energy Sector in Asia

Within the economy, energy sector is a driving force for economic and social development. As Asian economy is growing up quickly, the demand for energy is increasing rapidly. At current growth rates Asian energy demand is doubling every twelve years as compared to world average of every twenty eight years. The demand for electricity is growing even faster: two or three times faster than GDP for most of newly industrializing East Asian countries (Republic of Korea, Taiwan Province of China) i.e. 10-25 per cent per year, and up to two times faster than GDP for most of South Asia i.e. 5-l0 per cent per year (Thailand, Indonesia, Malaysia) [Branson C. and Ramankutty R.1993]. The high growth rate of electricity consumption indicates an intensification of the electrification programmes in the majority of Asian countries.

In Asia coal contributes with the large share in conventional energy consumption. Consumption of coal is concentrated in two countries namely China and India. For example, in 1992, China extracted 1,095 million tons of coal which was equivalent to 76 per cent of primary energy supply, India in the same year produced 112.4 Mtoe of coal. Coal finds popular use in Asia because it is available in many countries of the region other than China and India such as Indonesia, Thailand (lignite), Viet Nam and also in Australia. In those countries where coal is domestically produced, its use is usually being promoted by government policies as a means of self reliance.

Energy consumption in Asia is dominated by China and India. China alone consumes 61 per cent of all Asian conventional energy or 55 per cent of Asian wide energy consumption including traditional energy such as biomass. Combined China and India consume three fourths of the total Asian energy consumption. Apart from commercial fuels such as coal, oil, natural gas and electricity, traditional fuels like biomass still play very important role in Asian rural community.

1.3 Main Environmental Concerns Related to the Energy Sector

The spectrum of main energy related environmental problems covers the following aspects: (a) large loss of cultivated land due to development of large hydropower projects and possible change of regional/local biosystem and climatic conditions; (b) vast land area required for coal storage at the coal mines especially open pit mines; (c) water and solid waste pollution related to energy production and consumption; (d) air pollution and greenhouse gas emission from energy extraction, transportation, energy conversion and energy consumption. Among these issues the last one draws most concern because of its proven severe negative effects on human being, crops, livestock (or ambient biosystem in general) and global climate. Details about such impacts were reviewed by Bhatti N., Foell W. K. (1990) and Dawnson D.K. (1993). In literature, air pollution consists of the emission of constituents such as carbon monoxide, sulfur dioxide, lead, suspended particulates nitrogen and nitrous oxide into atmosphere, the presence of which in the atmosphere could cause damage to the ambient biosystem, acid rain and health hazard for people. Another phenomenon is greenhouse gas emission i.e. emission of gases which themselves are not directly harmful to the man and his surrounding but are destructive in long term by altering the earth climate. These are carbon dioxide, nitrous oxide, CFCs and methane etc,.

In Asia most serious environmental consequences related to energy sector are emission from transport sector due to combustion in vehicle's engines, emission from fossil fuel fired power plants, emission from industrial installations using fossil fuels for combustion and emission from household cooking stoves.

World Health Organization data indicates that twelve of the fifteen cities with the highest levels of the particulate matters and six of the fifteen cities with the highest levels of sulfur dioxide are in Asia (table 1.1). Of the seven cities worst ranked for air pollution by the Population Crisis Committee (PCC), based on a range of physical indicators, five are in Asia (table 1.1). In addition Asia is rapidly emerging as major contributor to acid rain and global warming.

Table 1.1. Air pollution in Asian cities

Cities of highest level of particulate matter	Cities of highest level of sulfur dioxide	Cities worst ranked by PCC
Shenyang	Shenyang	Calcuta
Xian	Seoul	Jakarta
New Delhi	Xian	New Delhi
Bejing	Bejing	Bejing
Calcuta	Malina	Shenyang
Jakarta	Guangzhou	
Shanghai		
Guangzhou		
Illigan City		
Bangkok		
Bombay		
Kuala Lumpur		

Source: WRI, IIED, UNDP 1988.

Transport contributes the most to air pollution in many Asian cities (Bombay, Bangkok for example). While the motor vehicle population in Asia is relatively small compared to world total, it has been increasing very rapidly at a rate above 10 per cent per annum in many Asian countries. Diesel vehicles and motorcycles powered by two stroke engines, both highly polluting technologies, represents a large share of vehicle population. In addition many vehicles have no pollution control equipment and fuel used are unsanitary with regard to lead and sulfur contents. Traffic congestion as a result of alarming increase in number of vehicles is the main newly emerging obstacle in Asian megacities, it puts an additional barrier on the way to curb transport air pollution.

Heavy dependence on coal in energy supply and consumption is one of the main characteristics of the Asian energy sector. The use of coal not only in power generation but also in many industrial enterprises is the main source of emissions of sulfur, nitrogen oxides and carbon dioxide and also particles. On the other hand burning of biomass for cooking creates indoor air pollution in rural areas throughout Asia.

Asian contribution to global warming is swiftly increasing, led by China and India. The Asian region accounted for about 20 per cent of the worldwide emission of CO_2 in 1985 and this share is expected to rise to 25-30 per cent by the year 2000. Incremental growth of anthropogenic carbon dioxide in Asia by the year 2000 is expected to more than offset any savings to be achieved by limiting emission in OECD countries to 1990 levels [Brandon C. and Ramankuty, 1993]. Data of 1993 (table 1.2) shows that, China alone accounted for 11.6 per cent of total worldwide carbon dioxide emission from fossil fuel (676 million ton out of 5,812 million ton carbon worldwide) and that the share of emission from coal in total greenhouse gas emission of China was 81 per cent (548 million ton of carbon). This huge share has not been changed since 1983 [John H. Walsh 1994].

Table 1.2. Worldwide Carbon Emission from Fossil Fuels
(Million tons of Carbon in 1993)

Country/Region	Source			
	Oil	Natural gas	Coal	Total
Canada	64	36.3	26.1	126.4
United States	658.2	303.6	500.7	1 462.5
Non-OECD Europe	277.5	340.3	379.0	996.8
European Union	469.1	141.9	231.4	842.4
China	119.8	8.2	548.1	676.1
World Total	2 608.9	1 035.8	2 167.2	5 811.9

Source: John H. Walsh "1993 Carbon Dioxide Fact Sheet" Energy Studies Review, Vol. 6 No. 2 1994.

Acid rain is the collective term used to describe the result of sulfur dioxide and nitrogen oxide emissions. At least two thirds of acid rain emission in Asia come from coal-fired power plants and industrial sources, the rest from residential cooking and heating. If cleaned and burned in modern plants with SO_2 and NOx emission controls, Asian coals would have a minimum impacts on the environment. But almost all power plants in Asia have no pollution control equipment other than particulate control. Sulfur and nitrogen oxide emissions have both local and regional impacts. Depending on heights of smoke stacks and prevailing wind conditions, the acid rain precursors can be carried hundreds of miles away from the emission sources. The major weather pattern in Asia is that, wind blows from the land to the sea in the winter and in reversed direction in the summer. Emission of SO_2 and NOx are thus carried out from China to the Republic of Korea and Japan, from Southeast China to Viet Nam, and from India to Bangladesh. Total sulfur dioxide emission in China is approximately 18 million tons per year, among which 7 million tons is from coal-fired power plants. China is responsible for two thirds of Asian SO_2 emission. India is in second place to China in term of coal use and sulfur dioxide emission. India emits about 3-4 million ton of SO_2 per year. Given the projected growth of energy consumption over the next two decades acid rain

Table 1.3. Emissions of SO$_2$ and Nox in Several Asian Countries
(Million tons/Year)

Countries or areas	1986		2000		2010	
	SO$_2$	Nox	SO$_2$	Nox	SO$_2$	Nox
Bangladesh	0.15	0.025	0.204	0.039	0.27	0.052
China	18.972	7.671	34.036	15.316	48.802	21.864
Hong Kong	0.274	0.111	0.397	0.162	0.588	0.249
India	3.181	2.83	5.386	5.516	8.796	9.252
Indonesia	0.78	0.712	1.85	1.701	3.184	3.131
Korea, DPR	0.587	0.628	0.92	0.938	1.275	1.249
Korea, Rep of	1.224	0.663	2.721	1.302	3.308	1.641
Malaysia	0.298	0.296	0.441	0.582	0.753	0.982
Pakistan	0.748	0.119	1.675	0.274	2.486	0.405
Philippines	0.403	0.202	0.815	0.438	1.339	0.734
Singapore	0.061	0.166	0.107	0.252	0.151	0.338
Taiwan Province of China	0.85	0.298	1.738	0.648	2.217	0.828
Thailand	0.627	0.495	2.616	1.508	2.999	3.523
Total	28.155	14.216	52.904	28.676	76.167	44.249

Source: Wesley K. Foell; Collin W. Green; "Acid Rain in Asia: An Economic, Energy and Emissions Overview" 1990.

precursor emissions will also increase. Foell and Green (1990) predicted that SO$_2$ emission in Asia will increase from 35 million tons in 1990 to 53 million tons in 2000 and to 76 million tons by the year 2010 if no substantial efforts to limit emission are taken. Based on this projection Asia will surpass both Europe and the USA in SO$_2$ emission by the year 2000 and will emit more SO$_2$ than the combined total from all OECD countries by 2010. A similar pattern is observed for NOx. (See table 1.3)

1.4   Measures to Mitigate Negative Impacts of Energy Utilization on the Environment

There are three main types of concerns regarding the consequences of emissions resulting from burning of fossil fuels: (i) direct negative impacts on human being due to lead content, CO content and dust & particulates in the air in urban centres (ii) the threat of acid rain deposition with its derived consequences (iii) and the potential of irreversible global warming. In order to put these effects under the control, a set of actions should be worked out. The recommended strategy is to mitigate what is unpreventable and to prevent what is unmitigatable. Based on that guideline the following two groups of emission reduction measures can be proposed:

Group 1: Controlling the level of emissions through the control of energy consumption level. This implies that energy consumption (or demand) should be rationalized. Rationalizing energy use will minimize the emission on the one hand and provide the service with satisfactory quality for the customers on the other hand. This simple statement implies a complex set of policy measures which are mutually interrelated and interacted between each others.

Measures in this group have mainly a non-technical character. They include energy efficiency and energy conservation promotion in both sides of the energy business: supply and demand. The energy conservation at the end use levels could be achieved partly through proper energy pricing, which preferably takes into account the externalities associated with producing and consuming particular energy commodity. It also could be achieved by implementing cost effective demand side management programmes, which will facilitate market penetration of efficient appliances. On the other hand, energy conservation at supply level could be materialized if the saving of energy can offset the costs of advanced technology investments, technologies that could produce and convert energies with higher efficiencies.

Group 2: Controlling the emission levels themselves. Once the emissions cannot be avoided, it is reasonable to think of the ways to reduce them. This group consists of mostly technical measures, the implementation of which will help to partially capture pollutants formed as a result of energy use. At the present time three stages of capturing pollutants have been developed with the so called pre-combustion, insitu-combustion and post-combustion technologies. These technologies are applied to power plants using fossil fuels, industrial installations and vehicle engines as well. Example of pre-combustion measures could be coal washing, coal cleaning or coal benefaction for power generation, or reduction of lead content in vehicle fuels. Fluidized bed combustion technologies help to eradicate formation of SO$_2$ and NOx in significant extend within the boilers; they are known as in-situ reduction measures. It is also possible to set one more barrier on the way pollutants go to the air, the so called end of the pipe technologies are also available for use; they include precipitator filters, flue gas desulfurization, denitrification and catalytic converters. Substituting environmentally dirty fuels by cleaner one also belongs to this group of measures.

In practice, a reasonable combination of measures from both groups would be the best strategy for environmental protection. Fuel substitution, for example cannot eliminate totally the use of a given fuel form, so fuel substitution must be applied in parallel with other measures such as the end of the pipe technologies. Similarly, the promotion of energy efficient (and therefore environment friendly) technologies without energy conservation measures from the consumer side will not bring the expected results.

How to determine an effective combination of measures is the essential task of the energy-environment planning.

1.5 Role of Energy Planning and Modelling in the Context of Sustainable Development

National energy planning is a complex process which permits to link a country's energy system with the rest of its economic and social system. The energy outputs produced by the energy sector (e.g. petroleum products, electricity) go to the society to satisfy its need. On the other hand, the energy sector requires capital, labor and other resources for its functioning, which are supplied by the national economy. Along with energy products, the energy sector also discharges undesirable by-products (e.g. pollutants) into the environment. Thus, the primary goal of the national energy planning is to achieve the optimal configuration of energy demand, energy supply and environmental protection given the socio-economic objectives and also the specific conditions of the country.

To accomplish such an important task of the energy planning, it is often necessary to resort to the use of modeling. The energy modeling objective is to group and represent all the activities (together with their complex interrelationships) of the energy sector in a simplified, consistent and comprehensive manner, through which the past trends of energy supply, energy consumption and associated pollution can be analyzed; future trends can be projected, and other useful relevant information can be derived. A well structured energy model usually allows for the simulation and optimization of the energy system with the incorporation of different constraints imposed either on the demand or on the supply side of the energy system such as: resource limitation constraints, technology availability constraints, financial constraints, and environmental constraints. A possibility of integrating various kinds of constraints into the models creates the flexibility for the planners to test their policy options and to assess the impacts of the policy measures on the energy-environment system. Thus, in environmental impact assessment study, energy models are essentially useful not only because they allow to evaluate the pollution level associated with each energy

scenario at the present time and in the future, but also because they can generate optimal development strategy for the energy sector, which satisfies the imposed environmental standards. By exploiting adequate energy models it is possible to simulate the environmental consequences of an exogenously defined energy scenario, or to find out an optimal energy scenario given the environmental objectives.

In that context, energy planning and modeling are important since they assist the planners and decision makers in assessing the extent to which the energy sector hamper the environment, in choosing the most suitable combination of energy-environment sound policies given a socio-economic scenario and other specific conditions of the nation.

1.6 Role of the Government in Environment Protection

The government plays also an important role in establishing the environmental laws, standards and regulations, creating the legal environment, within which all members of the society perform their activities, as well as in setting up the institutional and organizational framework to enforce laws, standards and regulations. Its role in coordinating national with international activities should not be underestimated. Moreover, the coordination between environmental protection policies and socio-economic development policies obviously belongs to the highest level decision making body of the nation.

2. Review of Energy-Environment Studies in Selected Asian Developing Countries

At the present time the science on energy environment interactions in Asian developing world seems to lag behind Europe and America. The state of the art in this field of study in Asian developing countries shows a lack of systematic approach. The most severe difficulty is the absence of regional consistent database and even at national level data is not always available for undertaking necessary analysis. This limitation of data availability precludes in some cases the use of complex models. The application of models is also limited because many Asian developing countries do not have quick access to models designed in developed countries of the world. In addition, sometimes, models applicable for industrialized world are not very adequate for the developing world due to many differences between them especially in database structure, methods of historical statistic records and also in the inner description of the energy-environment system which can be sometimes very far from the reality of the developing countries.

Given the fact that a small number of countries have carried out such kind of analyses and studies, available documents are at the present time quite limited and sometimes incomplete; it would be unwise at this stage to try to characterize the state of the art at Asian level. So it is better to look at some individual studies carried out by some representative Asian countries, in particular the cases of

China, India, Indonesia and Thailand will be specifically addressed in this document. A part from national studies, several regionally coordinated studies on energy and the environment issues will also be addressed by this analysis.

2.1 National Studies on Energy Environmental Problems

2.1.1 Energy Environment Studies in China

China is among the biggest coal producers and consumers of the world. Energy consumption of China is almost half of that of Asia. The carbon emissions from burning coal in China accounts for more than a quater of the total carbon emission from coal worldwide (Table 1.2 chapter 1). So any regional strategy to deal with air pollution and greenhouse gas emissions due to energy consumption must tackle China in order to be successful. China has carried out variety of studies in the field of environmental consequences of energy utilization especially on coal utilization.

In **"Study on the industrial energy system in connection with environmental impacts in PRC (1983)"** [9] the industrial centre of North China had been considered. This study developed a linear programming model, which allowed for minimizing costs of economic activities, subjected to a set of constraints including limitation on air pollution from these activities. In this study energy consumption was estimated under the assumption that it grows in linear relationship with economic development. Environmental consideration was incorporated through the introduction of limits on SO_2 and CO_2 emissions. The drawback of this model is its over simplification; technological solutions to emission reduction problem cannot be represented, energy conservation and energy efficiency as well as fuel substitution were not considered.

In 1991, Asian Development Bank financed a study for China entitled **"Environmental Considerations in Energy Development Project"** (ADB TA No. 5357-Regional). [10]

The report briefly reviewed the present environmental pollution situation in China. Air pollution in China is mainly of the smoke-dust type. The concentration of the pollutants in the air has two daily peaks: morning and evening reflecting the tangible influence of coal consumption in the residential sector on the air pollution. The average concentrations of the typical pollutants in 1989 were: 432 mg/m^3 for suspended particulate and 105 mg/m^3 for SO_2. The proportion of cities with SO_2 concentration above national standards were 34 per cent for northern region and 29 per cent for southern region. Other aspects of environmental pollution such as water, solid waste, noise and agro-ecological problem were also reviewed.

Energy consumption in China relied mainly on domestic coal, which accounted for about 76 per cent of primary energy supply. High quality energy forms like petroleum contributed only 17 per cent. As coal and biomass are the major energy sources, direct burning of great amount of coal and biomass has serious impacts on the ecological balance. Inefficient use of energy has also contributed substantially to severe environmental impacts.

Energy demand forecast was a core part of the project as it served as a basis for environmental consideration, and to determine investment strategy. Despite its importance the description of the model used for energy forecasting is not clearly defined. Although it was mentioned that the study used sectoral analysis approach for forecasting energy demand, the disaggregation of the economy into sectors and subsectors is not consistent with the international standards. Future energy consumption were projected for each of the 30 provinces, 8 economic subsectors and 9 fuel types (i.e.: coal, coke, petrol, diesel, fuel oil, natural gas, thermal, electricity and others). The projection was made for the years: 1995, 2000, 2010. The whole economy was disaggregated into three main subsectors: material production, non-material production and household. Material production sector grouped industry, agriculture, construction, transport and commerce. Further dissagration was not considered. This unconventional format for disaggregation is based on the accounting technique used in Chinese economy other than the one used in market economy.

The study concluded that sulfur dioxide spectrum in China has a clear regionally dependent characteristic. The SO_2 concentration was high in north, east, and south China where industry was most developed, it was lower in northwest and southwest of China. Pollution of smoke-dust is mainly caused by burning coal; such an emission is more serious in Northern region especially in winter season, when space heating is necessary. To estimate the volume of carbon dioxide emitted to atmosphere by burning mineral fuels, the emission coefficients were calculated: 0.66 (kg/kgce) for coal, 0.543 (kg/kgce) for fuel oil and 0.404 (kg/kgce) for natural gas. The volume of emission was obtained by multiplying emission coefficient to forecast quantities of corresponding fuels. Since the structure of the energy consumption was not expected to change significantly in the study, i.e. coal will continues to play a dominant role, the carbon dioxide pollution will increase steadily. Summary of the output of this report regarding to emission data is given in table 2.1

Table 2.1. Air Pollution in China, Non-Abatement Case
(million ton/year)

	1995	2000	2010
SO_2	22/20	29/24	45/34
CO_2	613/565	758/651	1097/849
Smoke-dust	21/19	27/23	42/32

Note: High economic scenario/Low economic scenario.

It was stressed that if some abatement technologies, such as desulfurization of smoke and gas, coal washing, removal of sulfur hydrogen were to be implemented, the sulfur dioxide and smoke dust emissions could be reduced substantially (table 2.2). Unfortunately, the way these measures should be taken into account in the model was not clearly specified in the report.

Table 2.2. Emission of SO$_2$ and smoke-dust Abatement Case
(million ton/year)

	1995	2000	2010
SO$_2$	18/16	24/19	36/25
Smoke-dust	14/12	19/15	27/16

Note: High economic scenario/Low economic scenario.

The report is also dealing with cost benefit analysis and multiple assessment of the energy supply development in China. Three energy supply scenarios were considered: base line scenario, intensive energy saving scenario and energy alternative scenario.

The model allowed for calculation of SO$_2$ and CO$_2$ emission, which permitted to compare the emission level of the different scenarios. The impact of the alternative energy scenario and of the intensive energy conservation scenario was the reduction of the SO$_2$ and CO$_2$ as follows: compared to the base scenario the emissions of SO$_2$ and CO$_2$ of the intensive energy conservation scenario would be 83.3 per cent and 86.6 per cent respectively, similarly the SO$_2$ and CO$_2$ emission in the alternative scenario corresponded to 83.5 per cent and 97.6 per cent.

Following the cost benefit analysis, giving the quantitative assessment to each scenario, the multiple assessment technique was performed in order to take into account for the unquantifiable factors. In this part of the analysis, an environmental hierarchy was set up and environmental impacts of energy production were given due weights, for example: at the first level the air pollution (meaning the SO$_2$ and dust emission) was assigned the weight of 0.35, CO$_2$ emission was given a weight of 0.2, at second level the SO$_2$ was assigned a value of 0.6 while dust took a value of 0.4 etc. Then the scoring system was established with the current situation being as the reference point i.e. centre (zero) value. Negative value indicated the increase of the concentration of pollutants in the atmosphere or increase of other negative impacts and vice versa. Based on this procedure the environmental impact of the energy supply scenarios can be quantified. This kind of information is supplementary to the cost benefit analysis. The ranking was based on both economic and multiple assessment. From the result of the ranking process, it was then concluded that the most wanted scenario was the intensive energy conservation one, followed by the base line scenario and then by the alternative energy supply.

2.1.2 *Energy Environment Studies in India*

As a big coal producer and consumer in the region, India is now facing the increasing threat of environmental consequences of its growing energy consumption and posing a serious threat to the region. To find the way to tackle the energy related environment problem, the Tata Energy Research Institute had conducted the study **"Environmental considerations in Energy Development"**. (1991) [43]. It examined all aspects of the energy utilization in India from energy resources, energy demand, energy supply projection to environmental impacts of the energy sector, and measures to combat them. The study also recommended different alternative energy development strategies. Economic analysis and overall assessment of these alternatives was carried out before making the final conclusions and recommendations.

Three economic-energy scenarios were considered:

* Business as usual
* Environment scenario I
* Environment scenario II

The first environmental sound scenario placed emphasis on energy conservation, energy efficiency of both supply and demand sides and technological progress.

The second environmentally friendly scenario was based on cleaner energy forms such as renewable energy forms, etc.

The energy demand projection used in this study was based on a kind of techno-economic method. The whole economy was divided into agriculture, industry, transport and residential sectors. The industry sector was further divided into 8 subsectors. The residential sector distinguished urban and rural household. Sectoral growths are first estimated then useful energy consumption norms applied to them. Next these useful energy demands are distributed over various fuel alternatives taking into account efficiencies of utilization, availability of various fuel types and present distribution pattern. The demand forecasts have been based on two socio-economic scenarios: 5 per cent of GDP growth and a population growth of 2 per cent till 1999 and 1.8 per cent thereafter; 6 per cent economic growth with population growth rate declining from 1.8 per cent to 1.4 per cent. The mathematical description of the model used was not available in the report.

In the framework of this research, the environmental impacts were considered separately for the energy sector and for the final users. From the supply side, the air pollution, soil erosion, land losses etc. were assessed. Based on the electricity demand projection, the level of air pollution from the power generation subsector was calculated for the period from 1990 to 2010. The CO$_2$ emissions from energy production and end-use were also calculated. The emission

44

from industrial subsectors such as fertilizer, iron and steel production, cement production were computed as well.

The study recommended a series of policy measures to combat the environmental consequences of energy utilization and several sets of policy, fiscal, investment, institutional and regulatory measures mainly related to the two abatement scenarios were proposed in the study.

The valuation of environmental impacts/damages from energy production and end use sectors is based on the so called "preventive expenditures" concept: the expenditure, which is accepted for environmental protection is taken as an indication of what society is willing to pay for the reduction in pollution. Thus if abatement devices are actually installed, one can assume that, the society's willingness to pay is greater or at least equal to the costs of abatement. For example, the cost per unit of pollutant removed is the amount the society is willing to pay to avoid the damage caused by each unit of pollutant. Estimation of the cost per unit of pollutant includes several steps:

- Calculation of emissions per unit of production with no pollution control in place,

- Calculation of emissions per unit of production with emission control,

- Estimation of pollutant reduction per unit of production,

- Calculation of annual levelized control costs per unit of production and cost per unit of pollutant removed. This latter value is used to place lower bound on environmental damage caused by these pollutants.

This research study, like the one of China used the multiple assessment technique to supplement the judgment of the economic analysis. It too assigned the weighted values to different factors then set up a scoring system, with which the ranking of scenarios was done. It was found that the combination of the alternative scenarios I and II was the best.

One of drawbacks of the methodology used in this study was as follows: while energy demand projection was based on an end-use approach, energy supply expansion was based on capacity and investment planning; this likely poses the problem of consistency between future demand and future energy supply forecasts. The strength of this study lays in its detailed economic assessment of the different alternatives.

2.1.3 Energy Environment Studies in Indonesia

Like any Asian developing country, Indonesia's environmental problems arise primarily from a rapid increasing population and industrialization. These two factors are mainly concentrated in Java island. The most

pressing pollution issues are: drinking water pollution, general pollution by waste and ambient air pollution. Energy sector bears most responsibility for the air pollution: CO, CO_2 SO_2, suspended particulate matters (SPM) and NOx. Air analysis showed that the lead concentration in the air in Jakarta is twice as high as WHO's limits and the city is listed both among megacities worst ranked by PCC and among those with highest SPM (table 1.1 chapter I). In the future if the oil reserves are to be depleted, electricity generation will likely be based on coal, which will accelerate the air pollution level. In Jakarta, the capital of Indonesia, the situation is exacerbated by a big vehicle fleet.

Indonesia has taken a serious approach to the problem of environmental consequences of the energy sector. In an effort to determine national strategy for the energy sector development and to assess its impacts on the environment, several consecutive studies at national level were carried out [2], [13]. In particular the problem of air pollution associated with energy use had been tackled in the join Indonesian-German project: **"Energy Use and Air Pollution in Indonesia, Supply Strategy, Environment Impacts and Pollution Control".** [13] The first phase of this project completed in 1988, devoted to the development of economic scenarios, energy demand projections and multi-objective energy supply optimization. The second phase, which ended in 1993, aimed to develop environmentally compatible energy supply strategies for the next 30 years. In the study, the project team used a package including several computerized models. Three submodels: DEMO, DEMI and MACRO, were utilized for modeling the future population growth, for macroeconomic scenario design and for energy demand projections. The core model was MARKAL. It employs linear programming with a least cost criterion subject to various constraints. The model generates the optimal energy supply strategy for each of the scenarios under consideration, satisfying a set of specified constraints including capacity constraints, resource availability constraints, environmental constraints, etc. The project went further on examining the impacts of air pollution on the environment with the help of dispersion and deposition models and of a risk assessment model. Two environmental scenarios were examined. The first one was named Doing Nothing Case (DNC) implying the assumption that no significant improvements (compared to present pollution situation in Java) in air pollution management would take place. The results, generated by the model for this scenario showed that the 1991 level of SPM emission in Java was already twice as much as the 1982 level of West Germany. In 1991 Java's SPM emission reached 0.8 million ton and will reach 2.6 million ton per annum by 2021. Among pollutants NOx emission will increase fastest, followed by SO_2. The annual NOx emission will overpass that of SPM from the year 2006 onward. In 2021 i.e. end of the study period anthropogenic emissions in Java under Doing Nothing Case will be 3.95 million ton for NO_2; 2.8 million ton for SO_2 and 2.6 million ton for SPM. Regarding emission by economic sectors, it has been found that transport and power generation will compete for the first place in NOx emission, with higher growth rate belonging to the power sector. Industry was found to be SPM biggest polluter while power generation will dominate SO_2 emissions. The second environmental scenario was more realistic. It was called Case of Reduced Emission (ERC). This scenario assumed that along with high economic and energy consumption growth, measures are to be taken to control air pollution. The ERC is based on the following scenario assumptions:

1. For power plants, industrial boilers and furnaces the German emission standards were taken as reference. For these standards, the experience and necessary technical as well as economic data were available to carry out the ERC case calculations. Moreover, the reduction technologies included:

- Flue gas desulfurization;

- NOx control during and after combustion;

- Effective dust control.

2. For middle distillates and kerosene, processed from Middle East oil, desulfurization was assumed. The maximum sulfur content was 0.1 per cent of weight and 0.2 per cent of weight for middle distillate.

3. Three reduction measures were postulated for the traffic sector:

- Equipment of gasoline-powered passenger cars and minibuses with three-way catalytic converters;

- Production of unleaded gasoline;

- Reduction of particle emission from the diesel engines of passenger car, minibuses, and trucks according to the state of the art in Germany in early 1990.

As the project was a joint study between Indonesia and Germany, experiences and standards of Germany were fully made use of.

The model results showed significant improvement compared to Doing Nothing Case (DNC). Annual emission of all pollutants of ERC case were reduced to below 50 per cent of the corresponding values in DNC case. For example, cumulative emission of SO_2 calculated for the period 1989-2013 in DNC case was 41.8 million tons, while the same variable in ERC case was 22.3 million tons. For NOx these indicators were 64.4 and 35.3 million tons for SPM: 56.7 and 35.6 million tons respectively. Effects of emission reduction on concentration and deposition were examined using the modules DEDIS and GIS. Application of the ERC case required also the estimation of additional costs incurred. The ultimate purpose of the cost calculation was to assess the economic effectiveness of the emission reduction strategy. If the costs were too high, the

competitiveness of the country's industries might be affected. In this study, the cost data used were based on the state of the art in Germany in 1990. The additional cost for clean environment in Java island was found to be very high. It was estimated that the ERC case would require $1.1 billion to $1.6 billion annually from 1999 to 2013 and even more after that. This huge increase in emission reduction costs is due to the sustained growth in capacity addition in all sectors of the Indonesian economy in the forecasted period.

As a part of the study, the carbon dioxide emission from fossil fuel utilization between 1991 and 2023, was estimated in line with the energy supply strategy proposed. As it was defined in this study, ERC case did not aim to tackle CO_2 emission, thus CO_2 emission estimations were almost the same for DNC and ERC cases. Study results showed that by the year 2018 the fossil fuel related CO_2 release in Indonesia will reach the 1991 level of Germany i.e. around 1 billion ton per annum. The per capita releases of fossil fuel related CO_2 in Indonesia by the year 2023 will be 4.2 tons per capita per year or the world average level for 1991. This result shows that Indonesia is not a big contributor to the greenhouse gas emission. Anyway if the country wants to combat the CO_2 problem, it needs more measures than just abatement technologies for SO_2, NOx and particulates control. The study stressed that, the most important CO_2 reduction measures in electrical power sector are related to an increase in efficiency. It reported that a one per cent increase in efficiency of electricity production would result in a CO_2 reduction of 2.1 million ton per year. Typical measures proposed to improve efficiency were (i) retrofitting old plants, (ii) decreasing transmission and distribution losses and (iii) introduction of new efficient plants. Indonesia had introduced recently several gas combined cycle plants which are highly efficient. Energy sources such as hydro, geothermal and even nuclear power are also option for CO_2 free electricity generation. In other sectors of the economy, final energy conservation is a key issue. Almost 70 per cent of electricity generated in Indonesia is consumed by the industrial sector; if the conservation of 5 per cent of the electricity consumption in the industry is to be achieved then the CO_2 emission would be reduced by 20 million tons per year compared to the Doing Nothing Case. Carbon tax could be introduced after macroeconomic and microeconomic side-effects are carefully considered.

This is an exceptionally well organized and conducted study. The project team conducted a series of the fundamental studies at national level before undertaking the environmental assessment of energy use. Macroeconomic development, energy resource analysis, energy demand projection have been done with the help of computerized models, ensuring a sound basis for the energy supply optimization by MARKAL, incorporating exogenously specified environmental constraints.

In the framework of the **AEEMTRC's "ASEAN 2020 programme",** [2] a study for Indonesia had also been carried out in 1993. The study utilized the EFOM-ENV model for energy supply optimization and environmental impact assessment. The mathematical tool used in this model is a linear programming software based on an energy reference network. The study considered three energy demand supply scenarios, with one reference economic development scenario: the baseline case (or non intervention) scenario, the oil reduced scenario i.e. considering limited oil supply in the supply mix and the environmental scenario imposing limits to different emissions. For each of the scenarios, the energy supply – demand pattern was generated, emissions were calculated to estimate the possible level of pollution including CO_2, SO_2, NOx and TSP matters associated with each scenario; the optimal economic costs of the energy supply system are computerized to permit the comparison between scenarios. At the present time the final report of this study has not yet been published.

2.1.4 Energy Environment Studies in Thailand

Among countries under review, Thailand is the only one, which shows a systematic approach to the energy-environment problem. At national level there are several studies overseeing the current and future overall environmental situation in Thailand and highlighting the national strategies for sustainable development such as: "Thailand National Report to the United Nations Conference on Environment and Development (UNCED)" (June 1992), "A National Strategy for the Global Climate Change: Thailand" (1993) [46] and the project carried out by the Thailand Development Research Institute in collaboration with the Thailand Environmental Institute: "Industrializing Thailand and Impacts on Its Environment" (1990). The last project consists of eight reports covering all possible aspects of environmental impacts of the Thailand's industrialization and urbanization plan. Three reports deal directly with environment implications of the development e.g., Report No. 3: "Industrialization and Environmental Quality: Paying the Price" [45], Report No. 5: "The greening of Thai Industry – Producing more and Polluting less" [47] and Report No. 7: "Energy and Environment: Choosing the Right Mix" [44].

"Energy and Environment: Choosing the Right Mix".

In this report a Reference Energy Network model was used for characterizing the energy-environment impacts. The focus was placed on air emission quantification associated to energy flows through the two main components of the energy system: sectoral end use demand and main supply/conversion facilities. The five key dimensions, around which important variables were calculated, included:

- Energy by fuel type,
- Energy by sectors,
- Pollutant types,
- Time,
- Geographical location of the regions.

The core of the model is the energy module and corresponds closely to the energy balance set up annually by the National Energy Administration (nowadays Department of Energy Development and Promotion – DEDP).

The model is structured in such a way that it is capable of taking into consideration the implications of various policy measures aimed at the reduction of air pollution from energy sectors. The policy measures from the supply side aimed at the rationalization of the national energy resources and fuel substitution can be tested through modification of sectoral fuel mixes. The impacts of changes in energy pricing and end-use efficiency improvements can be assessed through modification of sectoral energy intensities of the final consuming sectors. The effects of technological progress can be addressed through the modification of sectoral intensities of economic sectors. Furthermore, the evolution of technology standards, emission standards, fuel standards as well as other limitation on total emission imposed by the government can be assessed by altering the fuel specific emission rates or introducing new constraint for total emission.

Five scenarios were considered:

- Scenario 1: base case,
- Scenario 2: Emphasized fuel and technology – based pollution control,
- Scenario 3: Sectoral fuel shifts,
- Scenario 4: Enhanced energy efficiency,
- Scenario 5: Comprehensive environment response.

The study addressed mainly the economic sectors with high potential of pollution: transport and industrial sectors. It also looked at the formulation and dispersion of acid rain precursors, as well as inventory of CO_2 resulting from production and end-use of energy. According to the study, Thailand will be experiencing high emission level of sulfur and carbon. Most of SO_2 emission comes from the use of lignite and fuel oil in power generation. The government policy to encourage the use of lignite in power generation will raise, at a higher level, the share of SO_2 emission from lignite burning. In Thailand, emission of NOx, HC and CO are originated mainly from transport sector. Industry is the major source of particulates emission. The study concluded that the projected future emission level creates a bleak outlook and indicated disturbing trend for environment conditions in Thailand. The study recommended also a series of policy measures to address the problems arising from each scenario.

UNEP greenhouse gas abatement costing study (the Thailand case)

This study aimed at the estimation of the cost of CO_2 abatement measures. The approach used in the study consisted of the following steps:

i. Establishment of a reference scenario up to the year 2030 on the basis of available data on national demographic and economic forecasts, data on technologies and emissions;

ii. Evaluation of relevant GHG abatement technologies in all energy sectors and ranking of these technologies on the basis of costs and emission reduction levels;

iii. Calculation of abatement costs taking into consideration technical potential, feasibility of adopting these technologies using relevant social, political and economic criteria;

iv. Construction and analysis of abatement scenarios.

Three energy-emission scenarios were developed for the study: Reference scenario, Abatement I and Abatement II scenarios. The Reference scenario is the case in which little or no measures are to be taken to reduce CO_2 emissions. The two abatement cases correspond to two different levels of CO_2 abatement; the first one represents a moderate effort to reduce CO_2 by 25 per cent by the year 2030, the second one represents a more stringent situation demanding more determined efforts to cut down CO_2 emission by up to 50 per cent.

A spreadsheet model was developed to make projections of energy demand and supply up to the year 2030. This spreadsheet model allows for detailed disaggregation enabling the analysis of the effects of the technical substitution and efficiency improvements. Four economic sectors namely industry, agriculture, transportation, and residential/commerce were examined. After energy demand and supply were projected, the CO_2 emissions of the reference scenario were estimated. The possible CO_2 emission reduction could be achieved through implementation of several options. The study considered only energy related options i.e. demand side management measures to reduce electricity consumption in the residential, commercial and industrial sectors, fuel switching in the power sector; and mileage improvements in transportation sectors. Various energy conservation technologies were considered in the study, viz., efficient lamps, electronic ballast, refrigerators, air conditioners, industrial motors. In the power sector, the latest power development plan was used as a reference. Technologies included coal and lignite power plants with and without flue gas desulfurization equipment, natural gas combined cycles, nuclear power option, and conventional thermal power plants. The study calculated the incremental costs of abatement scenarios. The incremental costs were derived by comparing the costs and emissions of more efficient or less polluting technology with the technologies used in the reference case.

It was found that the least cost options to reduce CO_2 were those in the final demand side: efficient air conditioning in the residential sector would yield greatest negative incremental abatement cost. The power sector

showed a considerable potential for CO_2 reduction with fuel switching from coal to natural gas. The most expensive option was found to be the retrofitting of old cars of transport sector. The study found that about 120 million tons of CO_2 (equivalent to 16 per cent of total CO_2 emissions) could be avoided by the year 2030 under moderate scenario at a total cost of Baht 26 billion. Under a more stringent scenario, the CO_2 reduction could be as much as 29 per cent with a cost of Baht 88 billion.

2.2 Regionally Coordinated Studies

2.2.1 "Acid Rain and Emission Reduction in Asia"

This project was initiated in 1989 when a first workshop on Acid rain in Asia was held at the Asian Institute of Technology. This was a response to growing recognition and concern about acid rain problem in this continent. This workshop brought together a large number of international institutions dealing with acid rain problems. The participants were chosen to represent the entire spectrum of issues and expertise, ranging from energy technologies, all the way through the cause – effect chain to the ultimate damage of natural, man-made systems. As a result of its review of the current and future situation in Asia, the workshop concluded that acid deposition had the potential to cause significant damage in Asia. Based on the above conclusion, the workshop recommended the development of an intensified monitoring programme in Asia and the development of a programme for research on pollutant transportation/transformation and on impacts of acid deposition on the natural and man-made systems. In addition the participants strongly recommended that an integrated programme of assessment and policy analysis be developed for the purpose of analyzing long term strategies for acid rain problems at national and Asia wide levels.

The second conference on Acid rain in Asia was held in November 1990. It had the purpose of reviewing the problem more in depth and to lay out a detailed programme and plan of actions. During this conference, several papers were presented and discussed which provided further understanding of the current status and potential of the acid rain problem in Asia. Major results include: a survey paper (Bhatti et al, 1990), which gave a broad perspective of the issues; and the first Asia-wide estimate of acid precursors through the year 2010 (Table 1.3 chapter I) (Foell and Green, 1990). Based on discussions at this conference, a integrated policy analysis framework was proposed. The plan included personnel and resource requirements, time schedules, institutional statement of interest and responsibilities from approximately 14 institutions through Asia, Europe and America. The conference produced a proceedings containing all the papers presented at the conference. A major outcomes and follow up of this conference was the growing awareness of potential acidification and air pollution problem in Asia and the increased interest within national government, research institutions as well as from international community, including UNEP, ESCAP, ADB and the WB.

The third consecutive meeting was convened at AIT in November 1991 to further examine the current status of the problem, develop and refine a proposal for the first phase of a complete assessment methodology of acid rain impact of Asia. Especially important results of the third conference were the presentation of methods and some preliminary results of the first emission inventory, long range transport calculations and ecosystem sensitivity classification and maps in Asia.

In addition, the participation of the Asian Development Bank and the World Bank led to the development of a detailed work plan for the implementation of a project, which was later financed by the two Banks. This project focused specifically on policy model development for acid rain in Asia. A PC based software tool to assess consequences of emission reduction strategies was also selected; the RAINS model developed by IIASA for European countries was integrated in the formulation of the RAINS – ASIA project. The target of this project is to implement an integrated acid rain and emission policy analysis tool for the development of national and regional policy perspectives in this region. The model design includes the entire cause-effect chain from energy systems and emissions through to the ultimate impacts on natural and man-made systems.

This model consists of three main modules:

i.   Energy and emission module (ENEM);

ii.   Atmospheric module (ATMOS);

iii. Impact module (IMPACT).

The Rains – Asia model covers countries of East, South and South-East Asia, with particular focus on China, India, Thailand, the Democratic People's Republic of Korea and the Republic of Korea. The range of the model is 1990-2020 with a one year resolution. The results of the first phase of the project were summarized at the last workshop held in November 1994 in AIT Bangkok, Thailand [49], [50].

2.2.2 "Global Warming Issues in Asia"

The workshop on "Global warming issues in Asia" [4] was organized in September 1993 at AIT to bring together researchers of diverse expertise from different countries in Asia as well as recognized experts from overseas in order to catalyze the formation of multinational and multi-disciplinary working groups and provide an impetus for climate change research in the region. It gathered prominent experts from twelve Asian developing countries and nine developed countries of America and Europe.

Papers presented at the workshop dealt with various aspects of the problem: the modeling of the climate change and its impact, carbon dioxide emission related to energy in Asian developing countries, impact of agriculture, forestry on the global warming, policy and technical options to combat the climate change.

2.2.3 "Study on Environmental Indicators and Indices"

The study is a joint ADB – AIT/Harvard University project initiated in 1994 [53], [54], [55]. Its aim is to develop a usable set of Environmental Quality Indicators that can be utilized by the ADB as well as by decision makers in countries members to analyze the progress and performance of environmental quality management. The project team introduced an aggregated index: "environmental elasticity" (EE), which is defined as the percentage of changes in environmental quality with respect to one per cent of changes in the economic development for a given country. By looking at this environmental elasticity the policy makers can be able to judge toward what direction regarding environmental quality the country is moving, while pursuing the economic goals. So the EE index provides useful information for decision making in the future.

In calculating the EE index a set of initial environmental parameters are used, e.g.: water quality, air quality, solid waste, and forest covers, etc. Each of the parameters has several components, for example the air quality is made up by the combination of the concentrations of different pollutants such as particulate matters, SO_2, and NOx, etc. The aggregation of the variations of all components embodied within one parameter as well as the aggregation of the variations of all parameters into one general index is done by assigning some weight factors to each of them. The EE index relates the changes in the environmental quality (e.g. square kilometer of the forest cover) with the change of the economy (e.g. GDP per capita) over a given period of time.

A regional workshop was organized during June 28-30/1995 at AIT, at which the country studies from China, Nepal, the Philippines and Pakistan were discussed. It has been found that the new environmental index did well reflect the reality in these countries. Further research is to be done in order to make the environmental elasticity index not only qualitatively but also quantitatively reliable.

2.2.4 WEC – ADEME/AIT Project on "Cross Countries Comparison of Energy Efficiency Indicators"

One of the ways to combat the environmental pollution is the energy conservation and the improvement of energy efficiency in the demand sectors, which is the scope of the WEC – ADEME/AIT project on "Cross country comparison of energy efficiency indicators in Asian countries".

The project thoroughly analyzed the energy conservation situation in the past period from 1980 to 1992 in seven Asian countries, namely China, India, Indonesia,

Republic of Korea, Philippines, Taiwan Province of China and Thailand. The WEC study focused primarily on the impacts of energy demand management policies of the countries under consideration on their energy efficiency performance. An identical set of indicators, including Divisia index for the industrial subsectors, average fuel consumption per vehicle for different vehicle types and index of energy and electricity consumption per household, etc., was designed to provide a possibility for cross country comparison.

It has been found that, the energy demand management policies implemented in Asian developing countries differs from one to another. For some countries the policy is a coherent set of administrative, economic and legislative measures enabling to achieve step by step an efficient energy utilization (e.g. Republic of Korea, Taiwan Province of China and Thailand in some extent). Other countries have just started with initial policy measures such as: propaganda, public educational campaign to promote the energy conservation and efficiency, (e.g. Indonesia, India and Philippines), but the results of such initial policy measures in these countries, at this point, reflected in their poor energy conservation records.

In most of the countries only the industrial sector showed some achievement in energy efficiency. Other sectors did not show significant progress in energy conservation. Thus, there is still a significant potential for energy conservation in every sector in many Asian developing economies. If this potential were to be exploited, the energy conservation could be substantial and consequently the environmental pollution could also be reduced drastically in the future [15-22].

2.2.5 AEEMTRC – ASEAN 2020 Programme

The ASEAN 2020 is a long term energy supply/ demand study for ASEAN member states up to the year 2020. The project main objective is to provide a comprehensive assessment of the energy situation in ASEAN and to identify opportunities for regional action. This general objective is transformed into following operational objectives:

- to develop a consolidated database on ASEAN;

- to demonstrate a common methodology for energy analysis and forecasting for all member states;

- to under take a systematic analysis of the determinants of energy use in ASEAN;

- to review the main sources of uncertainties affecting energy supply and demand in ASEAN and put them into future scenarios;

- to identify and evaluate long term energy supply/ demand prospects in selected relevant scenarios;

- to analyze the relevance of various technological options under different energy policy objectives;

- to develop a regional framework for national energy programmes and policies;

- to estimate future emission levels under the different scenario assumptions and assess abatement options; etc.,.

With regard to the objectives of the study to analyze the possibilities of ASEAN countries to construct a reliable, low-cost, environmentally sound energy system with special emphasis on the opportunities of inter ASEAN and ASEAN-EC cooperation, three groups of basically different scenarios are defined for country studies:

- Baseline scenario (BASE) – a non interventionist

- Oil reduced scenario (OILRED) – reduced energy consumption and oil substitution

- Environmental scenario ENV – environmental constraints are imposed.

Several country studies have been completed (Thailand, Indonesia) as presented in previous section. The final study report is expected to be published in near future.

3. The Analytical Models in the Energy-Environmental Planning

After having reviewed some theoretical and practical aspects of the environmental problem in some Asian countries, and in several national and regional energy environment studies, in the first two parts of the present report, this third part will introduce computerized tools popularly used and most of the time needed in the framework of energy environmental studies over the world.

3.1 Overall Framework of Energy Environment Analysis

Nowadays, a number of computerized tools, based on different fundamental approaches and concepts, and relying on a range of mathematical algorithms, have been developed for carrying out the energy system analysis and comparative assessment studies of different options for the energy sector development. The objective of a comparative assessment for planning and decision making in the energy sector is to provide the framework for analyzing and evaluating all the social, economic, and environmental impacts of the various energy scenarios in order to allow a choice of a optimized solutions according to specific goals of the decision makers. The schematic presentation of that framework is sketched in figure 3.1 in which interrelationships of the trio Economy – Energy – Environment are shown. A development of the national economy requires the development of the energy sector, which discharges waste, pollution into the environment. The sustainability of the development requires an integration of external costs into the planning process as illustrated in the figure. The role of each component within the framework is discussed below:

Macroeconomic analysis: The macroeconomic analysis aims at providing a comprehensive description of the current structure of the economy and its expected evolution. This provides the inputs/outputs for the energy sector and an analysis of the impacts of the energy sector at macroeconomic level on the one hand and also the influence of the macroeconomic situation and economic policies on the energy sector on the other hand. Different types of models are available but disaggregated models often require extensive economic data bases. Since macroeconomic analysis serves essentially as a basis for energy demand projection mainly and, in view of underdeveloped database in many Asian developing countries, an aggregated model could be recommended for this purpose.

Energy system analysis: Energy system analysis serves to assess the energy system consisting of interrelated energy flows and technologies in a comprehensive and systematic way. The energy system models are usually based on a network representation showing activities from natural resource extraction to delivering energy to the final end users. Energy models allow to find among various alternatives the one that satisfies best the objective of the energy planning taking into account a set of constraints. The analysis may focus primarily on the demand side e.g. evaluation of secondary energy demand associated with a given level of economic activities, starting from the outputs of the macroeconomic analysis and incorporating elements like energy conservation policy, demand side management and fuel substitution policies etc. Afterwards the analysis will look at the energy supply needed to satisfy a given requirement under different conditions taking into account resource, technology constraints and eventually environmental constraints.

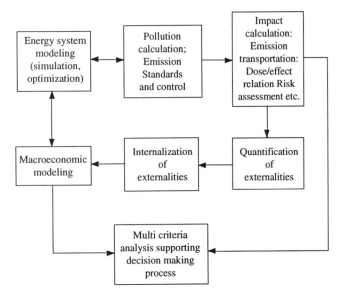

Figure 3.1 Framework for energy-environment planning

Pollution assessment: The accounting of the emissions and waste discharged into the air, water and soil is the first step necessary for further assessment of the negative impact of a given energy strategy. Following the straightforward calculation of a volume of pollutants, the analysis of the health and environmental impacts aims towards quantifying all the effects and to evaluate how they affect human well being at the present time and in the future. The quantification of physical impacts on the man and the environment consists of two main steps:

i. The analysis of pollutant transportation, potential chemical transformations; the evaluation of changes in concentration of the pollutants in the ambient air, water and soil quality; and potential intake by human beings;

ii. Quantification of the effects on the receptors, e.g. death rate, physical damage of the built environment, effect of climate changes, etc.

The valuation of physical impacts is required in view of the incorporation of externalities in the comparative assessment of the different alternatives of the energy sector development. The impacts may be valued by an estimation of social costs, i.e. the importance attached to these impacts by society. The economic valuation of impacts can be based on two types of methodologies i.e. the abatement cost approach and the damage function cost approach. The first one considers that the costs associated with emission reduction are a reasonable surrogate for damage values. The second approach is based upon a detailed assessment of the chain from emissions through concentration to physical impacts which are then valued. The evaluation ought to estimate the willingness to pay for, which is an indicator of the value of human health and environmental goods and the like.

Multi criteria decision supporting analysis: The previous analyses provide information intended to support the decision making process. However the outputs from previous analyses and modeling at this point include economic values, quantitative and qualitative indicators related to environmental impacts, risk etc. This kind of information could be passed on to the decision making body without further processing or an additional analysis should be made with the so called "decision aiding tools" in order to provide convenient procedures and transparency for the comparison of the alternatives, especially when the number of parameters is large. The decision aiding tool could be as simple as a matrix or a graphical display providing a convenient way to visualize, e.g. a list of the key parameters mentioned above. Or the decision aiding tool could be a computerized programme which permits to combine all economic values, quantitative and qualitative indicators related to environmental impacts, risk, etc. in simpler set of indicators ordering the results of each energy-environment scenario under consideration, so that the comparison between alternatives becomes easier. This decision aiding tool can enhance the capability to use more effectively the results of the previous analyses.

3.2 Model Classification

Before going into the detailed description of some models, a general classification of existing models would be helpful for understanding their need, their roles and their specificity in relation to the studies under consideration. For those models being described in this chapter the most famous one, four categories can be proposed as follows *(DECADES project, working paper No. 5)* [8]:

Category I: Energy Information Systems

These models consist of a database plus some peripheral tools for data analysis (e.g. CO2DB model of IIASA).

Figure 3.2 Simplified diagram of an Energy Information System

Category II: Energy System Models

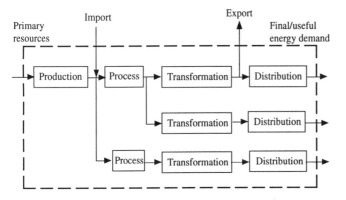

Figure 3.3 Simplified diagram of an Energy System Model

These models focus on the analysis of the energy supply system in a systematic manner. Some of the energy system models are extended to include parts or all of the energy demand analysis as well. Others provide additional features to calculate the impacts of the planned energy system on environmental, economic and social aspects (EFOM-ENV, MARKAL)

Category III: Modular package

These tools may consist of several different kinds of models: a macroeconomic component, an energy supply and demand balance, etc., but are integrated into one package. The modular structure provides the users with the flexibility

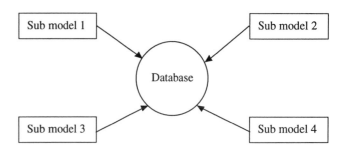

Figure 3.4 Simplified diagram of a Modular Package

to run any submodel needed for a specific purposes (e.g. ENPEP, LEAP, MESAP).

Category IV: Integrated Models

This category includes models consisting of an integrated set of equations simultaneously solved. These models usually cover energy-economy – environmental interactions (e.g. MICRO MELODIE, ESG)

3.3 Model Description

Following are the description, main characteristics, features and capabilities of nine selected models from the different categories presented above:

3.3.1 Category I: Energy Information Model:

1) The CO2DB model

Description:

The CO2DB model, developed by IIASA, has the purpose to select technologies, calculate the efficiency, costs and environmental effects of the energy conversion chain. It gives qualitative and quantitative description for CO_2 reduction purposes. The data bank contains general data, technical data covering physical energy flows, economic data (investment, operation and maintenance costs, costs of decommissioning of power plants); environmental data (emission factors and inventory) and miscellaneous data. The CO_2 technology data bank is a fully interactive software package designed to allow the user to enter, update, review and print information on CO_2 technologies.

Scope:

Objective:

To help in decision making and comparative assessments of different energy technologies based on technical, economic and environmental criteria.

Issues addressed:

- *Energy system analysis:* the model allows for resource use analysis with emphasis on the electricity generation planning

- *Environmental analysis:* This model deals exclusively with CO_2 emission. It also considers environmental impacts of different technologies in the power system planning.

Limitation:

- Analyses of the demand and the supply sides are not included in energy system analyses, water pollution and solid waste are not assessed by the model.

Future development:

- Other than CO_2 pollutants will be included in the data bank.

Technical characteristics:

- *User friendliness:* menu driven; on line help

- *Hardware:* IBM PC 386; Minimum 8 MB RAM, 25 MB hard disk; VGA color monitor.

- *Software:* DOS 5.0 and above db VISTA and Graphic C

3.3.2 Category II: Energy System Model

1) The MARKAL model

Description:

The MARKAL model, which was designed by IEA/ETSAP, is a flexible tool to represent the energy system from primary energy resources through conversion processes, to transport, distribution and end-use devices. Exogenously specified end-use demands are satisfied at the least total costs taking into account a wide variety of constraints. MARKAL is a dynamic optimization model employing linear programming.

Scope:

Objective:

- This model is used for target-oriented integrated analysis and planning.

Issues addressed:

Overall energy system analyses:

- Demand analysis: Optional level of detail for demand sector with possibility of modeling conservation technologies.

- Resource analysis: Detailed modeling of depletable and renewable resources is possible

- Supply side analysis: Detailed modeling is possible

- Demand/supply balance: Optimization

- Detailed electricity system analysis including generation expansion, transmission analyses.

Environmental analysis:

- The MARKAL permits a comprehensive treatment of air, water, solid waste pollution.

Limitation:

- Macroeconomic analysis is not included.

Future development:

- MARKAL – MACRO module for macroeconomic analysis.

Technical characteristics:

- *User friendliness:* Basic understanding of linear programming is required. User interface for data handling, model execution; menu driven on-line help; graphic output in DBF format.

- *Hardware:* IBM PC 386 (486 is preferable); 4 MB RAM, 30 MB hard disk; VGA color monitor.

- *Software:* DOS 5.0 and above OMNI and HSLP.

2) The MESSAGE III model

Description:

The MESSAGE III model is used for optimization of the energy system. However, other systems supplying specified demands of goods that have to be processed before delivery to the final consumers could be optimized. It consists of a demand data module, a supply data module, an optimization module, a result module and other supporting programmes.

Scope:

Objective:

The objective of MESSAGE include: resource extraction analysis; import/export energy planning; energy conversion analysis; energy transport and distribution analysis; final energy utilization analysis; environmental protection policies and investment policy.

Issues addressed:

Overall energy system analysis:

- Demand analysis: Demand elasticity and fuel substitutions;

- Resource analysis: Domestic renewable and exhaustible resources;

- Supply side analysis: Detailed evaluation of supply side configurations;

- Demand/supply balance: Optimization.

Environmental analysis:

- Focus on air pollution.

Limitation:

- The model does not include macroeconomic analysis. The assessment of pollution other than air pollution cannot be performed.

Future development:

- No plan for the time being.

Technical characteristics:

- *User friendliness:* Special training is required.

- *Hardware:* IBM PC 386 (486 is preferable) with coprocessor; 8 MB RAM, 300 MB hard disk; VGA color monitor.

- *Software:* AT&T UNIX 5.3 or higher; Sun UNIX or IBM AIX; Optimize MINOS, MOPS or OSL.

3) The EFOM-ENV model:

Description:

The EFOM-ENV model designed by ECN/CEC-DG XII is a techno-economic supply and demand model that simulates or optimizes the primary energy requirements and the related investments for energy production and consumption necessary in order to satisfy a given exogenous demand of useful or final energy. The techno-economic information is stored in a database capable of describing various modular structures of the energy system. Two operational modes are provided: simulation and optimization. They can be used alternatively on any defined structure. EFOM-ENV is a multi period linear programming model. Minimization of the total discounted costs of the energy system over the complete time horizon provides an optimal energy supply for a given useful (of final) energy demand. Many constraints can be implemented such as depletion rates of energy resources, penetration rates of technologies, and allowable emission levels. The model contains technological processes for extraction, transport and conversion of energy (e.g. electricity generation, combined heat and power production, refinery processes) and also for end use technologies (e.g. food processing industry, cement, iron industries). Abatement technologies are also available to reduce the emissions of pollutants.

Scope:

Objective:

- Energy and environmental analysis and planning.

Issues addressed:

Energy system analyses:

- Demand side analysis: Analysis of energy requirement at final or useful level; energy conservation measures can be investigated.

- Supply side analysis: All energy flows entering the system are modeled. Fuel substitution; conversion efficiency improvement; Technological substitution can be integrated.

Environmental analysis:

- All kinds of pollution (air, water, solid waste) can be calculated at national and any subsectoral levels. Cost of abatement scenarios can be derived.

Future development:

- A significant development of the EFOM-ENV is now being done by Energy Planning Central Consultant Team (Energy Technology Division, Asian Institute of Technology). This includes (i) a user-PC interface SHELL package which provides the user with facilities in data management (modification of the network, updating of data etc.), in running the model and for report preparation, (ii) the inclusion of a 6th keyword level, which permits to analyze energy system at the regional or provincial level, (iii) graphical presentation of the energy network and of model outputs.

Technical characteristics:

- *User friendliness:* A special user-PC interface i.e. EFOM SHELL has been developed by Energy Planning Central Consultant Team (AIT) to provide the user with a convenience for data handling, consistency checking, model execution and report generation;

- *Hardware:* IBM PC 386 (486 is preferable) with coprocessor; Minimum 4 MB RAM, VGA color monitor, graphic card;

- *Software:* DOS or UNIX; MINOS, MOPS or OSL.

3.3.3 Category III: Modular Packages

1) The ENPEP package:

Description:

The ENPEP package was developed for IAEA and is distributed by this organization. It is a set of micro-computer based energy planning tools that are designed to provide an integrated analysis capability. ENPEP begins with macroeconomic analysis, develops an energy demand forecasts based on this analysis, carries out an integrated supply/demand analysis for the entire energy system, evaluates the electricity system components in detail and evaluates the environmental impacts (emissions) and resource requirements (land, manpower, financial) of the proposed evolutions of the energy and electricty systems. ENPEP is structured in a modular fashion with each module having a specific objective. Each module can be executed independently or in a chain depending on the objectives of the study and the data available. The programmes were developed out of proven methodologies for energy and electricity planning. Thus, balances of supply/demand are determined for an energy network that describes all facilities of the energy system, and the analysis is carried out based on the equilibrium modeling approach of the IDES model. Energy and electricity demand forecasts are calculated by the MAED model (which is in turn based on MEDEE-2). Optimal expansion plans of the electricity generation system are determined by mean of WASP-3 model. Finally, environmental burdens and resource requirements of the energy/electricity system are calculated using an approach that permits treating each system component separately, allowing also to optimize the emission reduction devices that would need to be installed when environmental controls are imposed.

Scope:

Objective:

- Energy policy analysis;

- Energy tariff structure;

- Energy project investment analysis;

- Electric system expansion planning;

- Environmental policy analysis for energy system.

Issues addressed:

Overall energy analyses:

- Demand analysis: Detailed evaluation of the sectoral energy demands by sector, subsector, fuels and useful energy. The growth of the energy demand is determined by macroeconomic variables or other user-specified parameters (e.g. elasticities, energy intensities, etc.,). The package is able to carry out energy conservation and demand side management analyses;

- Resource analysis: Representation of renewable and depletable resource availability and costs;

- Supply side analysis: User-defined level of detail. Detailed evaluation of the power system configurations both current and future. ENPEP has special submodels to deal with the electric power sector (e.g. MAED which generates

electricity load from an energy demand module (MEDEE-2), and WASP III, which performs the generation expansion planning);

- Supply/demand balance: Equilibrium solution for total energy system, energy policy constraints can be imposed;

Environmental consideration:

- All environmental impacts can be computed both under base scenario (uncontrolled emissions) or under environmental scenarios (emissions with alternative control equipment implemented). Incremental costs of control is also computed. All kinds of pollution (air, water, solid waste, land loss) can be taken into consideration.

Future development:

- Continual improvement of computational algorithms; development of graphical user interface and development of a Windows version.

Technical characteristics:

- *User friendliness:* menu driven on-line help; graphical outputs;

- *Hardware:* IBM PC 386 (486 is preferable) with coprocessor; 2 MB RAM, 30 MB hard disk; VGA color monitor;

- *Software:* DOS 3.1 or higher.

2) The Long Range Energy Alternative Planning Package

Description:

LEAP – the Long-range Energy Alternatives Planning system, developed by Stockholm Environmental Institute – Boston, has the objective to provide a computer-based approach for fostering integrated, reliable and ongoing energy planning. It is suitable for performing energy assessment in developing as well as in developed countries, for multi-country regions and local planning purposes. LEAP provides an information bank, an instrument for long-term projections of supply/demand configurations and a vehicle for identifying and evaluating policy and technology options.

Scope:

Objectives:

- Energy policy analysis;

- Environmental policy analysis;

- Biomass and land use assessment;

- Preinvestment project analysis;

- Integrated planning.

Issues addressed:

Energy system analyses:

- Demand analysis: Detailed evaluation of the sectoral energy demands by sectors, subsectors end-uses and equipment. Growth of energy demands is determined by users-defined relationships for fuel shares, intensities, structural changes, equipment ownership;

- Supply side analysis: Detailed evaluation of supply configurations both current and future. Iterative calculation of demand/supply balance.

Environmental analysis:

- Environmental burdens computed as uncontrolled emissions, with alternative control equipment under alternative environmental regulations and with incremental cost control;

- The package permits comprehensive treatment of air, water, solid pollution.

Future development:

- Extend full fuel cycle analysis capabilities;

- Expansion of environmental database;

- Link to atmospheric dispersion model;

- Develop a Windows version.

Technical characteristics:

- *User friendliness:* menu driven on-line help; error checking; graphical outputs;

- *Hardware:* IBM PC 386; 640 KB RAM, 6 MB hard disk; CGA color monitor;

- *Software:* DOS 3.1 or higher.

3) The MESAP package

Description:

MESAP (developed by IER, University of Stuttgart, Germany) is a modular energy planning package providing energy analysts and planners with tools to perform a complex energy analysis. It consists of basic techniques for the energy planning, a set of tested energy modules and a data management and processing software. At the heart of the MESAP is a data management processing system (RSYST).

Scope:

Objective:

The objective of the package is energy and environment policy analysis with several modules performing following tasks:

INCA: comparative assessment of single technologies on an economic basis;

MADE: demand analysis;

MESSAGE: integrated energy system analysis;

WASP: least cost power plant expansion planning;

ENIS: energy information system on time series, energy balances and technology data.

Issues addressed:

Macroeconomic analysis:

- Country – specific econometric model;

Energy system analyses:

- Demand analysis: Analysis of the energy requirements at the useful energy or final energy levels with user specified degree of detail;

- Supply analysis: Technology oriented.

Environmental analysis:

- The package allows to calculate emission levels of all kinds of air pollution. Calculations of solid waste and land use are also possible.

Limitation:

- Assessment of water pollution is not included.

Future development:

- The demand model is to be expanded to a full scope simulation model covering both demand and supply analyses. The model will allow to consider hourly load curve of electricity in order to analyze renewable and cogeneration;

- Development of a General Equilibrium Model based on I/O technique and incorporating LP features to model the technical characteristics of the energy and environment system. The model is used for analysis of policy impacts of pricing and taxation strategies.

- Development of a central network database with graphical interface. All modules can access the database and allow the graphical representation in the network format.

Technical characteristics:

- *User friendliness:* Some modules are menu-driven (INCA, MAED), other are not (MESSAGE); error checking programme and executive menu shell are provided;

- *Hardware:* IBM PC 386 (486 is preferable); 30 MB hard disk;

- *Software:* DOS or UNIX. For MESSAGE III: MINOS LP solver is required.

3.3.4   Category IV: Integrated Model

1) The MICRO MELODIE model

Description:

MICRO MELODIE (CEA/France) is a macroeconomic model with detailed technological description of the energy sector, especially the electricity sector. The model also computes polluting emission such as NOx, SO_2, and CO_2. Economy, energy and environment are then described in a single framework, but for each topic a specific methodology has been developed. The model is adapted to analyze any energy policy modifying the cost structure of electricity.

Scope:

Objective:

- Objective of the model is to provide a tool for analysis of macroeconomic-energy – environment linkages, employing an econometric model with a technical representation of the energy sector.

Issues addressed:

Macroeconomic analysis:

- Country specific econometric model.

Energy system analyses:

- Demand side analysis: Analysis of energy requirements for sectors using econometric estimations of transfer costs and utility functions.

- Supply side analysis: Technological presentation of the electricity sector including coal, gas oil and nuclear fuel cycles.

- Supply/demand balance: Price equilibrium.

Environmental analysis:

- The model permits to calculate air pollution for NOx, CO_2, SO_2.

Limitation:

- Water pollution, solid waste, and land use are not included in the environmental assessment.

Future development: not yet planned.

Technical characteristics:

- *User friendliness:* Basic understanding of econometrics and economics are required;

- *Hardware:* IBM PC 386 (486 is preferable) with math coprocessor; VGA color monitor;

- *Software:* DOS; AREMOS II/X PC version 1.41 (WEPA).

2) The ESG model

Description:

The main purpose of the ESG (Swiss Federal Institute of Technology) is to generate consistent scenarios of economic development which simultaneously determines energy demand and supply as well as environmental impacts. The feedback between economic development, energy demand and energy supply is fully integrated into the model, i.e. an energy technology model is linked with a macroeconomic model.

Scope:

Objective:

- Coordination of macroeconomic, energy, and environmental policy.

Issues addressed:

Macroeconomic analysis:

- Input-output approach refined for ten sectors of the economy.

Energy system analyses:

- Energy demand analysis with demand derived from macroeconomic submodel, final demand is calculated by a demand function of disposable income and relative price structure;

- Supply side analysis with energy technology system defined by the users.

Environmental analysis:

- Emissions of air pollutants are aggregated and reported.

Limitation:

- Only global figures for water pollution; solid waste and land use can be calculated.

Table 3.1. Summary of the main characteristics of reviewed models and packages

	Model/ Organization	Category	Method	Data requirement	Energy analysis	Environment analysis
1	CO2DB/IIASA	Energy Information System Model (Category I)	Interrelation between database and comparison options	Energy inputs and outputs	Focus on generation expansion analysis.	CO_2 emission only
2	EFOM-ENV/CEC	Energy System Model (Category II)	Linear programming	Useful energy demand; base year energy balance; data on technologies; market shares of technologies and energy carriers, energy prices	Both demand and supply sides are integrated for analysis.	Flexibility for air, water, solid waste pollution calculation at user specified levels.
3	MARKAL/ IEA-ETSAP	Energy System Model (Category II)	Linear programming	Base year energy balance; useful energy demand; energy prices; data on technologies, fuel mix, efficiencies etc.	Both demand and supply sides can be analyzed with detail.	Analysis of all pollutant is possible.
4	MESSAGE/ IIASA	Energy System Model (Category II)	Linear programming	High data intensiveness	Demand and supply analyses are possible. Detailed modeling of electric system is emphasized.	Only aggregated estimation of air pollution (not detailed).
5	ENPEP/ IAEA-US DOE	Modular Package (Category III)	Simulation and Dynamic optimization depends on modules	Base year energy balance, energy prices, energy technology performance, international energy price projection electric system load, technological data etc.	Possibility for analysis of demand and supply side, strong capability for electric system planning.	Assessment of all kinds of pollutants is possible.
6	LEAP/TELLUS Institute	Modular Package (Category III)	Simulation	Base year energy balance, energy prices, energy technology performance, international energy price projection electric system load, technological data, biomass land use data, etc.	Both demand and supply sides can be analyzed with detail.	Assessment of all kinds of pollutants is possible with emphasis on biomass and land use.
7	MESAP/IER	Modular Package (Category III)	Econometric and simulation	Base year economic activities, energy technology characteristics, performance, costs, investment, energy prices, etc.	Both demand and supply sides can be analyzed with detail strong capacity for electric system planning.	Air pollution can be assessed with detail.
8	ESG	Integrated Model (Category IV)	Econometric method	Base year energy balance, economic data, input/ output tables, energy technology data, capital market data etc.	Both demand and supply sides can be analyzed.	Aggregated air pollution is reported.
9	MELODIE/CEA	Integrated Model (Category IV)	Econometric (for energy supply)	Input/Output tables; energy balances in physical and monetary units, technological and economic data of electricity sector, etc.	Emphasis on electric system planning.	Only air pollution is evaluated.

Note: This list is not exhaustive (many other models exist around the world) but the target was to present only the well known international models.

Future development: not yet planned.

Technical characteristics:

- *User friendliness:* Economic and technical knowledge necessary. Data collection is very labor intensive. Programming effort is required for economic submodel;

- *Hardware:* IBM PC 386 with math coprocessor, 12 to 16 MB RAM; 100 MB hard disk, VGA screen. Or any UNIX workstation, any main frame computer with dumb terminals;

- *Software:* DOS 3.0 up; FORTRAN 77; Graphical system for presentation purposes.

3.4 Summary

As it can be seen from above description, each model or package incorporates within themselves the main elements of comprehensive comparative assessment for planning and decision making such as:

- Macroeconomic analysis;

- Energy (or electricity) system analysis;

- A framework for accounting for emissions and other effluents born within the energy chain;

- Incorporation for environmental analyses;

- Decision aiding framework.

Although the general scope and the objectives of these models are similar, their structural complexity, employed concept, data requirements, and their capabilities are very different. Table 3.1 summaries the basic characteristics of these nine models and packages. From the table, it is can be seen that regarding the environmental impact assessment, MARKAL, MESSAGE, EFOM-ENV and ENPEP are found to be more adequate than the others. Among the four, ENPEP belongs to the modular package family, which usually requires very intensive database. MESSAGE model limits the pollution evaluation to the air pollution only, it does not allow for detailed evaluation of water pollution, solid waste pollution and land use impacts as MARKAL and EFOM-ENV do. The two models EFOM-ENV and MARKAL are equally powerful in handling the assessment of the environmental impacts and can be recommended for this purpose. The advantage of the EFOM-ENV model is in its flexibility: the structure of the energy system can be changed all along the planning process; technological processes can be removed or added. These features permit the modeling of many policy options for the emission reduction. Moreover emission levels can be calculated for each subsector and emission bounds can be put at any levels of the Reference Energy System (RES).

It is impossible to make a proper ranking among the models bearing in mind their differences in concepts, structures and capabilities. What model to choose for a specified energy-environment study depends upon the main objectives of the study, availability of data and other resources as well as specific conditions prevailing in the country or region concerned.

4. Conclusions

Although the number of studies carried out in Asian developing countries to assess environmental impact of energy production and consumption is still limited, by reviewing the existing ones it is possible to figure out broadly the state of the art of the scientific and technological knowledge on this subject in the region.

Most of the nations in this fast growing region of the world are aware of the negative impacts that they likely impose onto natural and man-made systems when utilizing energy to meet their increasing demand. As such, more and more efforts are being made in order to understand the nature of the problems and so effectively combat undesirable consequences of energy development.

The studies under review have a similar structure though the degree of detail and in depth in their analyses are different. They consist of following main parts:

- The first part of the studies usually deals with **trend of socio-economic development,** which summaries historical development of the country and puts forward socio-economic goals for the study period (GDP growth, population growth, urbanization rate, etc.);

- The second part considers possible energy supply and energy demand alternatives, to form the **energy development scenarios;**

- These studies often devote a part to review **current global environmental situation** of a given country. Depending on the study, this review may cover several or all of the following items: air pollution, water pollution, solid waste problem and land loss, forest cover and deforestation;

- **Estimation of likely environmental consequences** of energy development without abatement option is another part, which serves as a reference for later comparison and ranking of abatement scenarios;

- **Analyses of the abatement scenarios:** technological & policy option, and finally;

- **Feasibility of measures implementation** are recommended in most of the studies.

The focal goals of the different studies are different following the countries. Some of the studies look at overall environmental impacts (China, India). They explored all aspects of environmental implications of the energy sector: air pollution, land loss, etc. Other studies focused only on air pollution. In fact, air pollution and global warming are the most serious issues for a large number of countries at the present time.

In the studies under review, energy models are utilized at different level of complexity. For most of the studies, macro-economic goals are defined exogenously. Exception is the study on Indonesia, in which macro economic variables are integrated in the model.

For energy demand projections, all studies resorted to techno-economic (end-use) approach. Such an approach allows to account for the different energy demand trends of the various consumer categories. More importantly, end-use approach can take into consideration changes in efficiency, equipment innovation, effects of energy conservation, etc. For the energy supply system, planning was based on capacity investment expansion planning with demand being a given input. Total emissions are calculated based on emission factors and on the quantity of each energy form utilized. Some of the studies went further to examine and try to quantify the impact of acid rain deposition with dispersion and dilution models and dose response functions. Others limited themselves to the estimation of total quantity of SO_2, NOx and CO_2 emissions.

The limitations of the studies under review are: standards models are rarely used in the studies. This is probably because the scope of studies was so large that they could not go in depth in each of the above mentioned subjects. In fact to make a comprehensive and coherent study each of the above mentioned parts should be modeled separately using various software development. The Indonesian and the Thailand studies are example of such a methodology. On the other hand, software usually is not always made available to developing countries. Even when they are available the lack of the well-organized, comprehensive database and qualified operators precludes the successful application of the tools.

Given that situation in the region, it is urgent to introduce and disseminate a regional methodology and procedures for the incorporation of environmental consideration into energy development planning and policy making. The analytical tools of the methodology could be one of existing models popularly used for similar purposes in other countries. As it is highlighted in chapter III of the present study, models like MARKAL or EFOM-ENV are believed to be most appropriate for such a role.

As a conclusion the EFOM-ENV has been selected by EPCCT experts and a considerable effort has been done by this team to ensure a high level of user friendliness which permits to consider it as the most flexible and powerful tool at the moment to be used in the framework of an energy environment study and in particular in the framework of the Energy Environment Planning Activity (sub-activity EEP-3) of the Programme for Asian Cooperation on Energy and the Environment (UNDP/ESCAP/PACE – E/RAS/92/071).

PART III: THE IN-COUNTRY STUDY ON ENERGY-ENVIRONMENT PLANNING

1. Main Characteristics of the Design and Implementation of the In-Country Studies on Energy-Environment Planning

1. 1 Introduction

Scarcity of energy and/or financial resources, the increase of environmental concerns, and the overall burden on world energy markets, characterize the general situation that the developing countries of Asia have to face and which threaten their development.

To help these countries cope with these difficulties, Programme Element I of the PACE-E project and in particular the Sub-activities EEP1 to 3 will put a special emphasis on building up national capabilities in energy environmental planning. One of the major conclusions of the Regional Energy Development Programme (REDP) was the recognition that energy demand planning and policies were definitely the backbone of any rational and sustainable energy development strategy.

Based on this conclusion, the design and implementation of the Energy Environmental Planning Project of PACE-E have four (4) main objectives:

- To strengthen or to build up if necessary the in-country capabilities in energy environment assessment, in relation to energy planning and policy formulation;

- To upgrade the information base, analytical tools and forecasting models to carry out energy environmental studies and to prepare recommendations and decisions in this field;

- To support the establishment of institutional arrangements to ease the exchange of information among ministries, public agencies and companies, and to incorporate explicitly energy environmental issues in the formulation of energy plans and policies;

- To foster regional cooperation among the developing countries of Asia to harmonize and coordinate their efforts in the field of energy environmental assessment and management.

1.2 Design of the Energy Environmental Country Studies

The overall philosophy of this project is the combination of a strong involvement of the country in terms of manpower and working facilities, and a support from PACE-E in terms of methodological assistance and funding:

- A Central Consultant Team has been set up at the Asian Institute of Technology (AIT), based in Bangkok, Thailand, thanks to strong financial support from the Government of France and the United Nations Development Programme (UNDP), through which PACE-E and ESCAP provide financial support to all in-country teams;

- The Central Consultant will help the countries in designing and implementing their study plan and provide them with methodologies, analytical tools, databases and models software. Together with ESCAP and the Working Group on EEP (WG/EEP), they will assist the countries in establishing the In-Country Team and the institutional arrangements;

- The In-Country Teams, under the guidance of a Team Leader, will work mostly by themselves, benefiting only from the overall methodological support provided by the Central Consultant and from some very specific consultancy services (mainly software). The Team will have to report mainly to a national focal group, but also to the WG/EEP.

The condition of the success of the activity, taking into account its philosophy and the very limited assistance available from the Central Consultant, will be the design of a thorough, well targeted and consistent study plan.

This study plan is aimed at providing clear objectives, methodological tools to be used, tasks to be performed and human (and other) resources needed. The provision of such a plan is considered a prerequisite for the country to benefit from PACE-E assistance and UNDP funding.

One basic objective of this activity is to build up national capabilities to carry out, on a permanent basis, energy environmental studies, in the overall framework of energy planning and energy policy formulation.

In that respect, the constitution of the National Team is of a crucial importance, and must fulfill several requirements.

1.3 Establishment of the National Team

First, the Team should be located in a place where it could report very easily to decision makers involved in energy planning and energy policy formulation. This means that preferably the Team should be established within an energy planning office, ministry of energy or any technical body (or research institution) in charge of preparing energy and environment decisions. The purpose of such a location is to create the right conditions for energy environmental issues to be fully integrated in the preparations of energy plans and policies.

Second, the Team should involve professionals from various institutions and energy companies. As a matter of fact, one of the major problems of energy environmental studies is the difficulty to identify and to make available sectoral techno-economic and energy data which belong to the various ministries and companies. Another problem is to make energy environmental perspectives consistent with sectoral policies and with strategies of energy companies. The establishment of a multi-disciplinary team aims at overcoming these difficulties by enabling the information to flow across institution boundaries.

Third, the Team should include some very senior people (including the Team Leader), even as external in-country consultants. The philosophy is that the sectoral energy demand study should be carried out almost entirely by the Team, while the Central Consultant only provides general guidance and training. This has been considered a prerequisite for building up a permanent capability on energy environmental studies. In that respect, the role and competence of the Team Leader and in-country consultants are very important.

The establishment of the In-Country Teams should be very carefully discussed, from policy as well as from technical points of view, country by country, during implementation studies carried out by the Central Consultant and a representative from ESCAP.

1.4 Development of the Study and the Role of the Central Consultant

As already stated, the Central Consultant is expected to have a major role in defining and implementing the overall methodology of the energy environmental studies, but a minor role in the development of the national study itself.

The development of the study and the involvement of the Central Consultant Team could be as follows:

- The study will be initiated by a regional training seminar for the core people of the team; then, the in-country teams work by themselves, focusing first on data questions;

- Technical Advisory and Supervisory Missions (TASM) will be undertaken at the time of the in-country studies by the Central Consultant and a representative from ESCAP; following the conclusions of the TASM, the work of the In-Country Team will be readjusted and the need for additional assistance from the Central Consultant identified;

- Short technical missions by members of the Central Consultant Team will be performed in the countries when needed, for the harmonious development of the project;

- Conclusions and findings of the study will be included in the final reports of the studies that all In-Country Teams will have to write;

- A national seminar will finally be organized in each country, with the attendance of the Central Consultant and of a representative from ESCAP, where the final reports of the studies will be presented to decision-makers involved in energy planning and energy policy formulation;

- For enhancing this coordination and regional cooperation a regional workshop will be organized to present the results of the National In-country Studies.

1.5 Practical Implementation of the Energy Environmental Planning Projects

1.5.1 Regional Training Workshops

In connection with the implementation of these studies, it was decided to focus the PACE-E training activity on the various aspects related to the energy environmental planning projects (EEP1 to 3). Regional training workshops will be implemented by AIT and ESCAP.

To make these workshops consistent with the development of the energy environmental planning studies in the countries, they will be designed so as to fulfill several requirements;

- Their programmes (lectures, resource persons, practical exercises) will be established in cooperation with the Central Consultant;

- The attendance will be restricted to only representatives of the countries involved in PACE-E energy environmental planning studies;

- Each National Team involved in the workshop will present overview papers on the energy characteristics of the energy sectors and previous energy environmental planning studies in their country;

- The Central Consultant Team will be fully involved as team members and will present the methodologies and tools which could be used in the framework of the EEP projects.

The programme of these workshops will be designed and based on three (3) basic ideas:

- To tackle each of the methodological problems to be faced in the implementation of the energy environmental studies;

- To balance theoretical and methodological presentations, by resource persons with practical exercises and case studies;

– To broaden the scope of the methodological approach proposed by the Central Consultant together with other Asian experiences.

1.5.2 *Technical Advisory and Supervisory Missions (TASM)*

The purpose of the TASM is to review the work undertaken by the In-Country Teams, to give guidance for the work, and to evaluate the need for external assistance that could be fulfilled by the Central Consultant Team.

As a conclusion of each TASM, the Central Consultant will write a comprehensive technical report which will give very precise guidance for the follow-up of the study, according to the initial in-country study plan and taking into account the revisions decided during the TASM. This report will then be used as a reference to evaluate the progress of the study.

1.5.3 *Technical Assistance Missions*

Besides the Central Consultant, the Central Consultant Team comprises several project assistants in charge of developing and maintaining computer tools and databases and a multi-disciplinary expert team in energy issues (energy survey, database, energy supply and demand, environment).

The project assistants and the energy experts will have to be involved in missions to assist In-Country Teams in the implementation and correct use of the computer software provided by the Central Consultant Team.

These technical assistance missions remain limited and will not exceed, altogether, one (1) month of the total study.

In addition to these missions, the Central Consultant Team has to react on a regular basis, on progress reports and specific written requests sent by all In-Country Teams related to the various aspects of the study: database, analysis performed, results, and final reports.

1.5.4 *National Seminars*

The national seminars are considered as crucial events where the major findings and conclusions of the In-Country Studies will be reported to decision makers involved in the process of energy environmental planning and policy formulation.

Prior to the national seminar itself, the final draft of the report will be reviewed and commented upon by the Central Consultant.

The national seminar will be attended by the Central Consultant and a representative from ESCAP.

It will be recommended that the national seminars will be held in the national language in order to ease

communication between the In-Country Teams and the national attendance.

After the national seminars, a report will be written by the Central Consultant, to give a synthesis of the studies and recommendations for a follow-up.

1.5.5 *Regional meetings*

One of the overall objectives of PACE-E is to foster regional cooperation in the energy and environment field. In that spirit, regional meetings will be organized with representatives from the In-Country Teams (usually the Team Leaders) to review the progress of the various In-Country Studies and to make the Team Leaders share their experience, strengths and weaknesses with other Team Leaders and with other experts from Asia or elsewhere.

A first regional training will focus mainly on methodological aspects, both for In-Country Studies and for inter-country comparisons. Well-known international experts on energy and environmental studies will be invited to present their viewpoint on methodologies and to give their appreciation about the orientations taken by the various In-Country Teams.

A second regional meeting will be restricted to Team Leaders, the Central Consultant Team, and ESCAP officials. Each Team Leader will be requested to bring the national final in-country report and to present it during the seminar.

2. Proposed General Framework of the In-country Studies on Energy-Environment Planning

2.1 Objective

To assist interested member countries of the Working Group on EEP in integrating into their decision making process the appropriate methodologies for taking into account environmental considerations in energy planning activities and energy project evaluation and to enhance the institutional capacity of energy bureaus of the participating countries to address issues on energy and environment.

2.2 Development Problem

A review of existing methodologies and procedures for bringing in factors pertaining to energy-related environmental concerns into energy planning will be commissioned to AIT which will recruit a consultant in the second half of 1994. Once the consultant is on board, the regional study would be started in the second half of 1994 for a period of nine (9) months. After the review, the consultant will be fielded to a selected number of WG member countries to collect relevant information for making an assessment of basic difficulties (conceptual, methodological as well as institutional) for effective incorporation of environmental considerations in the energy planning process of those countries. Other considerations such as pricing and demand side management should also be taken into account. The regional study would culminate and recommend the formulation of alternative appropriate methodologies and required energy environmental data bases for the region, which would be discussed and disseminated at the Regional Training Workshop scheduled for August 1995.

The second part of this activity should consist of In-Country Studies. These studies are designed by some PACE-E countries and carried out during 1996 and the first three quarters of 1997 under the responsibility of each In-Country Team expressly formed for the purpose in the framework of the PACE-E project; common technical and advisory missions would be fielded to assist each In-Country Study. The reports from the In-Country Studies would be synthesized by the Energy Planning Central Consultant Team at AIT in the first quarter of 1998 to obtain a regionally aggregated picture on energy impact on the environment.

2.3 Methodological Approach

In the proposed methodology, the energy system is represented by an oriented network of energy and material flows from primary energy until final energy. This final energy is transformed further down to useful energy so as to satisfy a given exogenous demand. All the energy related processes are thus represented and characterized by techno-economic parameters such as capacity, flow, conversion efficiency, emission factor, input and output mix etc. The modular representation allows the description and modeling of various types of emission reduction and abatement technology as well as new environmental friendly technologies.

The methodology allows both simulation and optimization of the constructed network. In the simulation mode the flows, capacities, costs and environmental impact are computed with respect to given end-use demand and certain assumptions on market and technological considerations. Simulation is used for descriptive studies and for performing sensitivity analysis around an optimal solution produced by the optimization model. In optimization mode a linear programming (LP) problem is created, which can be solved by the standard LP softwares. The LP problem contains a set of constraints, which represent, among other things, energy and material balances in all parts of the network, flows, capacities, costs and allocation boundaries, permitted levels of environmental impact etc. In principle, the user can specify any additional constraint on any of the parameters of the network. This permits great flexibility in the adaptation of the methodology, a step often required in multi-country studies. Objective function of the LP problem is often, but not necessarily, chosen as the minimization of the total discounted cost. Other objective functions can be used, for example minimization of the imports, minimization

emission reduction cost etc. and any combination of these criteria.

The proposed methodology can be used to address the questions related to energy policies, questions related to the behavior of the energy producing sectors as well as of energy consuming sector and questions related to environmental impact of energy development. It is possible to evaluate the optimal use of existing resources and the impact of this production plan on the environment; it can also address the problem of the impact of the environment policies on the development of the energy system. For example it permits to answer the following questions:

- What is the minimum cost solution for the long term development of the energy sector, taking into account technical progress, development of new technologies, energy saving potential and environmental constraints; or

- What is the cost for implementing certain emission abatement policy for achieving a specified target?

The model used in the proposed methodology can give comprehensive outputs and customizable reports for multiple milestone years during the whole period under study on global and sectoral energy and material flows, associated incremental capacities, investments and operating costs, emissions of CO_2, SOx, NOx, etc. Various analysis can be performed based on these outputs, for example sensitivity analysis around optimal solution, cross country comparison etc. This methodology has been successfully applied to energy and environmental analysis and planning in around 20 countries in the world.

2.4 Main Considerations for the design of the In-country studies

This section summarizes some preliminary considerations and basic requirements, which found a consensus among Workshop's participants, and which could be included in the framework of the in-country studies.

a. Scenario design

The following requirements are taken into considerations when designing the scenarios:

i. Scenario should be designed in such a way that it helps to address the most important issues of the participating countries such as urban air pollution and greenhouse gas emissions;

ii. Scenario design should allow to take into account the specific conditions in terms of energy resources, priorities of energy development and environmental management of participating countries;

iii. Scenario design framework should be done at regional level to ensure comparability between the country studies;

iv. Scenario design must be realistic for practical implementation (status of the database).

b. *Comparability*

To keep the country studies comparable, the same framework should be applied:

i. Units:

Units of currency (national currency of 1991 constant prices plus exchange rate), energy (Ktoe, along with the usual metric units),

ii. Energy system structure:

A similar general structure is to be used in the In-country studies, which includes:

Supply subsystems with environmental modules:

- Coal subsystem;
- Gas subsystem;
- Oil subsystem (intermediate complexity);
- Electricity subsystem (central electricity generation and self electricity generation with combined electricity-heat production);
- Biomass;
- New and renewable technologies.

Final demand subsystems with environmental modules:

- Industry sector which can include:
  - Iron steel industry;
  - Cement industry;
  - Building material production industry;
  - Textile industry;
  - Food processing industry;
  - Paper industry;
  - etc.
- Transport sector.
- Tertiary sector including:
  - Commercial sector;
  - Urban households;
  - Rural households.
- Other sectors.

iii. A similar set of emission reduction technologies is to be adopted:

The emission reduction technologies which could be selected are as follows:

for emission reduction in Coal subsystem:

- Emission reduction from coal preparation;
- Hard coal desulfurization;
- Emission reduction from coking;
- Emission reduction from coal gasification;
- etc.

for emission reduction in Electricity subsystem:

- Wet limestone process;
- Spray dryer process;
- Dry sorbent process;
- Wellmann Lord process;
- Selected catalytic reduction;
- Selected non-catalytic reduction;
- Simultaneous NOx and SOx reduction process;
- Fluidized bed combustion technologies;
- etc.

for emission reduction in Industrial subsystem:

- Fabric filters;
- Electrical precipitators;
- Dual combustion and denitrification;
- etc.

for emission reduction in Transport subsystem:

- Primary measures;
- Exhaust gas recirculation for gasoline cars;
- Three way catalytic converters;
- Exhaust gas recirculation for diesel cars;
- Methanol cars;
- LPG (bivalent) cars;
- Layer charge;
- Lean burn engine;
- Thermal recombustion;
- NOx control;
- Pulsair;
- etc.

for emission reduction in Tertiary subsystem:

- Packaged gas boiler with atmospheric burner and stainless steel inserts;

- Flue gas condensing boiler with pulsation burner;

- Packaged gas with atmospheric burner and continuously regulated gas flow;

- Boiler with forced draught gas burner;

- Superstoichiometric pre-mixing burner;

- Blue flame oil burner;

- Yellow flame oil burner with stepped combustion ventilation;

- Yellow flame oil burner with recirculation of hot combustion gases to the flame root;

- Flue gas washing system (DFVLR – Absorption/ Reduction Process);

- Flue gas washing system (KROLL – Oxidation/ Absorption Process);

- Flue gas washing system (HERBST – Absorption/ Reduction Process;

- etc.

Country teams may choose to model the energy system with all or some of the subsystems presented above. Similarly, the emission reduction technologies will also be chosen by the In-country teams in relation with their own reality and technical availability.

2.5 The proposed structure of an In-country study:

The In-country study will include the following parts:

a. *Part I: General.*

i. A review on socio-economic development (population, GDP growth, per capita energy and electricity consumption, urbanization rate, percentage of population electrified, etc.);

ii. A review of present environment situation (deforestation, oil spill, topsoil burden in the coal mining area, discharging of wastes into the water resources, concentrations of pollutants in the air, water shed, etc.). It will be important to include particular information or data, figures about hazardous incidents, professional illness, cost of repair of environmental damages etc.;

iii. Explicit statement of the current government policies regarding energy development, energy efficiency and conservation, environmental management (environmental regulations, standards);

iv. Institutional arrangement of the energy sector with interfaces with environmental agencies and other institutions responsible for strategic development of the country.

b. *Part II: Case studies.*

Base case:

i. The definition of a baseline energy development scenario reflecting most expected socio-economic trends. This will provide information on final (or useful) energy demand as an input for the modeling in the EFOM-ENV;

ii. An Environmental Baseline Case (CASE – 00 or Business as usual case) represents the forecasted development of the economy and of the energy sector, taking into considerations the present status of the environmental management situation, without any other than already defined measures to abate the environmental impacts. This case is country specific because it is based on existing energy policies and environmental regulations of each country.

Possible alternative cases:

The following alternative cases are being proposed taking into consideration the results of the discussions among the participants and EPCCT team members during the last Workshop; however a choice will have to be made to limit the number of cases to be studied in the framework of this project:

i. Emission Reduction Case (CASE – ALT 1): This case considers a reduction of 3-10 per cent per year of the growth rate of all three pollutants (SO_2, NOx and particulates) compared to the growth rate of the baseline case levels.

The growth rate of the emission levels was chosen because the results of the EFOM-ENV optimization problem is sensitive to this parameter.

This case examines the influence of the imposed emission limits on the energy sector development and its total costs. For this purpose a set of available abatement technologies and policy measurements and/or scenarios are to be adopted by the respective participating countries;

ii. CO_2 Reduction Case (CASE – ALT 2): considering 1-5 per cent per year reduction of the growth rate of greenhouse gas emission in comparison with the growth rate of the baseline case. As CO_2 emissions are different from acid rain pollution, it could be wise to treat them separately;

iii. Energy Efficiency Case (CASE – ALT 3): This case emphasizes on the energy conservation and efficiency on both supply and demand sides:

- Reduction of losses in the energy supply (by processes, by sub-sectors, etc.) by 5-10 per cent per year of the current level as a result of the application of energy efficient technologies or retrofitting old technologies.

- Reduction of 1-3 per cent per year of the final demand (by processes, by sub-sectors, etc.) as a result of the application of advanced technologies (more efficient) in the demand side;

iv. Fuel Option Case (CASE – ALT 4): This case considers, for example a 1-5 per cent per year of reduction of coal in energy supply/consumption (or any other fuel). Any energy resource depletion policy can also be considered in this case;

v. Comprehensive Case: (CASE – ALT 5): Combination of the measures of all previous cases (or country specific case with due considerations of the country's policies on the environmental management);

vi. Other specific cases proposed by In-country teams could also be incorporated in the study to take into consideration specific aspects of the energy-environmental policies and targets of the countries.

c. *Part III: Case study analyses.*

The main analyses to be carried out in the framework of the study should include at least:

i. Description of the energy sector of the country (energy supply subsystems, energy demand subsystems);

ii. The model results showing the dynamics of the energy system within the planning period (additional capacities, fuel mix, etc.);

iii. Emission levels;

iv. Abatement costs;

v. Possible structural changes of the energy sector due to integration of the environment protection measures;

vi. The feasibility of assumed policy measures in a given country;

vii. Conclusions and recommendations.

2.6 Intended Impacts

In as much as all segments of society use energy and are impacted by the environment, all individuals can be regarded as benificiaries of the project's activities. However, the direct recipients of this programme will be policy makers, administrators and technicians dealing with energy planning and environmental concerns. In addition, representatives from the private sector and the academia should be included in the training activities of the programme to ensure in the future a follow-up of the projects as well as capacity to carry out training within the countries.

The project aims at enhancing the national capacity to analyse implications of energy development policies so that more environmentally sensitive policies could be formulated. It would greatly contribute towards the human resource development in the area of energy planning.

2.7 Implementation Plan (see also table on page 69):

July-September 1994	Recruitment of consultants and integration into EPCCT
October 1994-July 1995	Regional Study Review of Methodologies, Models and software developments
August 1995	Regional Training Workshop
October 1995-September 1997	TASM Missions
August-December 1996	In-Country Studies Definition-Institutional Arrangements
January 1996-September 1997	In-Country Studies Development
April-September 1997	National Seminars
October-December 1997	Regional Workshop
January-March 1998	Synthesis Report
April-June 1998	Publication of Reports

2.8 Country Coverage

Bangladesh, Cambodia, China, India, Indonesia, Islamic Republic of Iran, Lao People's Democratic Republic, Malaysia, Maldives, Myanmar, Mongolia, Nepal, Pakistan, Philippines, Republic of Korea, Sri Lanka, Viet Nam and Thailand.

2.9 Agencies

AIT in collaboration with ESCAP, the WG on EEP and APDC/APENPLAN.

2.10 Outputs

(a) Report reviewing existing methodologies and procedures for incorporating environmental considerations into energy planning and policy (Phase I of Regional Report);

(b) Report assessing status of environmental impact of energy systems and constraints to incorporate environmental considerations into energy planning analysis in ten (10) countries (Phase II of Regional Study);

(c) Synthesis report giving regional aggregated picture of energy systems impact on the environment;

(d)   Report of the Regional Workshop;

(e)   Thirty (30) policy maker from ten (10) countries informed on consequences of environmental impact of various policy options and investment alternatives in the energy sector;

(f)   Thirty (30) energy planners from ten (10) countries trained in environmental impact of energy, energy-environment modeling, and data base development (supply and demand systems, emissions analysis);

(g)   Improvement of energy production, supply and emissions data bases of the participating countries;

(h)   Country reports on energy impact on environment (soil, land use, water, air) and least cost scenarios.

2.11   Description of Activities

(a)   Recruitment of an external consultant in energy-environment analysis and integration into EPCCT;

(b)   EPCCT/AIT reviews state-of-the-art of the methodologies for energy-environmental analysis to be used and disseminated to the participants of this sub-activity;

(c)   EPCCT/AIT drafts Part I of Regional Report;

(d)   EPCCT/AIT undertakes missions to ten (10) countries for definition of ten (10) Country Studies and collects information about energy-environment studies and data;

(e)   EPCCT/AIT reviews national energy-environment studies, national data bases and scenarios of ten (10) Country Studies;

(f)   EPCCT/AIT carries out software modifications and prepares all methodological, training, user and technical manuals;

(g)   One week Regional Training Workshop on energy-environment methodologies and modeling;

(h)   Publication of conclusions and recommendations of Regional Training Workshop (Workshop Report);

(i)   EPCCT/AIT drafts findings and recommen-dations as report on Phase II of regional report;

(j)   Letters of agreement signed between ESCAP/AIT and Energy Ministries to specify terms for financing of Country Studies (see annex I and II);

(k)   First Advisory Missions by EPCCT/AIT to assist participants in ten (10) countries to define the scope of the Country Studies;

(l)   Second Advisory Mission by EPCCT/AIT to check on progress of the ten (10) Country Studies;

(m)   Third Advisory Mission by EPCCT/AIT to evaluate country reports, quality of data bases in (10) countries;

(n)   National seminars in ten (10) countries to publicize results of Country Studies, and promote utilization in policy making;

(o)   EPCCT/AIT prepares a synthesis report to be presented in the Regional Workshop;

(p)   EPCCT/AIT conducts Regional Workshop with thirty (30) policy makers from ten (10) participating countries;

(q)   Publication of conclusions and recommendations from the Regional Workshop (Workshop Report);

(r)   Publication of Synthesis and of National Reports on In-Country Study.

2.12   Activities completed as of October 1995

As of October 1995, the following activities have been completed:

(a)   A Draft Report on Energy-Environment methodological proposals has been prepared by EPCCT and has been presented during the First Regional Training Workshop on EEP3 (Phase I of the Regional Report – see **Annex**);

(b)   In addition, a Users and Technical Manual on EFOM-ENV is available and has been disseminated to the In-Country Study Teams during the First Regional Training Workshop on EEP3 (see **Annex**);

(c)   A report on Energy-Environment Methodologies and Models used in Asia has been prepared, which presents the experiences of Asian Countries in this field; this report has been finalized by the end of July 1995 and has been presented to the In-Country Teams during the First Regional Training Workshop on EEP3 (Phase II of the Regional Report) (see **Annex**);

(d)   A Training Guide Book on Energy-Environment Studies has been prepared at EPCCT; it proposes several application cases of the EPCCT proposed methodologies and proposes to the In-Country Teams a framework for the In-Country Study to be prepared between 1996 and 1997. This document has also been finalized by the end of July 1995 (see **Annex**);

(e)   A Regional Training on the EFOM-ENV model was held at AIT from 24 to 28 July 1995 with the participation of 10 participants from 9 countries;

68

(f) A Regional Workshop on the Review and Application of Methodologies and Procedures for Integrating Environmental Considerations into Energy Planning and Policy Analysis was held at AIT from 31 July to 4 August 1995 with the participation of 25 participants from 15 countries;

(g) The guidelines for the In-Country Study on Energy-Environment Planning.

2.13   Inputs

(a) The ten (10) interested member countries of WG/EEP will provide budgetary support for respective in-country experts/counterparts designated for this activity;

(b) Host facilities for the Regional Workshop will be provided by ESCAP or AIT in 1995. Alternate host countries for this Workshop will be Indonesia, Sri Lanka or Myanmar;

(c) AIT (i.e. the Energy Planning Central Consultant Team (EPCCT)) will act as the implementing agency for this activity in close consultation with ESCAP and the WG on EEP;

(d) The results of the APDC/APENPLAN EASES Project will be an important input for this sub-activity, as the scenarios defined in the framework of EASES should be integrated and eventually revised by the In-Country Teams in the framework of their In-Country Study;

(e) UNDP funding support for 8 w/m for the main consultant who is a specialist/expert in integrating environmental considerations into energy planning;

(f) UNDP funding support for international travel and DSA for thirty (30) participants of the Regional Workshop as well as to cover administrative costs at AIT and ESCAP;

(g) UNDP funding support to cover external costs of the main consultant in carrying out Technical Assistance (TASM mission) to follow up In-Country Studies;

(h) UNDP funding support to cover external costs of respective In-Country Studies;

(i) Funding support from France for the main consultant and his team comprising required specialists/experts (research associates); this funding will cover mainly the software developments carried out by EPCCT. In addition, this funding will support complementary TASM missions, secretarial, communication and publication works.

2.14   Project Review and Evaluation

The project will be evaluated on the basis of guidelines for self-evaluation as provided in the Evaluation Manual of the United Nations. Questionnaires will be used to collect feed-back, assess quality and relevance of presentations and evaluate workshops. The terminal report will provide information on the evaluation undertaken by the Secretariat.

2.15   Budget

The overall budget is as follows:

Project Number: RAS/92/071/A/01/53
Project title: Programme for Asian Co-operation on Energy and the Environment

Programme Budget Covering UNDP Contribution for AIT Execution of Sub Contract 21-01 Activity EEPI-III (AIT)

		Total	1993	1994	1995	1996	1997
21	Sub Contracts						
21-03	EEP III (AIT)						
	• Regional Training Workshop			67,500.00			
	• Consultants (specialists)		20,000.00	52,250.00			
	• In-country studies					100,000.00	30,000.00
	• Consultant TASM missions and training material				10,000.00	25,000.00	20,000.00
	• Regional Workshop						80,000.00
	• Publication of reports, Workshop Proceedings and training material						25,000.00
	• Miscellaneous				2,500.00		
	Total	364,750.00	20,000.00	52,250.00	12,500.00	125,000.00	155,000.00

2.16 Terms of Reference of the In-Country Study Team

1) Each participating member country would form an In-Country Study Team which would conduct the majority of the activities within the project. The Team should be initially coordinated and called for by the focal point of EEP (Energy Environment Planning within the framework of PACE-E). The Team should consist of various members which should influence the formulation of energy development policy such as officials from government bureaus such as the Ministry of Energy, Environment, Statistics Bureau. Participation of research institutes and NGOs are also strongly encouraged. Participants to the regional training workshops under EEP1, EEP2 and EEP3 should also constitute part of the Team.

2) Participants to the regional workshops are strongly advised to assist in the preparation for the national workshops on (1) methodologies on energy-environmental surveys; (2) methodologies on energy and environmental planning (demand and supply); (3) fuel switching potential and energy development scenario building; (4) training on necessary software to comprehend the methodologies, i.e., DBA-VOID, MEDEE-S/ENV and EFOM-ENV.

3) The Team is expected to receive the first advisory mission to identify environmental issues within energy planning for that specific country. The advisory mission should also define together with the Team to draw up a schedule to implement the national programme to train personnel, update energy database, make energy demand forecasts, and provide different scenarios of supply mix with careful considerations to environmental concerns.

4) The Team should also collect energy data and environmental data for DBA-VOID and update the energy environment database which becomes the basis of further activities.

5) The Team should conduct a mid-term national workshop to train personnel on methodologies and tools transferred by EPCCT/AIT, i.e., DBA-VOID, MEDEE-S/ENV and EFOM-ENV. The workshop will be assisted by EPCCT during the second advisory mission. The workshop should provide different supply mix options based on energy demand scenarios with due consideration to the environment.

6) The last advisory mission should be dispatched during the national seminar to discuss the results using the methodologies and tools produced by MEDEE-S/ENV and EFOM-ENV on the energy demand scenario, and supply mix and environmental impacts.

7) Upon completion of the national seminar and the last advisory mission, the Team should produce a synthesis report for publication.

2.17 Terms of Reference of the Asian Institute of Technology (AIT)

1) The Asian Institute of Technology (AIT), the implementing agency of the programme element Energy and Environment Planning (EEP) within the framework of the Programme for Asian Cooperation on Energy and the Environment (PACE-E) will also implement the proposed project.

2) AIT will provide the substantive advisory services in order for the In-Country Studies to: (a) identify areas to specific environmental issues concerning energy planning, (b) provide technical assistance in conducting national trainings and seminars, (c) provide technical assistance to develop the methodologies as well as tools and support all specialized software such as DBA-VOID, MEDEE-S/ENV and EFOM-ENV to the In-Country Study Team.

3) AIT will provide technical support so that the In-Country Team of the participating member countries could produce (a) an updated energy database, (b) make energy demand forecasts, (c) provide different scenarios of supply mix with due considerations to environmental concerns.

4) The AIT Team should conduct a minimum of three technical advisory missions per country.

5) The last technical advisory mission should coincide with the national seminar to discuss the results from the transferred methodologies and tools such as MEDEE-S/ENV and EFOM-ENV on energy demand scenarios and supply mix and its environmental impacts. The national seminar should discuss policy implications based on the results of the study. ESCAP staff members will also join during this mission.

6) Upon completion of the national seminars AIT will compile the results and publish them.

7) Finally, AIT should submit a terminal report including a financial statement upon completion of the project.

Programme for Asian Cooperation on Energy and the Environment (PACE-E)
(RAS/92/071)

WORKPLAN OF THE PACE-E PROGRAMME ELEMENT 1: ENERGY-ENVIRONMENTAL PLANNING
EEP-3

Activity	Responsible Implementing Agency/Institution & Collaborating Agency (ies) Institution (s)	1993 IV	1994 I	1994 II	1994 III	1994 IV	1995 I	1995 II	1995 III	1995 IV	1996 I	1996 II	1996 III	1996 IV	1997 I	1997 II	1997 III	1997 IV	1998 I	1998 II
EEP-3 Review of methodologies and procedures for integrating environmental considerations into energy planning and policy analytic effectiveness of E.I.A. guidelines for the energy sector in Asian developing countries	AIT/IEPE/ ENERDATA																			
• Consultant recruitment					July–Sept.														
• Regional study review of methodologies and models developments							Oct. 94–Junly 95												
• Regional training								Aug. 95											
• In-country studies definition								July–Dec. 96											
• In-country studies										Oct. 95–Sept. 97									
• Consultant TASM missions										Jan. 96–Sept. 97									
• National Seminars													April–Sept. 97						
• Regional Training																	Oct.–Dec.		
• Synthesis Report																		Jan–Mar	
• Publication of reports																			April–June

Latest update: 14 September 1995

BIBLIOGRAPHY

[1] **ADB/EPCCT – AIT (1995)** *Energy – Cum Electricity Demand and Supply Analysis* ADBT.A. No. 1628 PRC.

[2] **Asean 2020 Program (1993)** *Country report of Indonesia*, Report for the ASEAN-EC Energy Management and Research Center, ASEAN 2020 Program.

[3] **Asian Development Bank (1993),** *Environmental Issues Related to Electric Power Generation Projects in India,* Proceeding of the training workshop, Jaipur 4-6, March 1993.

[4] **Bhattacharya S.C. et al (ed) (1994)** *Global Warming in Issues Asia,* Proceedings of the Workshop on Global Warming Issues in Asia 8-10 September 1993, Bangkok, Thailand.

[5] **Brandon C., Ramankutty R., (1993)** *Toward an Environmental Strategy for Asia,* World Bank Discussion Paper No. 224.

[6] **Center for Economic Research, Swiss Federal Institute of Technology Zurich (1985),** *An Energy Scenario Generator Model for People's Republic of China* Project ZENCAP.

[7] **Dang G.V. et al, (1993),** *UNEP Greenhouse Gas Abatement Costing Studv: The Case of Thailand* AIT.

[8] **DECADES (1994),** *Computerized tools for comparative assessment of electricity generation options and strategies,* Project working paper No. 5.

[9] **Energy and Development (1983)** *Study on the industrial energy system in connection with environmental impacts in PR China.*

[10] **Energy Research Institute, State Planning Commission, PRC (1991a)** *Regional Study on Environmental Considerations in Energy Development Proiect PRC*, Part A: Final draft report, November ADB T.A. No: 5357-Regional.

[11] **Energy Research Institute, State Planning Commission, PRC (1991b)** *Regional Study on Environmental Considerations in Energy Development Proiect PRC,* Part B: *Economic Analysis of Three Alternative Scenarios for China Energy Development,* November ADB T.A. No: 5357-Regional.

[12] *Final Report of the Regional Training Workshop on Energy Surveys* (EEP1, PACE-E/RAS/92/071), 26-30 September 1994, Bangkok, Thailand.

[13] **Kleemann M. (1994)** *Energy Use and Air Pollution in Indonesia. Supply Strategies, Environmental Impacts and Pollution Control.* Avebury Studies in Green Research.

[14] **Lefevre T., Bui D.T., (1995)** *Studies on the environmental impacts of energy use in Thailand – A review.* Material prepared in the framework of the Regional Training Workshop on Review and Application of Methodologies and Procedures for Integrating Environmental Considerations into Energy Planning Policy Analysis, 31 Jul-4 Aug 1995, AIT, Bangkok, Thailand; ESCAP/UNDP/AIT/PACE-E Activity EPP-3.

[15] **Lefevre T., Chen X., Thanh N.C., Bui D.T., (1995)** *"Cross Countries Comparison of Energy Efficiency Indicators – Report on Korea",* ADEME/AIT Project, Bangkok, Thailand.

[16] **Lefevre T., Chen X., Bui D.T., Thanh N. C, (1995)** *"Cross Countries Comparison of Energy Efficiency Indicators – A synthesis report",* ADEME/AIT Project, Bangkok, Thailand.

[17] **Lefevre T., Chen X., Bui D.T., Thanh N. C, (1995)** *"Cross Countries Comparison of Energy Efficiency Indicators – Report on Indonesia",* ADEME/AIT Project, Bangkok, Thailand.

[18] **Lefevre T., Chen X., Bui D.T., Thanh N. C, (1995)** *"Cross Countries Comparison of Energy Efficiency Indicators – Report on The Philippines",* ADEME/AIT Project, Bangkok, Thailand.

[19] **Lefevre T., Chen X., Thanh N.C., Bui D.T., (1995)** *"Cross Countries Comparison of Energy Efficiency Indicators – Report on China",* ADEME/AIT Project, Bangkok, Thailand.

[20] **Lefevre T., Chen X., Thanh N.C., Bui D.T., (1995)** *"Cross Countries Comparison of Energy Efficiency Indicators – Report on India",* ADEME/AIT Project, Bangkok, Thailand.

[21] **Lefevre T., Chen X., Thanh N.C., Bui D.T., (1995)** *"Cross Countries Comparison of Energy Efficiency Indicators – Report on Taiwan",* ADEME/AIT Project, Bangkok, Thailand.

[22] **Lefevre T., Chen X., Thanh N.C., Bui D.T., (1995)** *"Cross Countries Comparison of Energy Efficiency Indicators – Report on Thailand"*, ADEME/AIT Project, Bangkok, Thailand.

[23] **Lefevre T., Chen X., Thanh N.C., Bui D.T., (1995)** *Analysis of the Long Term Energy Suppl Mix, A Technical Draft Report* prepared in the framework of UNDP/MALAYSIA project: "Malaysia 2020 – Study on Energy Policy Analysis and Planning of Malaysia to the year 2020" (not published, restricted document).

[24] **Duong Quang Thanh (1995)** *Long-term Optimization Strategies of CO_2 Emission Abatement: the Case of Electric Power Sector in S.R. Vietnam,* AIT Master Thesis ET-94.

[25] **Lefevre T., N.A. Tuan, Thanh N.C., (1994):** *Asean 2020 Country report of Thailand,* Report for the ASEAN-EC Energy Management and Research Center, ASEAN 2020 Program.

[26] **Yang Min (1993)** *The Economic Implications of Alternative Energy Policy Options for Controlling Carbon Dioxide Emissions: the Case of Northeast China,* AIT Master Thesis ET-93-11.

[27] **Debashis Dutta (1993)** *Planning of Energy Efficiency Strategies for the Abatement of CO_2 Emission: A Case of Bangladesh.,* AIT Master Thesis ET-93-13.

[28] **Lefevre, T.,** *Design and Implementation of Energy Environmental Planning* (EEPI to III) in the Framework of the Programme for Asian Cooperation on Energy and the Environment (PACE-E).

[29] **Hills, K.V. Ramani (1990)** *Energy System and the Environment: Approaches to Impact Assessment in Asian Developing Countries.,* Asian and Pacific Development Center.

[30] **ST/ESCAP/***Energy-Environment Planning in Developing Countries: Training Material Part I,* Bangkok, Thailand (1995).

[31] **ST/ESCAP/***Energy-Environment Planning in Developing Countries: Training Material Part II,* Bangkok, Thailand (1995).

[32] **ST/ESCAP/***Energy-Environment Planning in Developing Countries: Energy Saving and Interfuel Substitution Potential Evaluation for Developing Countries,* Bangkok, Thailand (1995).

[33] **ST/ESCAP/1520:** *Sectoral Energy Survey Guidebook – Part I – Methodology,* Bangkok, Thailand (1995).

[34] **ST/ESCAP/1521:** *Sectoral Energy Demand Analysis and Long-term Forecast for Developing Countries: Methodological Manual – MEDEE-S,* Bangkok, Thailand (1995).

[35] **ST/ESCAP/1522:** *Sectoral Energy Demand Analysis and Long-term Forecast for Developing Countries: Technical Manual (and Application Programmes) – MEDEE-S,* Bangkok, Thailand (1995).

[36] **ST/ESCAP/1523:** *Sectoral Energy Demand Analysis and Long-term Forecast for Developing Countries: User's Manual (and Application Programmes) – MEDEE-S,* Bangkok, Thailand (1995).

[37] **ST/ESCAP/1524:** *Information Management System for Analysis of Energy-Environment Data: Technical Manual (and Application Programmes) – DBA-VOID,* Bangkok, Thailand (1995).

[38] **ST/ESCAP/1525:** *Information Management System for Analysis of Energy-Environment Data: User's Manual (and Applications Programmes) – DBA-VOID,* Bangkok, Thailand (1995).

[39] **ST/ESCAP/1531:** *Energy Environment Planning in Developing Countries: Methodological Guide – EFOM-ENV,* Bangkok, Thailand (1995).

[40] **ST/ESCAP/1532:** *Energy Environment Planning in Developing Countries: Programmer's Guide – EFOM-ENV,* Bangkok, Thailand (1995).

[41] **ST/ESCAP/1533:** *Energy Environment Planning in Developing Countries: User's and Technical Guide – EFOM-ENV SHELL,* Bangkok, Thailand (1995).

[42] **ST/ESCAP/1534:** *Energy Environment Planning in Developing Countries: User's and Technical Guide – EFOM-ENV,* Bangkok, Thailand (1995).

[43] *Synthesis Report on Sectoral Energy Surveys in Asia and the Pacific Region,* Regional Training Workshop on Energy Surveys (EEP1, PACE-E/RAS/92/071), 26-30 September 1994, Bangkok, Thailand.

[44] **Tata Energy Research Institute (1991),** *Environmental Considerations in Energy Development,* India case study, Draft final report submitted to ADB.

[45] **Thailand Development Research Institute (1990),** *Report No 7: Energy and Environment – Choosing the Right Mix, Industrializing Thailand and its Impact on the Environment,* TDRI 1990 Year end Conference.

[46] **Thailand Development Research Institute (1990)**, *Report No. 3: Industrialization and Environmental Quality: Paying the Price, Industrializing Thailand and its Impact on the Environment,* TDRI 1990 Year end Conference.

[47 **Thailand Development Research Institute and Thailand Environment Institute (1993)**, *Preparation of a National Strategies on Global Climate Change: Thailand,* Bangkok, Thailand.

[48] **Thailand Environment Institute (1994)**, *Applying Polluter Pays Principle – Time for Action,* Bangkok, Thailand.

[49] **Walsh J. H.** *"1993 Carbon Dioxide Fact Sheet",* *Energy Study Review* Vol. 6 No. 2 1994 pp. 178-183.

[50] **Wesley K. Foell and Collin W. Green (ed) (1992)** *Acid Rain and Emission in Asia,* The third conference proceeding, Bangkok, Thailand.

[51] **Wesley K. Foell Deepark Sharma (ed) (1991)** *Acid Rain and Emission in Asia,* The second conference proceeding, Bangkok, Thailand.

[52] **World Bank (1994)**, *Indonesia Environment and Development: Challenges for the Future,* Report No. 12083-IND.

[53] **World Bank/UNDP/ESMAP (1991)**, *Assessment of personal computer models for energy planning in developing countries.*

[54] **Peter R., Xiang Yu (1995)**, *Pursuing a Sustainable Development: An Index for Performances,* Paper presented at the Regional Workshop Environmental Indicators and Indices, AIT Bangkok, July 1995.

[55] **World Bank (1995)**, *Monitoring Environmental Progress – A report on Work in Progress*, Environment Department.

[56] **Allen H., et al,** (1995) *Environmental Indicators: A Systematic Approach to Measuring and Reporting on Environmental Policy Performance in the Context of Sustainable Development*, World Resources Institute.

Annex:

LIST OF EEP/PACE-E PUBLICATIONS

[1] **LEFEVRE, T.,** Design and Implementation of Energy Environmental Planning (EEP1 to 3) in the Framework of the Programme for Asian Cooperation on Energy and the Environment (PACE-E), Bangkok (1994).

[2] Prepared and edited by **LEFEVRE, T., et al.,** Guide Book on Sectoral Energy Survey – Part I – Methodology (ST/ESCAP/1520), UN, New York (1995).

[3] Prepared and edited by **LEFEVRE, T., et al.,** Final Report of the UNDP/ESCAP/AIT Regional Training Workshop on Energy Surveys (EEP1, PACE-E/RAS/ 92/071), Bangkok (1994).

[4] Prepared and edited by **LEFEVRE, T., et al.,** Synthesis Report on Sectoral Energy Surveys in Asia and the Pacific Region, UNDP/ESCAP/AIT Regional Training Workshop on Energy Surveys (EEP1, PACE-E/RAS/92/071), Bangkok (1994).

[5] Prepared and edited by **LEFEVRE, T., et al.,** Sectoral Energy Demand Analysis and Long-term Forecast for Developing Countries: Methodological Manual – MEDEE-S (ST/ESCAP/1521), UN New York (1995).

[6] Prepared and edited by **LEFEVRE, T., et al.,** Sectoral Energy Demand Analysis and Long-term Forecast for Developing Countries: Technical Manual (and Application Program) – MEDEE-S (ST/ESCAP/ 1522), UN New York (1995).

[7] Prepared and edited by **LEFEVRE, T., et al.,** Sectoral Energy Demand Analysis and Long-term Forecast for Developing Countries: User's Manual (and Application Program) – MEDEE-S (ST/ESCAP/ 1523), UN New York (1995).

[8] Prepared and edited by **LEFEVRE, T., et al.,** Information Management System for Analysis of Energy-Environment Data: Technical Manual (and Application Programs) – DBA-VOID (ST/ESCAP/ 1524), UN New York (1995).

[9] Prepared and edited by **LEFEVRE, T., et al.,** Information Management System for Analysis of Energy-Environment Data: User's Manual (and Applications Programs) – DBA-VOID (ST/ESCAP/ 1525), UN New York (1995).

[10] Prepared and edited by **LEFEVRE, T., et al.,** Guide Book on Energy Environment Planning – Part I: Methodology on Energy Saving and Interfuel Substitution Potential Evaluation for Developing Countries, UN New York (to be published by October 1995).

[11] Prepared and edited by **LEFEVRE, T., et al.,** Guide Book on Energy Environment Planning – Part II: Training Material on Energy Saving and Interfuel Substitution Potential Evaluation for Developing Countries, UN New York (to be published by October 1995).

[12] Prepared and edited by **LEFEVRE, T., et al.,** Energy Environment Planning in Developing Countries: Methodological Guide – EFOM-ENV (ST/ESCAP/ 1531), Bangkok (1995).

[13] Prepared and edited by **LEFEVRE, T., et al.,** Energy Environment Planning in Developing Countries: Programmer's Guide – EFOM-ENV (ST/ESCAP/ 1532), Bangkok (1995).

[14] Prepared and edited by **LEFEVRE, T., et al.,** Energy Environment Planning in Developing Countries: User's and Technical Guide – EFOM-ENV SHELL (ST/ESCAP/1533), Bangkok (1995).

[15] Prepared and edited by **LEFEVRE, T., et al.,** Energy Environment Planning in Developing Countries: User's and Technical Guide – EFOM-ENV (ST/ESCAP/1534), Bangkok (1995).

[16] Prepared and edited by **LEFEVRE, T., et al.,** Guide Book on Energy Environment Planning in Developing Countries – Part I: Synthesis Report on Energy-Environment Studies in Asia, Bangkok (1995).

[17] Prepared and edited by **LEFEVRE, T., et al.,** Guide Book on Energy Environment Planning in Developing Countries – Part II: Training Material on Energy-Environment Studies in Asia, Bangkok (1995).

[18] Prepared and edited by **LEFEVRE, T., et al.,** Final Report of the UNDP/ESCAP/AIT Regional Training Workshop on Review and Application of Methodologies and Procedures for Integrating Environmental Considerations into Energy Planning and Policy (EEP3, PACE-E/RAS/92/071), Bangkok (1995).

V. ENERGY RESILIENCY: REGIONAL PROSPECTS*

1. INTRODUCTION

1.1   The structural changes in the world's energy economy, the discontinuities in the oil sector (in particular the repercussions of step-wise price changes), major political changes in the former Union of Soviet Socialist Republics and China, and the ever growing concerns and public debate over environmental issues have all contributed to the need for energy policies and strategies to be resilient to such rapid changes. Without such resilience, the fabric of society, economic well-being, and quality of life could easily be eroded. The increasing dependence at the consumer level on energy, particularly electricity, makes it ever more important for energy policy and strategic decisions to be geared to the protection of energy supply.

1.2   A review of events affecting the energy sectors of the world economy over the past twenty-five years, and the expectations and forecasts of those involved at governmental, academic and industrial/commercial levels, will show the wide differences between forecasts and reality. Where there has been a consensus view, that consensus has been far from reality; where there has been a range of forecasts, reality has frequently been outside their spread – the most notable example is the future price of oil, where organisations predicting the most likely future movements in crude oil prices over a five to ten year time horizon have tended to be overly influenced by recent history. In the increasingly uncertain world of the second half of the 1990s and the first decades of the 21st century the historical approach to energy planning through forecasting is inappropriate. It is inflexible and fails to take account of the future uncertainties.

1.3   In the future it will be necessary for the decision makers and planners in government, industry, and commerce to ensure that their policy and planning decisions reflect the uncertainties of the future. **The underlying premise of the Scenario Approach is that the future cannot be predicted;** but that there are ways to structure the perceptions of the future to draw out the most robust strategies under a wide range of uncertainty. This requires firstly that the **Predetermined Elements** be segregated from the unpredictable ones. The unpredictable, exogenous elements are then combined in a logical way into internally consistent visions of the future – those are the **Scenarios.**

2. THE CONCEPT OF ENERGY RESILIENCY

2.1   The factors that determine the demand and supply for energy are both complex and controversial. The description of the socio-economic and political elements that characterise the economic system, and the impact on them of government policies – for example taxation, employment, personal benefits, industry – are neither well understood nor can their interactions be predicted. When this uncertainty is coupled with the uncertainty of the future – in terms of government policies, individual countries' economic performance, natural disasters and successes, and the inter-dependence of the world's individual economies – it is apparent that any planning system that is based on traditional forecasting techniques is likely to provide some very misleading information to the decision makers who are seeking guidance.

2.2   Within this uncertain and unpredictable future, energy supply is one of the key factors in the achievement of the economic progress sought by most countries and their governments, and commercial/industrial organisations. Decision makers and planners need to ensure with a reasonable degree of certainty that their policies and strategies will enable their organisations to gain access to adequate supplies of energy for whatever future may occur. In other words, the decision makers and planners need to have a "resilient" energy plan.

2.3   On the basis of the above, resiliency in energy planning may be defined as follows:

> **"A Resilient Strategic Plan for Energy** is a plan that provides a high level of security for energy supplies, and their economic and environmental costs, in order to protect both the economic well-being and the planned improvement thereof, of the nation and/ or the commercial/industrial organisations concerned, recognising the uncertainties and unpredictable nature of the future global energy demand and supply sector, and its economic structure."

Thus a resilient plan must be flexible, and capable of responding to the unexpected and unpredictable changes (sometimes random) in both availability and relative cost of different energy supplies.

2.4   Some examples of resilient strategies that are readily recognisable around the world are:

- the provision of dual firing capabilities in some industrial and power generation facilities in the United States of America – particularly for using fuel oil or natural gas. The switch between the two fuels is substantial as the relative prices of them change;

---

* Prepared by Michael W. Clegg and Hans duMoulin. The chapter is reproduced in the form in which it was received.

- the ability to burn natural gas with coal in coal fired power stations – in order to meet the changing environmental standards in some countries;

- the wide range of power stations in Japan that provide flexibility in the provision of electricity – using nuclear energy and hydro, plus coal-, oil-, and natural gas-fired stations, the mix depending on the relative costs of primary energy inputs at any point in time.

By contrast, the production of electricity in France is reliant on nuclear energy for more than eighty per cent of output – so that **the electricity industry is not resilient** to, say, a failure in one of its plants that may require the shutting down of a large proportion of similar power stations.

2.5   Meeting the target of a Resilient Strategic Plan for Energy presents a challenge for energy planners and decision makers. It can be thought of as a problem of risk assessment and analysis – for all policies carry risk. If one decides to implement any policy and/or take any action then there will be some degree of risk associated with that action. It is generally accepted that as the degree of risk increases the investor will seek to obtain a higher return; at the same time, if an investment opportunity is offered with a higher reward than normal for the particular type of venture, then it is almost certain that there will be an above average risk. One of the key objectives of the detailed analysis that planners, technologists, and scientists undertake is to assess that risk, and seek to reduce it through a better understanding of the system in which the opportunity lies. For example, in the analysis of exploration farm-out opportunities, the Company receiving the offer may be able to achieve a more realistic estimate firstly of the acreage's potential through better technology (more advanced seismic or geological interpretation), and secondly, of the socio-political factors through superior knowledge compared with the Company offering the farm-out. This allows a more precise assessment of the risks and rewards to be made, thereby establishing a valuation that more closely reflects the perceived risks.

2.6   A word of caution, however. In the case of the exploration farm-out the target – an oil or gas reservoir to be discovered by the exploration well – either exists or does not exist. It will not be influenced by the actions of the explorers, the planners, or the decision makers. By contrast, the price of oil, or the demand for gasoline, or the economic growth of a country or region, over the next five or ten years is not fixed in any way – there are no targets to be discovered and reached. Indeed, the collective actions of all the participants in the energy sector – government law-makers, energy planners and decision makers, consumers etc – will influence the future movements of the price of oil. The economy of a country or a company can therefore be thought of as an Adaptive System – a system that adapts its responses to the exogenous variables that affect it; whereas the exploration prospect is a Deterministic System – one

that will not be affected by any exogenous variables (unless someone suffers a blow-out and some or all of the hydrocarbons escape into the atmosphere!!).

2.7   Economics is an art, not a science. At best it may be called "a behavioural science". But as economic predictions depend on, and indeed influence human behaviour, they are therefore by definition unpredictable. Thus the construction of strategic plans must recognise, and be based on, the fact that **an economic system is an adaptive one.**

2.8   An adaptive system is far more complex than a deterministic one and must therefore be approached in a different way from the deterministic one that attempts to forecast the way in which the parameters characterising the system will change in the future. The Scenario approach has been developed to deal with planning under uncertainty, and has been successfully applied in a wide variety of problem areas over the last twenty five years. It is well suited to the needs of the energy sector.

3.   THE SCENARIO APPROACH – THE BASICS

(i)   Forecasts and Scenarios – A Comparison

3.1   It is helpful in introducing the basic ideas of scenario planning to compare and contrast forecasts with scenarios:

FORECASTS	SCENARIOS
• Statistical analysis of probabilities and "expert" opinions.	• Archetypal description of a possible future.
• Authoritative statements, assumed to be best answers – tend to dictate the final decision.	• Assists the understanding but is background to the decision making process rather than an integral part of the decision itself.
• Conceals risks.	• Clarifies risk.
• Stands alone; to be considered, accepted or rejected on its own.	• Designed to be used in conjunction with other scenarios; of no value on its own.
• Removes much of the responsibility for the final decision from the individual decision maker.	• Does not remove responsibility from the decision makers.
• Based on the belief that future can be predicted.	• Based on belief that future **cannot** be predicted.
• Increasing complexity through the temptation to build large scale economic models.	• Simplifies the complexities of the system by identifying the certain and the uncertain elements.
• Fosters inflexibility.	• Encourages flexibility and response to change.

Figure 1

(ii)   The Principal Types of Scenario

3.2   The scenario concept was initially made popular for the business community by the Hudson Institute through Herman Kahn in the early 1970s. Even then scenarios were not new; they were first used by military planners and strategists. However these frequently fell into the trap of allowing themselves to be overly influenced by the past. In business, people often convince one another to adopt similar views on specific issues so that they may indulge in the luxury of consensus building. They are frequently influenced by a sub-conscious desire to prepare for the type of conditions they would like to face – for example an oil producer may well concede the prospect of oil prices staying low for the next two or three years but will then predict increasing prices thereafter to meet his own desires (the hockey stick phenomenon).

3.3   It is not easy to guard against such biased thinking, but carefully conceived scenarios can help to prevent the decision makers from falling into such traps. Different types of scenario can be developed to structure the thinking and avoid these traps. The principal ones are:

- **Archetype Scenarios** – an analysis of the extreme types of a system in order to understand fully the mechanics of a "pure" system. For example, a good understanding of the logic of oil producers with very large reserves compared with the logic of a consumer country with no indigenous oil resources could give very helpful insights when constructing the building blocks for the analysis of oil price movements.

- **Exploratory Scenarios** – the combination of important archetypes which will interact with each other. For example, the combination of oil price archetype scenarios with economic growth scenarios can lead to realistic cause and effect situations, reflecting the real life interactions. Care must be taken to ensure that temptations to assume symmetric relationships where the reality is asymmetric are avoided. It is tempting to assume, for example, that a low oil price scenario would lead to more rapid growth, reduced inflation, and higher demands for energy in the same way as the reverse effects had occurred when high oil prices ruled. The reality has been different – there is a hysteretic effect – which is not reflected in the classical energy or economic models of the system.

- **Phantom Scenarios** – these are scenarios of low probability but with consequences that are so significant that it is important for the decision makers and planners to be aware of them and have the results of the analyst's studies. Experience has shown that decision makers and planners can cope with more than two mainstream exploratory scenarios – sometimes referred to as the **Framework Scenarios.** These two framework scenarios will form the basis for the decision taking, but there is often a requirement to respond to a challenging "What if" type of question relating to an extreme, but low probability situation not dealt with in the main scenarios. If it is agreed that this is an important variant on the main scenarios with a potentially dramatic effect on the organisation or country, then a further test case, or "Phantom Scenario" should be constructed.

- **First and Second Generation Scenarios** – once an exploratory scenario has been developed, the analyst should consider what responses such a situation is likely to trigger. In other words one is obliged to take into account the perceptions of the decision makers both in government and private industry, in response to the state of the world outlined in first generation scenario work. These collective responses will influence the future and alter the first generation scenario into a more mature second generation scenario. This is a characteristic shared by all adaptive systems where a decision or an event can change the response of the system to other decisions. In fact, an economic forecast can affect the economy through the responses of industrial/commercial organisations and governments to such forecasts.

(iii)   Focused Scenario Planning

3.4   Scenario planning seeks to simplify the complex process of decision making compared with the forecasting approach – involving as it does the construction and validation of large models. Uncertainty is present throughout the system under study, so any reduction that can be achieved will be welcome, and the separation of what is certain or near certain from what is totally unpredictable is the first task. It will therefore be necessary to identify those factors (elements) that are deemed to be important in the system under consideration and separate out those that have some degree of certainty from the uncertain ones:

- **The Predetermined Elements** – those elements that are certain or almost certain to occur, for example the prediction that in the early years of the next century half of the population of the non-OECD world will be under twenty years of age, and have a significant impact on the structure of the work force;

- **Remaining Uncertainties** – those elements that do not have a clear predetermined outcome and will be the major decision variables or choices that will determine the future direction of the system under study.

It is also important to identify those issues that could significantly change the structure of the system under consideration and/or greatly influence the behaviour of the system. In particular:

- **The Driving Forces** – the broad, global events that will be the driving force for progress and change in the system. Examples are geopolitical re-alignment, economic dynamism, policy decisions at the national, regional or global level, increasing environmental awareness;

- **The Prime Movers** – the major players who can change the rules of the game, or the framework within which the system under study operates.

The elements to be considered in scenario construction will be determined by the needs of the decision makers. If the objective were to assist in the development of some form of national energy plan then the key factors would certainly include world oil prices, the energy resources of the country, the stage of development of the economy, the energy infrastructure, the environmental agenda. Socio-political factors would also be important, although difficult to quantify.

The assessment of the relative importance of the critical variables in the future, and their ranking, will allow the use of a tree matrix approach – a useful technique for relating say, the consequences of high or low oil prices for the economic growth in a country – see Figure 2.

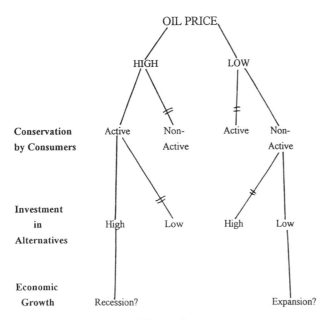

Figure 2

This is a highly simplified example of a tree matrix in first generation scenario work. Government decision takers may wish to influence the behaviour of consumers and investors. Such responses can be readily superimposed on this matrix and could change the direction of, for example, energy conservation. This may be encouraged even in the low oil price case, particularly if separate scenario analysis were to indicate that renewed upward price pressure is a

feature of all scenarios – in other words an ex-post predetermined factor.

(iv)   Scenario Quantification

3.5   For some decisions, qualitative scenarios may well provide sufficient input for the decision maker; for others the decision makers may well require quantitative input – partly because they may have been used to receiving such information when forecasting was the dominant planning tool, and partly because the nature of the decisions may involve comparisons of profitability for different strategies. Economic parameters can be quantified – in the energy world these are generally demand and supply, with some constraints on the energy and oil price conditions. In carrying out these calculations it is important to ensure that the required sets of assumptions are self-consistent and follow logically from the underlying structure of the scenario.

(v)   Option Planning and Testing

3.6   Once the quantification process has been completed, comparisons can be made for each scenario, and profitability, net present value, accountant's returns on investments, or pay-back periods for investments can be calculated – depending on the criteria used by, or helpful to, the decision makers when seeking to distinguish between investment options.

3.7   For the purposes of illustration, some examples of evaluations performed on a series of three scenarios, where the net present values (NPVs) at a 10 per cent discount factor for an investment of $1,000 have been calculated under a series of scenario assumptions and a series of different decisions are shown in the matrix below in Figure 3. This demonstrates how one can construct the spectrum of opportunities and their risks for a variety of decisions.

		SCENARIOS	
Investment – $1,000		MAIN	PHANTOM
	X	Y	Z
Decision A	100	50	Nil
Decision B	(50)	(120)	(300)
Decision C	750	(50)	(90)
Decision D	750	(750)	(40)
Decision E	100	150	(5,000)
TOTAL	1,650	(720)	(5,430)

Note that without the results of the Phantom Scenario the "disaster" case may have been missed – either accidentally or deliberately!

Figure 3. Quantitative Scenario Testing NPV of individual Investment Decisions at 10 per cent Discount Factor

In addition to identifying the value of a set of decisions under each scenario, this analysis opens up the prospect of discovering new strategic options that may not have been considered previously. Given a set of scenarios that are outside the control of the decision maker, one may ask the question – what strategies would be the most rewarding ones, and the most resilient to future changes in the system structure?

(vi)   Risk and Resilience

3.8   The broad objective of the analysis discussed so far has been to show how the risks and rewards of decisions may be linked together. They provide insights into the consequences of an adverse scenario occurring and seek to provide the basis for the decision maker to balance the perceived risks against the potential rewards. The final decision on this is the judgmental view of the decision maker, taking account of the risk portfolio of the corporation or government ministry.

        The simple matrix in the previous section illustrates the dangers of single line forecasting – for the selection of a "middle-ground" forecast would have concealed the true scale of the risk associated with the Phantom Scenario "Z". The weighting of the outcomes by some probabilistic (subjective) assessments of the likelihood of Scenario Z's occurrence would have obscured the true consequences of that Scenario. If the analyst had only presented the averaged results to the decision maker then the full potential impact of the adverse scenario outcome would have been lost. The scenario approach allows the decision maker to address the question – What if this bad outcome occurs, how will my company (or the nation's economy) be affected? Can the organisation withstand the shock? A positive answer may mean that the Decision E can be well justified under Scenarios X and Y for strategic reasons.

3.9   It is important to note at this point the distinction between the roles and responsibilities of the Decision Makers and the Scenario Analysts. The Scenario Analyst is in an advisory position, providing the Decision Maker with the analytical tools required to assess the risks that his organisation can afford to take and to achieve the organisation's agreed policy on the risk profile of its spectrum of investments. (Most sensible private investors will do the same – by having a spread of investments that cover many different risk categories, some gilt-edged securities, some Blue-chip companies, some speculative stocks and some readily available cash. The balance between these will vary from investor to investor, and will reflect the risk aversion of the investor). The Scenario Analyst is, however, responsible for the preparation of the Scenarios and must be selective in the choice of scenarios for in-depth analysis. No decision maker will wish to be confronted by a large number of different scenarios and the analysts will not want to carry out the detailed analysis for more than two or three scenarios. Feedback and dialogue between the scenario creators and the decision makers is therefore a necessary element in the scenario-creation process.

3.10   The scenarios will provide a basis for the evaluation of the resilience of certain strategies – by assessing their robustness under each of the scenarios, and the potential

penalties to be incurred should one of the phantom scenarios lead to a disaster situation.

4. CONSTRUCTING THE SCENARIOS

(i)   The Global Framework

4.1   Energy policies, and the strategies required to achieve those policies, cannot be created in a vacuum – whether the entity establishing the policy is a company, a national government, or a regional grouping of States. They must be set within a wider framework as the energy sector of the economy is an international one and the actions of one nation, or group of nations, could have a significant impact on the policy and it's implementation. In particular, the crude oil, oil products, and coal markets are international, and natural gas is still mainly regional but moving towards an international market, although the high costs of transportation will always constrain a fully international market in gas. This wider, global framework will be derived from a "Global Scenario" to which the Archetype and Exploratory Scenarios will contribute.

4.2   The developer of the scenarios, therefore, will first have to understand the mechanics of the "pure" systems through the construction of "Archetype and Exploratory Scenarios" (see Paragraph 3.3 above) – although for many aspects of the system the relevant mechanisms may already be well understood. They will, however, provide some of the basic building blocks of the First and Second Generation Scenarios that provide the assistance to the decision maker. As examples of the archetype scenarios the assessment of the behaviour of energy rich countries compared with those countries having no indigenous resources has already been mentioned. The response of countries, at different stages of economic development, to environmental issues could provide insights into the realistic ways for responses in the energy sector to environmental pressures.

(ii)   Defining the Parameters

4.3   The global framework required for **building scenarios for the development of resilient energy plans** will set the broad parameters within which the more localised and restricted scenarios will be written. Thus the global scenarios will take into account the following key factors introduced above in Section 3:

The Pre-determined Elements:	**Growth in world population. Location of the bulk of the world's oil and gas reserves** (very low probability of dramatic changes) – resource base is fixed.
The Driving Forces for Energy Markets	**Geopolitical Realignments** – for example the move for Eastern European countries to join the European Union; the growing strength of the Asia Pacific region.

The Dynamics of Economic Growth – the new patterns of world trade; expanding global links; technology revolution and communications – age of instant information.

The Environmental Factor – political pressures; global dimension; economic and logistical problems of response.

The Prime Movers

In Global Political and Economic Issues – primarily the United States and Japan, but with European Union possibly gaining in importance; Saudi Arabia also important force in energy/economic area.

On Environmental Issues – "grass-roots", populist movement; OECD if it wishes to have high profile for political ends.

Once these key elements have been identified, and the necessary archetype scenarios formulated, the global scenarios can be constructed. As with all scenario exercises the objective is to postulate a view of the future that is internally consistent, and incorporates the generally accepted inputs on the Predetermined Elements, Driving Forces, and Prime Movers. But note! – by **"generally accepted"** is meant generally accepted by the governmental decision makers and the General Management of an organisation. Without that agreement the final scenarios may be challenged (and rejected) on the basis of the fundamental assumptions. This highlights the need for consultation and dialogue at an early stage of scenario formulation – but not to the extent that the scenario builders are coerced into accepting the prejudices or biases of the decision makers!

4.4   Brainstorming has proved very successful in identifying some of the above key elements – predetermined elements, driving forces and prime movers. This involves a small (not more than ten) people sitting around a table and thinking aloud about these factors in the context of constructing the global framework scenario. The planners, decision makers and analysts must all actively contribute and be prepared both to challenge and respond when challenged on the logic of their propositions. This is particularly useful in seeking out the group's views on the Driving Forces – a factor that can give rise to much debate. Far better to have this dissent at an early stage in the scenario building process than later.

(iii)   Defining the Uncertainties

4.5   The Uncertainties must also be identified, and the assignment of parameters or values to these will be major determinants of the structure and character of the system in the future as represented in the scenario. There is a difficulty in ensuring that the chosen set of parameters for each scenario is indeed internally consistent, and this requires a certain amount of analysis to identify which uncertainties are independent, and where they are not, what the nature of the

linkages is. For example, consider a fundamental decision that must be made early in the scenario-building process – what sort of a world are we looking to have in the future:

- **World I** – a peaceful co-operative world in which there are genuine attempts by the industrialised nations to stimulate the Developing Countries' economies through the transfer of technology and investment; or

- **World II** – a world of three major power blocs – United States, European Union and the rapidly growing East Asia/Pacific Rim bloc – each looking inwards, maximising their own welfare and giving low priority to the nurturing of economic growth in the Developing Countries outside these three blocs, unless the economic benefits to the power blocs were significant.

These two options could well be the starting point for creating the global scenarios – and each will have a great impact on many, if not all, of the parameters that will define the structure and character of the scenario. Indeed, there will be very different pictures of the world emerging from these two broad characterisations of the future. In World I it is reasonable to assume there would be a good measure of collaboration on environmental matters, a joint approach to dealing with polluting emissions, and a joint (global) response on greenhouse gas emissions; whereas in World II there would be little success in joint collaborative efforts on curbing emissions and consequently a marked deterioration in air quality in many countries, poor efforts and responses on improving nuclear power station safety, and negligible effort on mitigating the effects of greenhouse gas emissions.

4.6   If these global scenarios form the framework for the development of resilient energy policies and plans for a particular country then they should contain sufficient detail on the global energy sector to enable the broad parametric constraints for the energy sector to be determined for use in the national or regional scenarios. These constraints provide the basis for determining how the global behaviour of the energy sector will impact on the national energy sector. Of course, if the country is self-sufficient in energy the interaction may be small; but almost certainly the external, global oil scene will interact with the indigenous industry in most countries – if only to influence the value of its exports or imports.

The Predetermined Elements, Exogenous variables and Driving Forces should all be listed. In addition to the points discussed above, World I and World II might also include:

- Economic Growth;

- Economic Policy as it reflects on relations with other countries – liberal or protectionist?

- Life-styles and infrastructure – including roads, public transport, buildings etc.;

- Ecological concerns, and the responses to the issues of today;

- Government responses – interventionist, *laissez faire,* mixed response;

- Key global energy issues – scarcity or abundance of resources; OPEC strategy; energy prices; emissions/climate consequences;

4.7　Once the global framework has been set, the first and second generation scenarios for the country can be developed. The predetermined elements, driving forces and prime movers will need to be identified within the broad framework specified for the global scenarios – they will have to be consistent with World I or World II as described above in Paragraph 4.5. Next must be considered the key factors that have a direct impact on the energy sector, and those attributes of the system that are affected by the energy sector. These should be listed in descending order of importance in a similar way to those in the global scenarios, although the emphasis will be on the country specific aspects rather than the global perspective.

(iv)　Energy Issues – Some Key Factors

4.8　On the energy issues, some of the factors that will need to be considered are:

- Available indigenous energy reserves, and the prospectiveness of the country for finding additional energy resources;

- Current demand for energy and the main parameters for determining future changes in energy demand; the scope for energy saving; fiscal and pricing controls on the energy sector;

- Reliance on imports of oil and/or coal; or is the country a net exporter of oil and/or coal?

- Attitudes of the local people and the government towards nuclear power;

- Availability of renewable technologies and their scope for growth in the country concerned?

- Energy storage facilities – Underground caverns for oil, LPG, or gas; electricity generation capacity and current surplus/deficit;

This information is basic to the quantification procedures that may be required later to allow commercial assessments to be made.

4.9　The first generation scenarios, when complete should each give a consistent picture of the future for the economic/ political/social environment in which the decision makers will have to implement their decisions once they have been made. One very important point made earlier in this paper

must be repeated – **these scenarios are not forecasts.** They are descriptions of possible worlds in which the company or country may be embedded in the future – they are usually very different and reflect diverse assumptions about the global future.

4.10　Their difference is their strength – for the insights that are given about the possible behaviour of the system when different policies and strategies are evaluated can be most valuable, especially when looking for resilient energy strategies. Once the scenarios have been endorsed by the corporate management (or appropriate ministry) the planners and decision makers will examine the opportunities available in the energy sector and evaluate them within the scenarios that have been agreed.

The diversity and range of the scenarios will allow the outcomes of investment decisions and/or policy initiatives to be compared and contrasted under the different scenarios. Those decisions that are attractive and acceptable under all scenarios are said to be "robust" – and are **resilient** to the range of futures identified in the scenarios.

Inevitably the management/ministry will question the analysts on the possibility of very different outcomes in the future from those identified in the scenarios. For example, suppose that the consequences of global warming could be established unequivocally within the next five years, and there was a very strong mandate (including economic penalties for nations failing to take the agreed actions) from the majority of nations to reduce the consumption of coal in power generation. How would this affect the strategy agreed by a country internally which was based on its robustness under a variety of scenario assumptions – but would be a disaster under the scenario described above? This is an example of a situation requiring another scenario to be established, a Phantom Scenario. In general the analysts would almost certainly have done this in their initial work – but new suggestions of this type may well come up late in the planning process. The analyst must be prepared to respond, unless it can be easily demonstrated that the proposal has no foundation in fact or logic.

4.11　As noted in Paragraph 3.8, if the Phantom Scenario yields a "disaster" for the organisation then the question must be asked – How does this impact on the organisation? Can the "shock" be handled? Some assessment could also be made of the probability of the event occurring, and whether or not such an event (collapse of the market for national chemical manufactures, say, due to new, cheaper technology and products offshore) elsewhere in the organisation's sphere of activity, or other events having a strong correlation with the chemicals market, will compound the "disaster" to the extent of bankrupting the company or damaging a nation's economy.

4.12　In developing options for a Resilient Strategy for Energy, based on the first generation scenarios there will be a number of "events" that need to be taken into account in assessing the ability of the Resilient Strategies to respond – in other words that they are really **resilient.** Such events will vary according to the nature of the organisation developing the strategies, but the following list reflects some of the more common ones:

- A major political upheaval in the Persian Gulf area leads to considerable disruption to crude oil and oil product supplies with associated shortages and increases in price;

- Economic growth in the OECD fails and a major recession ensues; international trade falls dramatically and commodity prices plunge;

- A failure of a nuclear reactor results in major shut-downs of similar reactors around the world for safety checks or as a result of public pressure;

- Technological advances in battery-powered cars make them competitive with gasoline-powered vehicles;

- The Chinese economy collapses causing a deep recession within the Asia Pacific Rim.

These may all seem to have low probabilities today, and the timing cannot be predicted anyway, but considering the implications of such events is part of the task of the scenario analyst.

4.13   The final step in creating the scenarios that the decision maker must have available in order to determine the "best" resilient energy strategies, is to look at the impact of these decisions at the global level via the global scenarios, and at the regional/country level. If the effect is significant then the internal consistency of the scenarios may be compromised – and second generation scenarios must be constructed. These will be modifications of the original scenarios, that may or may not be significantly different from the first generation.

5. ENVIRONMENTAL UNCERTAINTIES

5.1   In considering the environmental uncertainties that may face all planners and decision makers in the future one must distinguish between the issues that are primarily local or regional and those that are global. The first category includes issues such as

- **air quality** – the impact of emissions into the atmosphere, particularly those arising from the use of fossil fuels as sources of energy leading to acid rain, smog in cities etc.

- **water quality** – as it is affected by the disposal of household and industrial effluents; and the run-off from agricultural land where certain fertilisers have been in use;

- **radio-active emissions** – with concerns arising from the safety of nuclear reactors to the storage of radio-active waste, especially the long-life isotopes;

- **the disposal of toxic chemicals** – a growing problem as specialist disposal facilities are increasingly rejected by local communities;

In the second category – the global problems – many of those problems identified above are becoming global in some sense. For example the emission of nitrous oxide has an impact on the local/regional air quality, but is also a "greenhouse gas" and a contributor to global warming.

The spread of nuclear power is also a global problem should there be a catastrophic failure in a reactor anywhere in the world. Even were that to be avoided the wider concern involves the proliferation of nuclear material with the possibility that it could facilitate atomic bomb making by terrorists. The recent commissioning of re-processing facilities for spent nuclear fuel in a number of countries, yielding higher grades of plutonium suitable for bomb making, has added to the growing disquiet over nuclear power for electricity generation.

5.2   The growing trend for the energy consumer is to increase the share of electricity in the final consumption of energy – because it is clean to use, convenient, easy to control, and necessary for the modern world of computers. The problem is that many ways of manufacturing electricity lead to environmental problems or environmental opposition – for example nuclear power (mentioned above), coal or oil burning that lead to emissions of greenhouse gases; and hydro-electric schemes that are attracting increasingly aggressive environmental opposition.

The other key area where Archetype Scenarios and/ or Phantom Scenarios may well be required is in the Transportation Sector – one of the fast growing sectors for energy consumption, particularly in the Developing countries. It is also one of the highest profile sectors for almost everyone is affected as a road user whether on public transport or in private cars or motor-cycles. The principal issues here are emissions and congestion – the latter also contributing significantly to pollution. Technology could well cause some fundamental re-thinking in this area as super-efficient cars, electric cars, fuel cells and modern electronics for route selection and road pricing are amongst those areas receiving large amounts of research effort.

5.3   Such issues as those described above represent just a few of the possible environmental problems that the analysts, energy planners, and decision makers may have to consider. It is the analysts' task to weed out the less important issues before submitting the final version of the scenarios to the decision makers – but some new issues may always be brought forward later.

5.4   The Scenario Planning approach can help the Decision Makers to reach more robust policies and strategies. Their construction is not easy; but the potential benefits to organisations in coping with the uncertainties inherent in the energy system when selecting appropriate policies and strategies could be very rewarding.

WORLD
(Excluding Centrally Planned Economies)
ESTIMATES OF OIL DEMAND

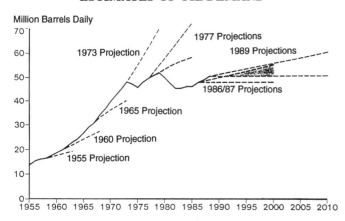

6. REFERENCES

H. DuMoulin – "The New Role of the Corporate Planner" – Paper presented at Eighth Annual International Conference on Winning Strategies for the 1990s, Amsterdam, October, 1988.

H. DuMoulin – "Analysis of Profitability and Risk" – Chapter 9 in Petroleum Resources and Development, Edited by Kameel Khan, Published by Belhaven Press, London.

M. W. Clegg – "Energy Balances in an Uncertain World: A Scenario Approach for the 21st. Century – Paper presented at 6th Annual APS Conference, Nicosia, Cyprus, September, 1992.

M. W. Clegg and H. DuMoulin, (Joint Coordinators) – MID-90's RESUME, ETE 21, Energy, Technology and Environment – A Circle to Promote Rational Action for the 21st Century. Private Report, 1995.

VI. REGIONAL COOPERATION IN ENERGY*

Technical cooperation among developing countries of the Asian and Pacific region in the area of development and management of energy resources is without any doubt a highly desirable thing. For several reasons, however, efforts towards those ends have met with considerable resistance and obstacles.

The benefits of regional energy linkages are obvious. One is the sharing of energy resources and increase in energy trade. The linking of transmission lines across borders would enable countries to make more efficient use of existing capital investment in power plants and to share existing hydropower resources. This would be especially desirable among countries with different time zones. An added benefit would be the reduction of emissions from fossil-fuel plants owing to the more optimal use of hydropower resources. Thus far, only limited power linkages exist in the region. Similarly, the establishment of a regional network of natural gas pipelines would enable countries of the region to share natural gas resources while at the same time enhancing energy trade and environmental quality. Both types of networks would also stimulate regional economic growth and cooperation.

Unfortunately, neither of these have been developed extensively in the region, presumably because most countries of the region have so far been largely concerned about the energy supplies within their respective borders. The only regional energy trade of international significance is the trade of oil products centred in Singapore on account of the refinery industry established in the island republic.

Another reason for the lack of energy linkages in electric power transmission lines and natural gas pipelines is the as yet relatively low level of energy consumption and the large distances involved between the consuming centres within the region. Compared with Europe, where energy linkages have been established since before the Second World War and have further flourished since the war, the continent of Asia is very much larger: about three times as vast, and more, if Australia and New Zealand are included.

International collaboration, however, could be conducted at the level of exchange of information and experience on energy development and management. In this more limited form of regional energy cooperation, ESCAP has accomplished modest milestones in cooperation with other United Nations agencies such as UNDP, FAO and UNIDO, and in collaboration with donor governments such as Australia, France, Japan and the Netherlands.

Since ESCAP's inception in 1947 (then known as the Economic Commission for Asia and the Far-East) until 1992 developing countries of the region have found useful the forum called the Committee on Natural Resources, one of the legislative committees established by the Commission. In 1987, the Committee was renamed Committee on Natural Resources and Energy. In 1992, the Commission adopted a thematic programming approach, as distinct from the previous sectoral programming approach, and restructured the legislative bodies. Energy development and management then became the concern of the Committee on Environment and Sustainable Development. Both committees would normally meet annually so that reports could be prepared for the annual session of the Commission.

In 1993, an ad hoc expert group meeting was called to discuss various topics of importance for the region, inter alia the area of energy development and management, in order to provide input for the first session of the Committee on Environment and Sustainable Development. One of the papers prepared by the secretariat for the ad hoc expert group meeting was entitled "Progress and functioning of the regional energy working groups" (annex I).

As stated in annex I, since 1993, ESCAP has acted as the main executing agency of the UNDP-funded Programme for Asian Cooperation on Energy and the Environment (PACE-E), with co-funding from the Governments of Australia and France. In the nearly two years of execution, a total of 19 events will have been organized by 1 October 1995, with the number of participants totalling nearly 500. A table listing the number of participants by country is provided in annex II.

In accordance with the terms of the PACE-E project document, the six regional energy working groups have been renamed as follows:

1. Working group on energy-environment planning.

2. Working group on coal development and utilization.

3. Working group on natural gas and petroleum development.

4. Working group on rural energy and environment development.

5. Working group on conservation and efficiency.

6. Working group on electric power system management.

In the area of new and renewable sources of energy, ESCAP since 1993 has continued to initiate and implement

---

* Prepared by the ESCAP secretariat for the Senior Expert Group Meeting on Energy Resiliency and the Integration of Environment the Energy Policy and Planning, Bangkok, 4 to 6 October 1995.

regional activities, in particular projects on wind energy development and utilization funded by the Governments of Australia and the Netherlands, and the Asia-Pacific Renewable Energy Symposium '95 (APRES '95) funded by the Government of Australia.

Senior experts participating in the Senior Expert Group Meeting on Energy Resiliency and the Integration of Environment in Energy Policy and Planning are requested to provide their considered opinion on how best to achieve a sustainable regional energy cooperation in the region in the above areas. In view of funding constraints for participation in regional meetings on energy development and management, it is suggested that the public utilities and agencies operating in the regional countries might be called upon to represent their countries in the various regional energy working groups, for example, coal companies/agencies in the working group on coal development and utilization, oil and gas companies or agencies in the working group on natural gas and petroleum development, and power/electricity utilities in the working group on electric power system management. The energy ministry or agency would still deal with the remaining three working groups on energy-environment planning, on rural energy and environment development, and on conservation and efficiency. The working group on energy-environment planning could retain the role of the coordinating working group.

Another idea worthy of pursuit is the possibility of convening a ministerial-level conference on energy in 1997. The last time that this was proposed was in 1986, when the fall in oil price removed the justification for such a meeting. It may be opportune to take stock of a regional view of the energy sector, at a time of an "oil-glut" situation tempered by calls to undertake more sustainable paths in an environmentally conscious world. Developing countries of the region, however, are being driven by the realization of an overwhelming need to eliminate poverty, and thus always mindful of the need still to expand the energy infrastructure.

Annex I

PROGRESS AND FUNCTIONING OF THE REGIONAL ENERGY WORKING GROUPS

Note by the secretariat for the Expert Group Meeting Preparatory to the First Session of the Committee on Environment and Sustainable Development held in Bangkok from 30 September to 2 October 1993

A. Background and rationale for regional cooperation

1. Developing countries of the ESCAP region are aware that energy sources are crucial to their economic development. Energy resources of the world are, however, unevenly distributed, and the ESCAP region is currently a net importer of energy. Even though energy production has been steadily increasing in the past decade or so, the region's energy consumption has also been increasing at a rate commensurate with dynamic economic developments.

2. Several subregions of the ESCAP region have excellent prospects for regional energy cooperation based on their energy resource endowments. The subregion of North-East Asia has vast resources of coal, oil and gas still to be tapped and used for the benefit of the region as a whole. The demand for energy is already very much present in the region: Japan and the Republic of Korea are dynamic economies with few of their own energy resources. The far-eastern part of the Russian Federation and the north-eastern and north-western parts of China are energy resource-rich areas with considerable potential resources waiting to be tapped. The subregion of South-East Asia also has considerable resources, although not in the same league as North-East Asia, of natural gas and hydro-power potential. The economies of this subregion is also experiencing dynamic and vibrant growth with prospects for further industrialization and development, thus requiring large inputs of energy. Subregional collaboration would enhance their collective security of energy supplies and increase the efficiency of their energy systems. Similarly, the subregion of South Asia could advantageously use the resources located within the subregion, such as natural gas in Bangladesh and the eastern part of India, hydropower potential in Bhutan, India, Nepal and Pakistan, and oil and gas resources in Afghanistan, the western par of India, the Islamic Republic of Iran, and Pakistan. The western part of the South Asian subregion could conceivably also be connected to the energy resource-rich countries of the central Asian republics.

3. The type of subregional energy cooperation and collaboration envisaged above cannot be realized in the medium term. Such endeavours and efforts require very long lead-times and are usually a response to pressures exerted by economic realities, such as those pertaining in the European countries where such collaboration exists in all energy sectors. However, a beginning has to be made. Perhaps ESCAP could provide the forum to encourage discussion and dialogue on this topic.

4. One form of collaboration between developing countries is exemplified by OPEC, formed by petroleum producing and exporting countries with specific aims and purposes relating to the area of petroleum exports. It was formed more than three decades ago. The oil crisis of 1973 displayed the strength of OPEC, so much so that in 1974 the member countries of OECD formed its own organization, the International Energy Agency (IEA), to counterbalance OPEC. Since then, both organizations have dealt with the overall energy problem, although each one had been established to deal with petroleum questions. The reason is, of course, that petroleum is an important and valuable commodity, and its use is principally as a source of energy, which is important for the economy. OPEC members are from developing countries only, even though some developed countries had been petroleum-exporting countries before 1960 and since the 1970s some other developed countries became petroleum-exporting countries. IEA consists of members only of developed countries, most of them oil-importing countries; developing countries are not eligible for membership, even though many developing countries are also oil-importing countries. (The Republic of Korea may soon become a member.)

5. Clearly, both institutions have their *raison d'être*. Members recognize the need for the institutions and support and sustain their existence. It is equally clear that both were established to deal directly with questions of supply and demand for petroleum and petroleum products. But both institutions are also engaged in the conduct of studies, pertaining not to only the specific area of petroleum but also to the overall energy problem, as well as areas closely related with energy.

6. Another example of an organization serving the interests of developing member countries is in Latin America, OLADE, the Latin American Energy Organization. OLADE is governed by a board, consisting of the ministers of energy of its member countries, and its secretariat is supported by contributions from its members.

7. For Asia and the Pacific, there is no question about the wide scope for regional cooperation in energy. Despite

the large disparities in stages of economic development, the great variety in natural resource and energy endowments, and the stark differences in human resources, developing countries of the region could fruitfully collaborate in exchanges of information, assist each other in meeting training needs, and benefit from transfer of know-how and experience in energy development and management, in areas such as energy planning, the coordination of policies, the energy trade such as in petroleum products, in gas and electricity networks, and also in environmental mitigation measures. Such collaboration could later develop into regional energy cooperation. However, developing countries of the region are constrained by lack of foreign exchange and lack of funds in general to undertake a sustained effort of regional cooperation in energy. In the Asian and Pacific region countries still require a source of grant funds to enable them to participate in a series of meetings, as would be called for in a regional cooperation programme covering the energy sector.

8. Thus, in 1988, after more than five years of implementation of two regional programmes in energy, namely the Biomass, Solar and Wind Energy Programme, funded by the Government of Japan with supplementary assistance from the Government of Australia, and the Regional Energy Development Programme (REDP), funded by UNDP with supplementary funding from the Governments of Australia and France, it was decided in two separate ESCAP forums to establish networks of regional energy working groups. The first was the network of the regional working groups on new and renewable sources of energy, with each working group dealing with only one specific area of new and renewable energy such as biomass, solar, geothermal and wind, and the second was the network of six regional energy working groups within the framework of REDP, each dealing with one specific topic or energy type: natural gas, coal, energy planning, energy conservation, electric power or rural energy planning. It was felt too premature to establish a fully-fledged energy organization, as many countries were unable to contribute the funds necessary to support such an institution. The countries intimated that grants, such as from UNDP and bilateral sources such as Australia, France, Germany, Japan, the Netherlands and Norway, should be available to enable them to develop cooperative programmes.

B. Establishment by ESCAP and UNDP of regional energy working groups

1. Working groups under the REDP framework

9. The third session of the Tripartite Review Conference of the Regional Energy Development Programme, held in Kuala Lumpur in August 1989, approved the work programme for phase IV of REDP for implementation during the period 1990-1991. The work programme was divided into six subprogrammes: energy planning, natural gas development, coal development, energy conservation, electric

power development, and rural energy planning and development. Each of the subprogrammes comprised several activities, of which at least one in each subprogramme was to conduct a regional seminar or workshop. During the conduct of the seminar or workshop, normally of three-to-five days duration, a special session was devoted to discussion in working groups of topics or questions of interest to member countries. The seminar or workshop participants acted as working group members representing their respective countries.

10. The working groups had the following aims and immediate objectives:

(a) To promote and develop a cooperative arrangement for regional cooperation to strengthen the national capabilities of the participating member countries in a specific area of energy;

(b) To promote and operationalize technical and economic cooperative programmes among participating member countries through (or as a result of) implementation of working group activities.

11. Six working groups within the framework of REDP were established during the period 1990-1991. The Working Group on Rural Energy Planning and Development met during the Executive Seminar on Rural Energy Planning and Development, held in China and Thailand, in October and November 1990. The State Planning Commission of China acted as the coordinator of the Working Group. The Working Group designated China, the Philippines and Sri Lanka to form a subgroup entrusted with the task of developing project profiles based on the programme outlines agreed by the Working Group. For this purpose, a meeting was organized on a TCDC (technical cooperation among developing countries) basis in Beijing by the State Planning Commission. The draft project profiles were circulated among members and then finalized and submitted by China to the Tripartite Review Conference of the Regional Energy Development Programme, at its fifth session held in Kuala Lumpur in August 1991.

12. A similar procedure was followed by the other working groups. The Working Group on Natural Gas Development met during the Executive Seminar on Natural Gas Development, held in Indonesia and New Zealand in February 1991. The designated coordinator was the State Gas Corporation of Indonesia, whose President Director presented the proposed project profiles on natural gas to the Tripartite Review Conference at its fifth session. The Working Group on Energy Conservation discussed a cooperative programme for the period 1992-1996 during the Regional Training Workshop on Energy Conservation in Small and Medium-scale Industries, held in New Delhi in March 1991. The Energy Management Centre of the Department of Power under the Ministry of Energy, India, is the Coordinator of the Working Group.

13. The fourth working group formed was the Working Group on Coal Development, which discussed a future programme in conjunction with an executive seminar held in Australia. The Joint Coal Board of Australia acted as the coordinator of the Working Group and its representative submitted a proposal to the Tripartite Review Conference at its fifth session. Subsequently, the Working Group on Electric Power Development was convened during the Regional Workshop on Economic Load Dispatching and Demand Management in Electric Power System Management, held from 29 July to 2 August 1991 in Malaysia. The Department of Electricity Supply of the Ministry of Energy, Telecommunications and Posts of Malaysia is the coordinator of this working group. The sixth and last working group was the Working Group on Energy Planning, which was formed during the fifth session of the REDP Tripartite Review Conference. The REDP Senior Coordinator assumed the responsibility as coordinator of the working group and finalized the project profiles based on the work programme outline agreed upon by the working group.

14. The establishment of the six regional working groups has proceeded smoothly. The response of the countries of the region has been very encouraging. For example, 17 countries have indicated their interest in participating in the Working Group on Energy Conservation and 15 countries are participants in the Working Group on Electric Power Development. Technical support for all working groups has been provided by the ESCAP secretariat through REDP and the Natural Resources Division. The Division of Industry, Human Settlements and Environment has also provided support to the Working Group on Energy Conservation. Additional support has also been provided by the Division of Statistics and the Development Planning Division.

2. Regional working groups on new and renewable sources of energy

15. The formation of the working groups on new and renewable sources of energy followed a procedure analogous to the REDP working groups, with working group discussions conducted during a session of the regional seminar or workshop on a particular topic of new and renewable sources of energy. The aims and objectives of the working groups were also similar. However, there were differences. The principal activity was not funded directly by UNDP through ESCAP but by a bilateral donor country, or by UNDP through another agency. There was no equivalent of the REDP Tripartite Review Conference to review and endorse the proposals from the working group. Unlike REDP, which was established for the benefit of Asian member countries (because Pacific island countries at that time obtained UNDP grants through the Pacific Energy Development Programme), activities were open to all member countries of the ESCAP region.

16. The first Working Group formed was the Working Group on Wind Energy Development and Utilization, effected in conjunction with the organization of the Regional Expert Group Meeting on Wind Energy Technology in China, held in November-December 1990. China agreed to host the secretariat of this working group. The second working group to be established was the Regional Working Group on Geothermal Energy Development and Utilization, which was set up during the International Workshop on Geothermal Energy Training, held in the Philippines in November 1991. Both working groups succeeded in formulating work programme outlines for their future work.

17. The establishment of other working groups is being considered. Among these are a regional working group on solar photovoltaic technology, a regional working group on solar thermal energy development and utilization and a regional working group on biogas production and utilization.

3. Regional cooperation by means of technical cooperation among developing countries

18. The type of cooperation effected through the working group mechanism is known as TCDC. This terminology is applied to a particular form of cooperation, namely technical exchange through mutual visits with local travel and subsistence costs being met by the host country and international costs provided by an international agency. This type of cooperation has been conducted by ESCAP, with supplementary funds from bilateral donor countries or from UNDP.

19. Such TCDC cooperation through ESCAP is already being effected in the area of new and renewable sources of energy. The three-country new and renewable sources of energy subprogramme of REDP has been successfully implemented to the satisfaction of all three participating countries, China, the Democratic People's Republic of Korea and Mongolia. The Liaoning Province Energy Research Institute of China is the coordinator. The subprogramme has been mutually beneficial in that exchanges of information and experience have been effected on various new and renewable sources of energy technologies and applications in countries with similar climates and agro-systems. Another series of activities pertained specifically to solar photovoltaic systems for remote villages. The donor country supplying the solar photovoltaic systems was Thailand, and the beneficiary country was Myanmar. Similar exchanges have recently been implemented in wind energy technology between China and Sri Lanka, and between China and Thailand, and also in charcoal production between China and Vanuatu.

20. In the future, such exchanges should be initiated and discussed during meetings on project activities being undertaken by ESCAP.

C. Functioning of the regional energy working groups

21. The experience of the implementation of energy activities during the period 1990-1992 in respect of the

regional energy working groups has been very satisfactory. The networks have been established and each of the working groups have succeeded in formulating work programme proposals for the future (in the case of the REDP working groups, for the period 1992-1996, in conformity with the period of the fifth programming cycle). Leadership has been provided by the coordinating country through the host of the secretariats of the working groups. The host countries have also contributed funds for the organization of the main activities as well as for the working groups.

22.   The foundations for a potential blossoming of regional cooperation in energy have thus been laid down. However, there remains much work to be done. The countries of the region that are already at a more advanced stage of development are eager to share their experience with other countries at a lower stage of development. Countries at the beginning of their economic reform programmes are enthusiastic about applying the analytical methods and methodologies commonly used for market economies. Old challenges remain, such as the vulnerability of oil-importing countries to oil price fluctuations or the rationalization of tariff structures, and new challenges have emerged, such as the incorporation of environmental considerations in energy planning. Regional cooperation in energy effected through the regional cooperative mechanisms reported in this note provides the necessary bases on which to meet these challenges.

23.   UNDP has now agreed to launch with ESCAP a new programme on energy and the environment: Programme for Asian Cooperation on Energy and the Environment (PACE-E). The programme will make full use of the working group "infrastructure" already built, with some modifications: (a) the participating countries will be requested to form "national focal groups" on energy and environment, instead of simply designating a "national focal point" to act as the national counterpart for the programme; and (b) the names of the working groups have been reformulated in the project document to reflect the energy-environment interrelationship.

24.   The launching of the PACE-E activities, probably in September 1993, will coincide with the convening of this Expert Group Meeting. It was suggested that the experts should discuss the possibilities for regional cooperation that could conveniently be realized in the coming years. It may be desirable to have a meeting of senior experts at policy level to discuss a possible future cooperating and coordinating mechanism to oversee and guide the activities of all working groups in the field of energy: thus, all areas of energy development and management could be coordinated by the same forum without any duplication.

25.   The secretariat invites the experts to deliberate on these issues and to make recommendations to the Committee on Environment and Sustainable Development accordingly. The principal activities envisaged are coordination of the energy development and management activities under the subprogramme on environment and sustainable development, execution and implementation of PACE-E, consideration of Asia Energy Efficiency 21, and TCDC activities in selected areas not covered by the above.

Annex II

NUMBER OF PARTICIPANTS IN UNDP/ESCAP PACE-E ACTIVITIES, 1993-1995

Country or area	EEP-1[a]	EEP-3[b]	CDU[c] 1(a) 6-week CPU & EP Course	CDU 1(b) 4-week CT & EP Course	CDU 2 2-week executive seminar	CDU 2 1-week senior executive seminar	CDU 3 4-week CT & EV Course	CDU 4 4-day CT & E Workshop	NG & PD-1	REED-1	C&E 1	C&E 2	C&E 3[d]	C&E 4	C&E 5[e]	EPSM-1 Review meeting[f]	EPSM-1 Regional workshop[g]	EPSM-2 Consultative meeting[h]	EPSM-2 Training workshop[i]
Bangladesh			1				1			1	1				1				
China	1	1	1	2	2	2	2		2	21		1		1			1		
Cambodia	2	1					2										1		1
Hong Kong	1		1		2	2				1		7	1	1	1				
India	1	1	1	2	2		1		2		2	1	1	1	1	1	1		1
Indonesia	1	1	1	2		1	1		2	1	1	1	2		3	1	2		
Islamic Republic of Iran	2	1							2										
Republic of Korea	1	2	1	1	1	2	2				1	1	5	3	1		1		
Lao People's Democratic Republic	2	1	1				1			1					1				2
Malaysia	1	3	1	1	2	2	2	36	1	1	1	1		3	9	1	11	2	2
Mongolia	2	1	1	1			1			1	1		1						
Myanmar	2		1						2		1						1		
Nepal	2	2	1	1	1		1		1	1			2		2		1		1
Pakistan	1	2	1	1	2	1			2			1		1	1				
Philippines	1	1	1	2		1	1		2	1	1	1	1	1	1	1	1		2
Singapore					1				1			1			2				
Sri Lanka	2	2	1		1	1					1			1			1		1
Thailand	3	3	1	2	2	5	1	101	2	2	1	1	1	6	4	2	1	1	
Viet Nam	2	2	1				1		2	1	1		1		1		1		3
Grand total	26	24	15	15	13	17	15	137	20	33	12	14	15	18	29	6	23	3	13

a In addition, 4 participants from Pacific countries.
b In addition, 1 resource person.
c In addition, 4 participants from non-ESCAP countries.
d In addition, 2 resource persons.
e In addition, 4 resource persons and consultants, one participant from the Pacific and three resource persons from outside Asia.
f In addition, 8 resource persons and consultants.
g In addition, 9 resource persons and consultants.
h In addition, 3 resource persons.
i In addition, 7 resource persons, 2 consultants and 6 observers.

VII. COUNTRY REPORTS

1. CAMBODIA: ENERGY, ELECTRICITY, RENEWABLE ENERGY*

Cambodia is a South-East Asian country is the gulf on Thailand on the South China Sea bordered by the Lao People's Demorcratic Republic to the North, Viet Nam to the East and Thailand to the West. The population of Cambodia is now over 9 million inhabitants, distributed over a surface of 181.035 km^2. The population is unequally divided among 21 provinces, which are divided in 170 districts, 1.570 communes and 13.305 villages.

The almost 20 years of war has put Cambodia behind in achieving the democratic and economic rewards she so richly deserves. There are so many things to do to achieve this goal. One of the most important is to create an Environment that attracts economic development to the country and, of course, one of the most important parts of the economic development formula is the availability of Power. Not only for industry but for the people to carry on normal lives. Power is the key to Cambodia's development.

I Would like to inform you that power (Energy, Electricity, Renewable Energy etc.) in Cambodia is the responsibility of Ministry of Industry, Mines and Energy.

Energy policy of the Royal Government of Cambodia there are:

* To provide an adequate supply of low cost energy for home throughout Cambodia.

* To ensure a reliable, secure electricity supply at prices which facilitates investment in Cambodia and development of the economy.

* To encourage exploration and develop environmentally and socially acceptable uses of energy resources needed for supply to all sectors of the Cambodian economy.

* To encourage efficient use of energy and to minimize environmental effects rising from energy supply and end use.

All the commercial energy used in Cambodia is imported. There has been no development of fossil fuel resources and very litter is know of them. Exploration for oil and gas is being undertaken in the Gulf of Thailand and the results so far have been very encouraging and we are confident that we will find commercial quantities. However, it will be some time before it will be developed and decisions have to be made as to whether it will be used as a premium fuel or used in trade for other commodities.

And the further more, according to research and collecting document that we just started on Renewable Energy (Solar Energy, Wind Energy, Mini-Micro hydropower, Biogas, Biomass) done by the recently formed Ministry of Industry Mines and Energy, and the results show that:

There are a lot of Natural Energy Resources in Cambodia like: Sunlight, Wind, Water, Biogas, Geothermal, Rice husk etc., that could be develop easily in a due to make an intelligent use of these resources, especially Solar, Wind and Mini-Micro hydropower. In the mean time, we received new information saying that: there are many meter cubs of Silicon (Million m^3), a long revere's depth and bark. It is the main natural resource needed to produce the Solar panel.

In addition, the Royal Government is actively encouraging private sector investment in generation (IPP-Independent Power Producers). We have already negotiated a contract with an investor for our second IPP project. The first move we have made to encourage inventors, not just IPPs but for all investors is to set up a favorable investment environment.

---

* Speech by Dr Sat Samy, Senior Expert and Coordinator of SEA and Renewable Energy, Energy Department, Ministry of Industry, Mines and Energy, Phnom Penh. This report is reproduced in the form in which it was received.

ESTIMATED PROJECT ON RENEWABLE ENERGY FOR RURAL DEVELOPMENT IN CAMBODIA
(SOLAR ENERGY, WIND ENERGY, MINI-MICRO HYDROPOWER, BIOGAS AND BIOMASS)

Most Urgently

No	Province	Districts	Communes	Villages	Groups	H'holds	Population	Area in km²	Hospital	Pagoda
1	Banteay Meanchey	7	58	1 114	4 209	67 585	389 861	9 937	37	147
2	Battambang	8	66	481	6 412	100 810	533 582	11 377	67	175
3	Kompong Cham	16	193	1 713	14 804	240 731	1 345 582	10 498	188	472
4	Kompong Chhnang	8	69	538	3 380	59 913	304 008	5 520	41	165
5	Kompong Speu	8	86	1 275	4 630	87 975	465 457	7 017	54	158
6	Kompong Thom	8	81	718	5 692	82 589	469 712	13 700	78	187
7	Kompot	8	95	476	5 579	86 060	454 269	5 209	122	155
8	Kandal	11	147	1 090	9 639	156 443	841 544	3 591	153	286
9	Koh Kong	7	30	119	359	13 300	69 688	11 160	26	45
10	Kratie	5	48	248	2 153	33 804	196 647	11 094	51	74
11	Mondul Kiri	5	21	87	172	4 037	21 449	14 250	18	3
12	Phnom Penh	7	96	496	3 569	111 413	667 814	267	31	85
13	Preah Vihear	7	9	197	826	14 554	86 460	14 800	57	250
14	Prey Veng	12	116	1 138	9 626		885 170	2 966	129	393
15	Pursat	5	44	440	2 844	50 389	254 587	12 692	49	104
16	Ratanak Kiri	9	50	243	657	12 761	66 764	11 373	11	10
17	Siem Reap	14	108	917	5 357	90 284	556 120	15 270	87	184
18	Sihanouk Ville	3	21	82	856	19 973	107 006	868	19	18
19	Stung Treng	5	34	129	598	11 259	63 598	11 000	42	23
20	Svay Rieng	7	100	690	5 730	80 457	413 329	4 883	87	180
21	Takeo	10	98	1 114	8 674	116 271	636 404	3 563	110	257
TOTAL	A=21	B=170	C=1 570	D=13 305	E=95 766	F=1 440 608	G=8 829 051	H=181 035	I=1 457	J=3 371

NOTE:

1 – A = 21 (Electricity demand) (±3%)

2 – B + C + D = 170 + 1,570 + 13,305 = 15,045 (Lighting for Administration) (±5%)

3 – C = 1,570 [Pumping (Irrigation)] (±2%)

4 – D = 13,305 (Depth, Pumping) (±3%)

5 – F = 1,440,608 (Lighting, TV, Pumping) (±50%)

6 – I = 1,457 (Lighting Vaccine, Pumping) (±20%)

7 – J = 3,371 (Lighting, TV, Pumping) (±10%)

"SOLAR ENERGY APPLICATIONS"
CAMBODIA

No.	Application		Priority			Time			Comments
	Place	System	High	Medium	Low	Present	Future		
							Short	Long	
I	City, Province, District.	Street Lighting	√		●	√			
		Road sign		√			√		
		Alarm system			√			√	
		Administration	√			√			
		Communication	√				√		
		Leisure/Camping			√			√	
II	Village	Water supply	√			√			
		Battery charger		√			√		
		Chool	√				√		
		Clinic	√			√			
		Pagoda	√			√			
III	Domenstic	Lighting	√			√			
		TV/Radio	√			√			
		Ventilation		√			√		
		Water pumping	√			√			
		Refrigeration			√			√	
IV	Farm	–	√			√			
V	Irrigation	–	√			√			
VI	Minigrid	–		√			√		
VII	Handicraft	–		√			√		

2. ENERGY DEVELOPMENT IS INDONESIA*

Overview of Energy Situation

1.   If we observe our national energy situation, then we will find that there are at least four indicators. Below is detailed description of energy indicators.

2.   The **first** energy indicator is the very high growth of energy consumption. In the last decade, the world energy consumption has only been growing at around 2 per cent per annum, while Indonesia energy consumption has grown at a rate around 8 per cent per annum. In the same period, energy consumption in Asia Pacific which includes Japan, South Korea, China, Taiwan and ASEAN has grown at annually about 5 per cent. The fast rate of this energy consumption, also happens in the electricity sector, even the rate is faster, it was recorded that the growth of electricity consumption was about 15 per cent per annum, even it ever reached 17 per cent per annum during the First Long Term Development Plan I (PJP-I). Below is a detailed description of energy consumption during PJP-I.

3.   The utilization of energy since REPELITA I (The First Five Year Development Plan) has increased substantially. The growth of primary energy consumption during REPELITA I was 12.71 per cent, during REPELITA II 14.98 per cent, REPELITA III 7.74 per cent, REPELITA IV 5.46 per cent and REPELITA V 8.21 per cent. The high growth of energy consumption as indicated above was due to the increase of development activities in almost all sectors and the fulfilment of a better standard of living of the society. Subsidies in energy prices have also caused an increase in energy consumption. The growth of energy consumption during REPELITA II was the highest, in line with rapid growth in economic activities. These rapid growths decreased during REPELITA III and REPELITA IV, but increased again during the first two years of REPELITA V mainly because of higher growth of consumption in the industrial and transportation sectors.

4.   Rapid increase in oil consumption was observed during the First Long Term Development Era (1969/70-1993/94); with a growth rate of 8.12 per cent annually, oil consumption has increased significantly from only 43.9 million BOE to 286.1 million BOE. Oil consumption growth, however, was lower than that of total energy growth which reached 9.57 per cent annually during the same period. This indicates that the government's policy on energy diversification which promotes the use of non-oil energy sources to replace oil has been to some extent successfully implemented.

5.   During the First Long Term Development Era, natural gas consumption has increased rapidly from 3.07 million BOE in 1969/1970 to 94.84 million BOE in 1993/1994, growing at 15.36 per cent annually. The share of natural gas has substantially increased from 6.1 per cent in 1969/1970 to 21.12 per cent in 1993/94.

6.   Though the rate of coal consumption increases rapidly, but the role of coal in domestic energy mix is still insignificant. At the end of the first long term development, its share only reached 7.99 per cent.

7.   The utilization of hydro power shows a significant increase. In 1969/1970, the utilization was only 2.39 million BOE and increased to 27.88 million BOE in 1993/1994, or growing at 10.76 per cent annually.

8.   Other alternative sources of energy are currently being developed including geothermal, solar, wind, biomass and biogas. However, the development is mostly still at the demonstration stage, except for that of geothermal energy which is located at Kamojang, West Java, and Dieng, Central Java with an installed capacity of 143 MW. The share of geothermal energy to the total commercial energy consumption has increased from only 0.07 per cent (143.0 thousand BOE) in 1982/1983 to 0.80 per cent (3,610 thousand BOE) in 1993/94. The primary energy consumption is presented in Table 1.

Table 1. The Primary Energy Consumption during PJP-I
(million BOE)

Year	Oil	Natural gas	Coal	Hydro Power	Geo Thermal	^Total
1969/70	43.9	3.1	0.7	2.4	0.0	50.1
1973/74	70.6	3.2	0.6	4.2	0.0	77.6
1978/79	129.9	20.7	0.7	3.8	0.0	155.2
1983/84	170.3	42.7	1.1	11.6	0.4	226.1
1988/89	190.1	69.9	19.9	20.2	2.0	302.1
1993/94	280.4	85.4	32.5	28.0	3.6	429.9

Source: Repelita VI Departemen Pertambangan dan Energi.

9.   The **second** energy indicator is that the oil share in national energy supply has been successfully reduced, although we still consider it high and needs further decrease. At the start of the five year development plan (early Repelita I) the oil share in energy supply was yet very high, i.e., around 87 per cent and in the last year of PJP-I the share of oil had been successfully reduced to around 65 per cent. Oil also still plays a significant role in the government's foreign exchange earnings.

---

* Speech by Mr. Zuhal, Director General, Directorate General of Electricity and Energy Development, Ministry of Mines and Energy, Jakarta. This report is reproduced in the form in which it was received.

10. The growing concern over oil depletion and the disturbing premonition that in the not too distant future the country may have to change its current status from an oil exporting country to a net oil importing country have forced the government to hasten the implementation of energy conservation and diversification measures. If, for instance, the rate of oil consumption is assumed to increase at 6.1 per cent annually, while the production rate is assumed to decrease at 8 per cent annually, then the country might become a net oil importing country by the year 2000. If, however, the consumption rate can be slowed down to 2.8 per cent annually, the country's likely chance to become a net oil importing country could be extended to the year 2008.

11. The imbalance in the energy use pattern has also characterized the energy utilization of the country. It is apparent that renewable as well as non-oil energy resources have not been utilized commensurate with its availability and potentiality. To some degree, the government's efforts to diversify the use of energy for domestic needs have gained support, especially from the industrial sector which has utilized coal and natural gas and the household sector which has utilized Liquid Petroleum Gas (LPG) to replace the use of kerosene and fuel wood.

12. The **third** energy indicator is the energy intensity which remains high. It means we consume too much energy to produce a certain quantity of national product compared to other countries. This shows that the technology we use is not yet energy efficient technology. For the future needs, such a condition needs to be changed through a more effective implementation of energy conservation policy.

13. During the first Long-Term Development era, the income per capita increased, but not as rapidly as the energy consumption did. This means that the level of productivity of the utilization of energy was still low, which was caused by higher energy consumption in the household sector, compared to that in the industrial sector.

14. The **fourth** energy indicator is Indonesia per capita energy consumption which is still low compared to other countries mainly the developed countries. If we relate this fourth energy indicator with the third energy indicator, then we can conclude that commercial energy consumption in Indonesia is not evenly distributed. Big customers are still wasting the energy, whilst many small customers still cannot be reached by commercial energy supply, especially in rural areas remotely situated faraway from the reach of commercial energy supply.

Prediction of Energy Situation

15. How does the energy situation trend look like?. The fast implementation of development and the big population need the support of energy. Energy is needed for the growth of activities of industry, services, transportation and households. In the long run, the role of energy will be more developed particularly to support the industry sector and those of related activities. Industrialization during Phase II Long Term Development (PJP-II) is expected to change the economic structure and society structure fundamentally, in which the industry sector will become the backbone of Indonesia economy.

16. Based on the past experiences and the prediction of influential condition, the challenge faced by energy sector in the period of second phase of long run development is even bigger. I record that there are at least four main challenges we are facing, namely to meet the ever increasing energy need with the relatively still high growth rate, oil consumption, provisions of fund and environmental problems.

17. Energy demand during this period depends much on the growth of the economy and population, the structural changes in the economy, substitution from traditional to commercial energy resources, and efficiency of energy utilization. It is expected that the rate growth of energy demand will remain on the high side, although somewhat curbed as a result of energy conservation efforts. The share of coal will increase appreciably, especially to meet the demand in the power sector, both public and private. Rural energy supply is also expected to increase significantly, as well as the utilization of new energy such as biomass, solar energy and wind energy. Guidances, regulations and implementation of energy conservation will be continually expanded to encompass all energy users.

18. During PJP-II, economic growth is projected to be around 7 per cent per annum, the continually lower population growth so that in the last year of PJP-II it is expected to become 0.9 per cent per annum, per capita income of Indonesia will multiply 4 times of the present level.

19. Based on that economic development target, our office is trying to forecasts the final energy consumtion during PJP-II. Based on our forecast the energy need in the year of 2010 will be around 985 million BOE or in other words in that period of time, the average rate of energy need is around 7.41 per cent per annum. To meet the energy, Indonesia will need primary energy be around 1.484 million BOE. The projection of the final energy demand and primary energy is presented in the Table 2 and 3 below.

20. As has been explained above, although its share continually declines, in absolute term, the consumption of petroleum is still quite high. Meanwhile, it is almost certain that Indonesia will become a net oil importer. This situation is a challenge which is not easy for the energy sector to replace the oil consumption with non-oil energy. Therefore, energy diversification must be enhanced.

21. To meet the ever increasing energy need as mentioned above, huge amount of fund is needed considering that

Table 2. The Projection of Sectoral Energy Demand 1995-2010

in million BOE

Year	Resident	Industry	Transportation	Total
1995	80,146	133,971	127,507	341,624
2000	100,024	194,184	193,987	488,195
2005	123,697	281,459	291,095	696,252
2010	151,437	407,960	424,742	984,139

Table 3. The Projection of Primary Energy Demand 1995-2010

in million BOE

Year	Nuclear	Oil	N. Gas	Coal	Hydro	Geothermal	Total
1995		306,782	104,755	52,377	29,930	4,988	498,833
2000		421,600	143,961	71,981	41,132	6,855	685,529
2005		544,547	227,720	148,513	59,405	9,901	990,086
2010	11,872	727,153	341,317	311,637	81,619	10,388	1,483,986

Note: BOE (Barrel Oil Equivalent).

energy development is a capital intensive activity. As an example, in Repelita VI the investment needed for electric power sector only is more or less 50 to 60 trillion rupiah. Whereas the development fund which can be provided by the Government is more and more limited. Consequently, the challenge is how to develop financing sources in order to be able to support the energy development efforts continually.

22. With the ever increasing people's welfare, the demand for environmental awareness will be higher. Meanwhile as we realize that energy development is an activity possessing high risk of environmental damage. Therefore, energy sector development requires to continually apply clean-environment-energy technology.

Energy Potential and Barriers Toward its Development

23. In general, Indonesia gains benefit from its nature which is rich of both fossil and non-fossil energy resources. It doesn't mean, however, that the country will not be lack of energy. For oil, for instance, it has limited reserves and no more of oil will be left in the near future if the consumption growth can't be restrained. The shortage of oil will lead to the changing of Indonesia's status from an oil exporting country to an oil net-importing country.

24. The hydrocarbon resources potential of Indonesia is currently estimated at 84.4 billion BOE, consisting of oil resources 66.7 billion BOE, and natural gas 266.7 TSCF. The current country's oil reserves is about 9.47 billion BOE and gas reserve is about 114.8 TSCF. The current production rate of oil is about 1.5 million barrels per day (including

condensate). Oil is still expected to play an important role in the future (especially during the next 10 to 20 years), albeit with decreasing reserves and production capacity.

25. Coal deposit is approximately about 36 billion tons which is expected to be sufficient to fulfil energy needs for long-term use, but 60 per cent of the total potential is the low rank coal with low caloric value.

26. On the other hand, the development of coal still faces several problems like the implementation of general planning on regional space lay-out (RUTR) and coordination among cross-sectoral institutions. In addition to that, today's growing environmental concerns has restricted the government programme to promote utilization of coal which produces more severe environment impacts than those of other fossil fuels cause green-house effect. Therefore, the clean coal technology should be applied to enhance its role in the future, but it needs high investment cost.

27. The current potential of hydropower that can be utilized for generating electricity is about 75,624 MW consists of 15,804 MW in Sumatera, 4.531 MW in Java, 22,371 MW in Irian Jaya, 674 MW in Bali and Nusa Tenggara, 430 MW in Maluku, 10,203 MW in Sulawesi, and 21,611 MW in Kalimantan. Hydropower is one of prospective renewable energy alternatives that can be expected to fulfill future energy demand.

28. The utilization of hydropower is not yet maximum, because about two-third of the total potential is located outside Java island, namely Irian Jaya and Kalimantan with lower electric power demand, whereas, at about 4.5 per cent is only located in Java island.

29. Though geothermal potential is relatively big, is approximately 16.000 MW of which 7,800 MW, in Java and Bali, 4,900 MW in Sumatera, 1,500 MW in Sulawesi and the rest, 1,800 MW spreading over West Nusa Tenggara, East Nusa Tenggara, Irian Jaya, Maluku and other islands. It still faces several constraints such as the location of most geothermal sources is distant from the load centre, the steam price is relatively high compared to other conventional energy, and its deep well sources (more than 1,000 meters).

30. Although the potential of some sources of renewable energy such as biomass, city waste, biogas, solar power, wind power, small-scale hydropower, geothermal is substantial, these energy haven't been utilized commensurate with its potential, because economically these resources still can't compete with conventional energy. The utilization of these resources to fulfil energy needs especially in rural and remote areas should be done in a sustainable way.

31. New and renewable energy such as biomass, solar energy, wind energy, small-scale hydropower and small-scale geothermal power haven't been utilized commensurate with its potentialities.

National Energy Policy and Strategy for Development

32. The development of the energy sector in the Second Long Term Development era is directed towards guaranteeing self sufficiency in energy. The main goals of energy development include enhancing the welfare of the society and meeting their energy need. Therefore, efforts should be made in developing and maintaining the reserves of energy; diversifying the use of energy; using energy more efficiently and wisely; and developing and promoting the utilization of renewable energy sources.

33. The objective will be achieved through several efforts inter alia as follows:

    a. To guarantee the availability of energy for domestic energy need;

    b. To improve the quality of service;

    c. To guarantee the long term sustainability of energy supply;

    d. To guarantee the availability of energy for export;

    e. To conserve and preserve the environment.

34. To achieve the above mentioned long-term policy objectives, a set of policy measures, designated as intensification, diversification and conservation, has to be implemented.

35. **Intensification** : intensifying survey and exploration activities to identify the potential of economically exploitable energy resources (to develop and maintain reserves of

energy); **Diversification** : diversifying the use of energy for domestic consumption, aimed at decreasing the role of oil and increasing the development and utilization of other potential, non-oil resources, renewable sources of energy included, with due consideration to the economic, social and technological aspects; and **conservation** : using energy more efficiently and rationally, aimed at safeguarding the sustainability of energy supply and achieving a more balanced development in the pursuit of equity in economic growth, and at protecting the environment.

36. The development of electric power subsector is aimed at pushing economic activities and raising social welfare both in urban and rural areas. To achieve these objectives, the government should guarantee continues and adequate supply of electricity; efficient utilization of energy sources for electricity generation; less use of oil and more application of environmentally sound technology; implement rural electrification programme utilizing local energy sources and invite local cooperatives to participate in the programme.

Energy

37. Development in energy utilization has so far been directed toward more rational and efficient utilization of energy, in line with increasing energy needs resulting from national development. Energy consumption however, is expected to grow faster in the future. Therefore, well conceived and coordinated policy and strategy for energy utilization is needed to assured that Indonesia's energy needs are met with adequate quality of service and at a price that is within the reach of the society. Meeting our energy needs, however must be accomplished with a minimal negative impact on the environment.

38. During the Second Long Term Development Plan, energy development will be directed to assure our continued self-sufficiency in energy supply. Our strategy will focus on preserving and diversifying energy sources, rationalizing and increasing the utilization of renewable energies. Energy extraction, conversion and utilization processes can be harmful to the environment. Therefore, all energy activities must follow our national environmental protection policy to minimize any negative environment impacts.

39. To achieve the goal of resource sustainability and to minimize negative environmental impacts, energy conservation, alternative and renewable energies and clean energy technologies shall be given priority.

40. The use of new and renewable sources of energy, such as geothermal, hydro, biomass, solar, wind energy, needs to be intensified while taking into consideration the economic and technical feasibility, applicability and detrimental environmental impacts. Rural energy developments need to be increased especially through the utilization of locally available energy resources. Increased participation and contribution of the local people and cooperatives are also required.

41. The growth of energy consumption needs to be reduced through conservation. Conservation should be applied to oil and non-oil energy source use. Appropriate regulations and measures combined with the application of more energy efficient appliances and technologies, conversion and energy management training for energy users, should be used to reduce the growth in energy consumption.

Electric Power

42. The development in the electric power sector is directed toward accelerating economic activities to improve the welfare of people in urban and rural areas. The installation of electric power generation facilities can be done by government, private sectors and cooperatives. Power sector management must be done efficiently and must guarantee continuous and adequate supply of electricity. Electricity price must be acceptable to consumers, but it also must cover the suppliers cost of service, including transmission and distribution costs, to assure sustainability of supply. Efficient utilization of energy sources for electricity generation is a vital element in the planning of electric power sector in the country.

43. Electricity generation plan is based on the least cost criteria, but must incorporate decreased use of oil and greater application of environmentally sound technologies. Based on that policy, during the last two decades the role of oil fired power plants has been decreasing, being replaced by coal and natural gas fired thermal power plants. The use of coal, of course, is subject to Indonesian environmental regulations, which are more stringent than in may be other countries.

44. The implementation of rural electrification programme is being intensified to encourage economic activities and improve the welfare of rural people. Rural electrification will be increased through the utilization of local energy sources, such as microhydro, wind energy, solar energy and biomass. This will help support our energy diversification programme, shifting away from oil dependence and simultaneously, encouraging the use of more environmentally benign energy sources.

45. In line with the objectives of policy of the electric power development, the main elements of the strategy are, inter alia, as follows:

a. Electric power development is a part of National Development Programme. Therefore, its activities have to be in conformity with the national development programme meaning that every stage of electric power development activities should support the achievement of the goal of National Development, either in improving the welfare of the people or in increasing the economic growth.

b. In the pursuit of fair distribution of the result of national development programme or of the wealth of the country, domestic electricity need should be met, especially the need for electricity in rural areas.

c. Electric power development is an integral part of national energy policy which consists of a set policy measures designated as intensification, diversification and conservation. Therefore, every stage of the development should be in line with those policy measures.

d. In the development and installation of electric power generation plant, the utilization of domestic products as well as services should be pursued to the maximum extent possible.

e. The development of electric power sector should support and be commensurate with the policy of environment preservation, regional development and other national development policies as well.

Action Programmes

46. To meet the increasing energy demand during PJP-II especially in Repelita VI, action Programmes have been set, namely:

a. Reduce the share of oil and increase the share of alternative energies in the domestic energy supply mix. It is planned that at the end of REPELITA VI, 30 per cent of kerosene consumption in household sector will be replaced by coal briquettes.

b. National energy conservation programme will be intensively implemented, so that at the end of REPELITA VI, national energy consumption will be reduced by 15 per cent of the projected consumption in that year (12.75 per cent reduction in households; 14.5 per cent reduction in transportation and 17.75 per cent reduction in the industrial sector).

c. Increase renewable energy utilization especially biomass, wind, microhydro and solar energy, so that at the end of REPELITA VI, the utilization should be able to reach commercial stage and should have more significant role in the total energy supply mix.

d. Rural energy development should be coordinated through the establishment of rural energy planning and rural energy supply programme using local energy sources in remote or isolated areas.

47. Electric power development programme during the REPELITA's of the Second Long-Term Development Plan will be directed toward meeting national demand for

electricity. To achieve this objective, numerous electric power generation, transmission and distribution projects will be implemented. The construction of the facilities will be financed and implemented by the government, private sectors and cooperatives. During REPELITA VI, approximately 9.460,1 MW of electric power generation plants, 10.548 kms of transmission lines, 133,317 kms medium voltage distribution lines, 30,406 MVA of sub-stations, and 21,817 MVA of distribution sub-stations will be built with government and PLN financing. The private sectors will finance the construction of 2,945 MW of electric power generation plants.

48. Rural electrification during REPELITA VI is expected to add 18.619 villages to the total electrified villages. Accordingly, the total number of villages electrified at the end of REPELITA VI, will reach 48,500 or approximately 70 per cent of the total number of villages in Indonesia.

49. Other energy programmes, for example, efficiency improvements, reduction of distribution losses, implementation of Demand Side Management (DSM), improvement of quality and reliability will be carried out with greater intensity. Human resource development programmes through both practical and theoretical training, research and development will also be enhanced.

50. Efforts to reduce environmental impacts caused by energy sector activities, especially those caused by electric power sub-sector through the Analysis of Environmental Impacts (AMDAL) and public training, e.g on the effects of electromagnetic radiation on human health, will be expanded.

51. The participation of private sector in electricity supply through solicited and unsolicited projects will be expanded. The private sector will also be given opportunity to contribute in the local content of power projects. International cooperation (bilateral as well as multilateral ASEAN, or other multilateral cooperation) will be expanded to share expertise and information.

3. DEVELOPMENTS RELATED TO NATURAL GAS IN THE PHILIPPINES*

The recent discovery of the country's first commercial size gas field, the Camago-Malampaya in Northwest Palawan with an estimated reserves of 3 to 4 trillion cubic feet, marked the beginnings of a natural gas industry in the Philippines. Following the successful appraisal drilling of the second well in May 1993 by the contractor (a consortium of Shell Exploration B.V. and Occidental Philippines, Inc. or Shell/Oxy) in May 1993, the government immediately pursued the creation a market for the gas to ensure the economic viability of developing the Palawan gas fields. At the same time, it also spearheaded the development of an efficient gas industry structure that would optimize investments in infrastructure and encourage further field discoveries and market expansion.

Gas Market and Delivery Plans

With the assistance of the United States Agency for International Development (USAID), the Department of Energy commissioned a study last year to identify market options for the Camago-Malampaya gas. Analysis of projected fuel requirements in both the power generation and industrial sectors indicate that there is more than sufficient potential demand in the country's biggest island grid of Luzon. The power generation sector alone can accommodate the projected initial production of 400 cubic feet per day to fuel the combined-cycle capacity additions of about 3,150 MW between year 2,000 and 2003. The gas is planned to be transported by a 480-km offshore pipeline to Batangas and then a 110-km onshore pipeline to Sucat, Metro Manila.

In line with the government policy to have the state-owned National Power Corporation slowly move out of power generation and to encourage the private sector to share the market risk, the DOE allocated the 3,000 MW demand as follows: 1,500 MW for independent power producers that would sell to MERALCO, the country's biggest electricity distribution utility which currently sells about 65 per cent of the country's power supply; 300 MW for the Texaco cogeneration project in Sta. Rita, Batangas; and, 1,200 MW for IPPs that would sell to NPC.

Both NPC and MERALCO are now soliciting proposals for power plants for their repective gas allocations.

NPC has concluded an agreement with TEXACO for the establishment of a gas-fired 300 MW cogeneration plant at Sta. Rita, Batangas. If has also conducted an initial bidding for a 1,200 MW project wherein seven (7) bidders submitted proposals for a greenfield plant and only one for the conversion of the mothballed Bataan Nuclear Power Plant. The lowest price bidder was Consolidated Electric Power Association (CEPA), a subsidiary of Hopewell Holdings, Ltd. Which already has about 2,000 MW existing power projects in the Philippines, but CEPA's bid was disqualified due to its proposal to use equipment unacceptable to NPC. The rest of the bids are also unacceptable because the price difference is too big – at least P42 billion ($1.6 billion) for the 20-year cooperation period. Thus, NPC decided to hold a rebidding for the project.

The power projects for the 1,500 MW MERALCO allocation, on the other hand, will be put up by First Gas Holdings Corporation (FGHC), a consortium between First Philippine Holdings, Inc. and British Gas (Global) plc. FGHC is currently evaluating bids for its 440-MW gas-fired power plant to be located in Sta. Rita, Batangas and expects to award the turn-key contract in October 1995. For the rest of its allocation, it has proposed the conversion to gas of the Sucat/Tegen oil-thermal power plants located in Metro Manila, and is keenly awaiting NPC's approval.

Meanwhile, NPC and FGHC are now negotiating with Shell/Oxy for a long-term gas purchase agreement which is expected to be concluded by December.

The Camago-Malampaya or what is now also known as the Philippine Gas Project (CMGP or PGP), including the gas production facility, transmission pipelines and power plants, shall entail an estimated total capital investment of US$ 5,003 million, making it the single biggest integrated infrastructure project so far in the Philippines.

Development of Policy, Regulatory, and Institutional Framework

The overwhelming response of the private sector to the government's initial efforts to promote natural gas development in the country has inspired the policy towards structuring a private sector-oriented gas industry.

Issuance of Policy Guidelines

To provide an initial framework for the development of the natural gas industry, the DOE issued Department Circular No. 95-06-006 on June 13, 1995. The circular broadly defined the policies of the Department on natural gas, basically stating that the Camago-malampaya discovery shall serve as a catalyst for a natural gas industry, initially

* Paper submitted by the Philippine Delegation to the *Roundtable on Notable Energy Developments* during the *11th APEC Regional Energy Cooperation Working Group (REC WG) Meeting* held on October 2, 1995 at the Howard Plaza Hotel, Taipei, Taiwan Province of China. The Philippine delegation was composed of Ms. Flordeliza M. Andres, Assistant Secretary for Policy and Programmes, Department of Energy; Mr. Froilan A. Tampinco, Manager, Corporate Planning, National Power Corporation; and Ms. Maria Rafaela C. Masangkay, Senior Science Research Specialist, Department of Energy. This report is reproduced in the form in which it was received.

supplying power generation requirements but paving the way for industrial and other end-user markets. The policy statement also outlined its ultimate vision of a competitive and private-sector dominated industry, with the national government's role to be limited to encouraging further resource exploration and development and ensuring access to transmission pipelines by various suppliers and end-users.

Setting up of the Gas Office

In June 1995, the DOE issued Department Order No. 95-05-12 creating an Ad-hoc Gas Office to provide a focus for the expeditious implementation of the Camago-Malampaya Gas Project (CMGP) and likewise prepare the groundwork for the development of a full-scale natural gas industry. The initial operation of the Gas Office (GO) is being supported through the ongoing USAID Technical Assistance to the DOE. Former DOE Undersecretary Rufino Bomasang was appointed as Senior Adviser of the GO.

The GO is currently compiling environmental and safety standards of neighboring countries to serve as basis for the preparation of draft Philippine gas regulations which will later be presented in public consultations. The proposed gas regulations will also address other regulatory and policy issues associated with the CGMP such as the following:

1. *Third party use of the pipeline* – the DOE's policy is to allow open access to pipelines by all users and producers;

2. *Ownership of the gas* – under the Service Contract for gas exploration and development, the gas belongs to the state until it is sold; and

3. *Buyer of the gas* – it has been agreed that NPC and First Gas Holdings shall be the gas buyer superseding the earlier agreement indentifying NPC as the sole buyer.

Creation of Philippine Gas Project Task Force

In July 1995, President Ramos signed Executive Order 254 creating the Philippine Gas Project Task Force (PGPTF). This is an inter-agency committee headed by the Secretary of Energy with the heads of relevant government agencies and private sector representatives as members. The creation of the PGPTF demonstrates the government's commitment to the expeditious development of the Camago-Malampaya Gas Project (CMGP) in recognition of its important role in the overall Philippine energy plan. PGPTF will provide overall coordination for the CMGP, address key institutional, policy, and regulatory issues, and in the process help ensure expeditious implementation of the CMGP.

The Task Force has two sub-committees, namely, a) the sub-committee for regulatory and policy matters and b) the sub-committee for safety and environmental matters. Through these sub-committees, the DOE GO which also provides secretariat support to the PGPTF, shall implement the resolution of policy and regulatory issues to expedite the on-going negotiation between the gas sellers and gas buyers.

Manpower Training

With funding assistance from the Australian Agency for International Development (AUS AID), six DOE personnel attended a month-long training programme on natural gas management and regulation in Australia which started on June 26, 1995. The trainees shall serve the Gas Office either on a full or part-time basis. Likewise, the USAID sponsored the participation of DOE and NPC officials in a Gas Negotiations Workshop in Kuala Lumpur conducted by Peter Ross of Barter and Petroleum Services of the United Kingdom.

Other Activities and Future Prospects

Upstream Development

1. *Review of the Proven Gas Reserves in Camago-Malampaya*

The Asian Development Bank (ADB) is funding a small scale technical assistance (TA) project for an independent third party evaluation of the proven gas reserves at Camago-Malampaya. The TA aims to guide the National Power Corporation (NPC) in its negotiations with Shell/Oxy and the DOE in its overall supervision of the Philippine gas industry. To-date, a list of potential consultants who will conduct the independent review has already been drawn by the Bank. The evaluation is expected to start by September and the consultant's report should be available by November of this year.

2. *Manila Bay Drilling*

Geologists have spotted a gas-bearing site in the Manila Bay area with potential reserves of as much as 2 TCF. This is potentially very significant to the Philippine gas industry because it is very close to possible markets in Metro Manila and vicinity. A very significant development was the entry of British Gas (partner of First Philippine Holdings in First Gas Holdings, the buyer of 50 per cent of Camago-Malampaya Gas) into the Manila Bay consortium led by Cophil. British Gas paid one million U.S. dollars for an option to acquire 25 per cent interest in the Geophysical Survey and Exploration Contract (GSEC 72).

3. *Delineation of Octon Field in Palawan*

Drilling of Octon-3 well to delineate the Octon oil-gas-condensate field discovered in 1991 at offshore

Northwest Palawan, was started in June to define the reserves more accurately and hopefully increase the oil reserves to warrant commercial development. While the field is known to have condensate and gas basides oil, the gas reserve of about 180 BCF (0.18 TCF) is not big enough to warrant a stand alone gas development including a pipeline to the Luzon market.

The well, however, failed to flow oil and the well has been plugged and abandoned with the oil reserves remaining sub-commercial (below 10 million barrels) and it is now unlikely that Octon will be developed as an oil field. The Octon field, however, can be viable as a gas field if and when the Malampaya project goes on stream, making a "gas highway" available for smaller gas fields.

4. Possible LNG Projects

Officials of Alcorn Petroleum and its partner Nissho Iwai reiterated their proposal to the Gas Office to put up LNG receiving facilities and serve potential markets in the Bataan-Zambales area and possibly even Metro Manila. They are currently preparing a formal proposal to the DOE.

Experts from Trans Energ and Sofregaz of France submitted the results of its Prefeasibility Study of an LNG Import Project, which among others established that a natural gas project supplied by imported LNG can be a technically and economically viable project for the island of Luzon, mainly for power generation, as a supplement to Malampaya gas development. The experts revealed that with a market that can absorb a minimum of 2 billion cubic meters per year (about 200 million cubic feet per day, or a power plant of 1,500 MW capacity) and LNG project can be viable. However, the study says that this is only possible if the government liberalizes the prices of coal and petroleum products and privatizes the energy sector, particularly the electricity sector, to promote more competition. Such policy directions are already being pursued by DOE.

5. Revival of CPC (Taiwan Province of China) Interest

With the remaining funds from the RP-Australia Seismic project, the Gas Office Senior Adviser visited Taipei on September 26, 1995 and met with senior officials of the Chinese Petroleum Corporation (CPC). The CPC is a state-owned oil and gas monopoly which used to be active in the Philippines but pulled out in 1991. The CPC officials expressed willingness to review new exploration data on the Philippines, especially those generated from the RP-Australia Seismic Project, and look at old potential gas areas such as Central Luzon and Cagayan Valley which may now be attractive in the light of the natural gas development programme.

Market and Distribution Network Expansion

1. Study on Natural Gas for Transport

The DOE together with the Department of Science and Technology and the Philippine National Oil Company is pursuing a study on the feasibility of using natural gas as an alternative to diesel fuel for transport use. The project is funded by the New Zealand government as part of the ASEAN-New Zealand cooperation programme on energy. Activities in the project included participation of DOE personnel in a natural gas vehicle workshop in New Zealand, continuation of data gathering on bus operations and coordination with the Department of Transportation and Communication on possible involvement of local bus companies in the project.

2. Transborder Distribution Networks

The realization of plans to construct transborder gas pipelines such as the Trans-ASEAN gas pipeline will greatly enhance the country's prospects for more discoveries and expansion of the gas market to other parts of the country. This is particularly true in the case of Mindanao which is part of the Brunei-Indonesia-Malaysia-Philippines East Asia Growth Area or BIMP-EAGA.

4. SRI LANKA: SCIENCE AND TECHNOLOGY FOR SUSTAINABLE DEVELOPMENT: ENERGY SECTOR*

1.0 Introduction

The per capita energy consumption in Sri Lanka, inclusive of all forms of energy, currently stands at 0.36 TOE per annum (TOE = 41.84 GJ). This is below the world standards but is comparable with many other developing countries in the region. The growth oriented development path, together with increasing population and improved living standards needs increasing inputs of energy. This can no longer be rationally supported in a resource constrained country like ours. As such the challenge today is in sustained economic growth, managing within limits the harnessing of natural resources, hopefully resulting in the preservation of the natural environment which sustains the life on earth.

Sri Lanka though an Island, cannot be in isolation with regard to the preservation of the environment even within the now fashionable parameters of sustainable growth. We have been and will be dependent, very significantly, on imported fossil fuels in whatever form, for the sustenance of the economy. This brings Sri Lanka into close contact with constraints in the exploration and utilisation of fossil fuels. Even if our contribution to the emission of effluents by burning fossil fuels is insignificant, we have to be mindful of immediate local impacts of fossil fuel usage, by curtailing effluent discharges in the process of burning fossil fuels.

The environmental consequences of large dams and reservoirs constructed for our hydro power generation cannot also be disregarded. Further more these large reservoirs are also concentrated in the central hilly region and the effects on the surrounding areas is also of great concern. The inundation of large areas of productive and most fertile land for hydro power generation alone can no longer be pursued.

In the above context Sri Lanka is concerned about the preservation of the environment for the future generation, while the energy needs of the present population for its very sustenance cannot be denied. With this in view the energy planner in Sri Lanka has a multiple role in meeting the energy demand at least cost to the economy, while preserving the environment.

2.0 The Economy

The economy has had a moderate growth in the past five years and is expected to grow on the average of about 6 per cent in the next five years. The rapid industrialisation envisaged is to be the leading factor in the economy. This is quite evident from Table 2.1.

This industry-led economy is expected to continue well into the foreseeable future.

The main thrust of the economic reforms undertaken by the Government in the immediate past with the prime objective of a sustained growth is as follows [2].

1) Achieving macro economic stability.

2) Improving the effectiveness of welfare programmes.

3) Creating an environment suitable for private sector and export oriented development.

Table 2.1. Growth Rates of GDP by Major Sectors at Constant prices

	Percentages						Average
	1991	*1992*	*1993*	*1994*	*1995*	*1996*	*92/96*
1. Plantation Agriculture	-5.7	-5.6	5.3	3.4	1.0	2.2	1.2
2. Other Agriculture	5.5	1.6	3.1	4.7	3.2	3.3	3.2
3. Mining, Manuf. & Constr.	5.0	7.1	6.8	8.8	8.8	8.9	8.3
4. Services	6.1	5.9	5.5	6.5	7.2	7.7	6.6
5. GDP	4.8	4.5	5.3	6.4	6.7	6.9	6.0
GDP at (1991) Constant Market prices : Rs. Billion	375.3	392.2	413.1	439.8	469.0	500.9	–
GDP deflator (per cent)	11.3	10.9	8.1	6.0	5.0	5.0	7.0

Source: Public Investment 1992-1996, Dept. of National Planning, Sri Lanka [2].

---

* Prepared by W.J.L.S. Fernando, President, Sri Lanka Energy Managers Association K.S.Fernando, A. Abeywardane and D.A.U. Daranagama. This report is reproduced in the form in which it was received.

The economic policy as envisaged by the Government in the medium term will continue to focus on structural adjustment and stabilisation. It is also predicated that with the recovery of the economies of the developed world, there will be a positive influence on Sri Lanka's export earnings, tourism and migrant worker remittances among others.

It is clearly evident that with rapid industrialisation in the medium term, the demand for energy will undoubtedly increase.

3.0 Energy situation in the Country

The domestic indigenous resources namely Biomass and Hydro constitute more than 80 per cent of the primary energy supply in the Country. This however does not mean the contribution in the form of useful energy it has the same importance as the shares indicate. A significant component of the biomass consumption in the domestic sector is mainly for cooking with very low efficiency of conversion. As such, the contribution of biomass as an energy source in the national economic activity is not very significant.

Sri Lanka has no proven reserves of fossil fuels. A small quantity of peat has been located in the vast extent of marshy lands to the North of Colombo. A recent feasibility Study [3] has indicated that the quality and extent of the reserve could not prove to be commercially viable for extraction and use in power generation.

As stated earlier, Fuelwood and other biomass including agro residues and hydro electricity are the main indigenous primary sources of energy supply in the country. Crude oil is the main primary energy import. Coal and refined petroleum products such as LPG, Diesel and Kerosene are also imported in small quantities.

The gross and the useful energy supply is shown in fig. 3.1. Hydro Electricity supply has been adjusted to reflect the energy input to a thermal plant to produce the equivalent amount of electricity (oil replacement Value: 1 kWh = 0.24 x 10^{-3} TOE).

As stated earlier, the per capita energy consumption including traditional non commercial energy sources in the country is 0.36 TOE. The consumption of energy by sectors of all forms of energy and commercial energy is shown in fig. 3.2.

3.1 Basic Energy Demand Characteristics

Per capita total energy consumption in Sri Lanka was 0.3 TOE per annum during the period 1972-1981 and thereafter steadily increased to 0.338 TOE in 1990 and had reached 0.36 TOE by 1992. As a result of high oil prices the per capita commercial energy consumption dropped from 0.090 TOE in 1972 to 0.073 TOE in 1976, but increased thereafter to 0.099 TOE in 1987. Per capita electricity consumption, however, has been increasing steadily from 64 kWh in 1972 to 153 kWh in 1992.

The overall energy intensity (computed as TOE per million rupees of GDP at constant 1982 prices) has been declining from 65.9 in 1972 to 44.4 in 1990. However, the energy intensity for electricity has increased from 3.3 to 4.8 during the same period. The period 1972-1990 has also witnessed an increase in the consumption of diesel and LPG but petrol consumption has remained almost constant while kerosene shows a drop in demand.

The demand for fuel types is also being influenced by the relative prices of fuels. For example, the relatively sharp price increase of kerosene, and pricing kerosene above furnace oil after 1983, has reduced the demand for kerosene as a substitute for furnace oil in the industry.

The provision of electricity to more households and the reduction of subsidies for kerosene is also seen as contributing factors for reduced demand for kerosene in the household sector. The fact that there had been a 200 fold increase in the consumption of LPG during the last two decades also points to a large scale transition from kerosene to LPG for cooking in the household sector.

This transition seems to be driven mostly by the convenience but it is also sensitive to the relative pricing policy of alternatives.

The share consumption of electricity in the domestic sector has steadily increased from 8.7 per cent of total sales in 1972 to 23.1 per cent of total sales in 1992. This can be attributed to extensive rural electrification work undertaken by the CEB. The share of industrial consumption in the same period has dropped from 54.4 per cent of total sales to 36.7 per cent of total sales. Consumption in the Commercial Sector has increased its share in the total consumption from 12 per cent to 19.6 per cent in the same period. The GDP Electricity index has declined over the period 1982-1992 from 56 Million Rs/GWH to 47.5 Million Rs/GWh. The above suggests that in the past decade, the consumption of electricity has shifted from productive sectors to non-productive sectors. A detailed analysis however is not available.

There is a high degree of uncertinity of statistics and information available with respect to supply and demand patterns of biomass energy particularly due to the complexity and diversity of its production and use. There have been ad-hoc surveys carried out since late seventies to estimate the biomass consumption in the country.

The total firewood and biomass consumption in 1989 is 4.64 = M ToE (4) Out of this total demand, 83 per cent is used for household cooking purposes by approximately 93 per cent of the population. The balance 17 per cent of the total is used in the industry. Almost 33 per cent of the industrial consumption of firewood is in the tea industry while the rest is consumed in Brick and Tile industry (13 per cent), Coconut industry (11 per cent) Tobacco industry (10 per cent), Rubber industry (6 per cent) and the rest in other sectors including the commercial sector.

3.2 Issues and Options related to the Energy Sector

(a) Electricity

The electricity demand growth is expected to be over 8 per cent per annum for the next 20 years. This is based on a forecasted national economic growth of approximately 5 to 6 per cent per annum. The elasticity of demand of electricity to economic growth is estimated to be 1.5. This indicates that with a higher growth rate of the economy the demand growth of electricity can even reach 10 per cent.

The system load factor is currently at 56 per cent and is expected to increase up to 58 per cent by the year 2005 with more industrialisation. A pricing policy to shift the demand from the peak hours to off peak hours is essential. The time of the day tariff offered by the CEB should be vigorously pursued on a rational basis to achieve this.

The current system losses stand at around 18 per cent of generation. This is fairly high. To reduce the system losses to a more acceptable level of 12 per cent by the year 2004 as planned, a transmission and distribution loss reduction programme should be launched.

Demand side management programmes such as improving the efficiency of the end-use devices and equipment, has a high potential for conservation. Lighting alone currently consume about 20 per cent of the total demand of electricity. A more realistic project should be undertaken to introduce more efficient light systems. However, techno economic considerations should be studied and resolved before large scale introduction of such systems.

It is evident that the future capacity expansion will be mostly from thermal plants. This would result in large scale gaseous, and particulate emissions and warm water discharges etc. It has been seen that this is inevitable in meeting the growth in the demand. Such projects should be so located after careful consideration of the environmental impacts. It is further recommended that a thermal options study be undertaken, giving consideration to the latest developments in technology with enhanced efficiencies of thermal power plants.

Even with a vigorously pursued rural electrification programme in the last two decades only 1/3rd of the population have access to the grid electricity. Other decentralised options to meet rural energy needs should be examined and vigorously pursued. This would not only lead to easing the burden of extension of the national grid on one hand and also would ease the burden on the centralised power sources.

(b) Petroleum Products

While the refinery's aggregate throughput is greater than the total consumption of petroleum products, its production slates differs significantly from the mix of product demand. Eventhough running crude oils with higher middle distillates in the refinery to try to meet the demand for middle distillates (kerosene, AVTUR and diesel) there are deficits deficit of these products with a need for supplementary imports while at the same time producing a surplus of Naphtha and fuel oil which has to be re-exported.

Present refinery capacity utilisation is in the range of 37,000 barrels per day. A production rate of higher than 37,000 barrels per day is not maintained continuously because this would produce other products (Naphtha and fuel oil) in excess of the local requirement. However, if the excess products could be successfully used locally or sold through exports, this spare capacity of the refinery can be utilised to advantage.

One of the factors which deter the operation in this manner is the fact that an export rebate is not given to the CPC for the export of refined products. Crude oil is taxed in the region of 35 per cent as custom levies. To compete in the export market CPC has to sell at the international price which would obviously be about 35 per cent lower than the price at which CPC can sell without loss.

The annual demand for LPG has been rising rapidly. Earlier, when the LPG demand was lower than the normal capacity for LPG production at the refinery, supply posed no severe problem. However, demand started to exceed the production and marginal quantities of LPG had to be imported from 1983 onwards. Imported LPG costs (CIF) about double the international market price due to the high freight costs, which is of the same order as the purchase price.

A study has been carried out by CPC which indicates that an additional 18,000 tons per year of LPG, which is currently used as refinery fuel gas, could be recovered by using fuel oil in place of refinery fuel gas.

Use of LPG in the transport sector to replace petrol should be discouraged. This will lead to producing even more excess Naphtha, which is exported at a lower price, and increase LPG imports at higher prices, thus burdening oil import bill even more.

The transport sector depends entirely on petroleum products for energy and it accounts for over half of all petroleum consumption. Auto diesel is the predominant transport fuel accounting for 66 per cent of energy requirement in the sector. This reflects both the relatively extensive public transport network and the long standing policy to price auto diesel well below petrol.

This policy has become a cause of some concern since the liberalisation of import regulations for private automobiles in 1978. This relative price differential has lead to a larger share of diesel driven motor cars. This trend will have an adverse impact on the already worsening refinery imbalance problem. This is evident from more than doubling of diesel consumption during the last two decades.

With increasing use of petroleum fuels in the rapidly growing transport sector environmental pollution is expected to accelerate during the decade. To combat this problem either consumption has to decrease or the pollutants released to the atmosphere should decrease with time.

What can be practically achieved is to decrease the levels of potential pollutants, namely, sulphur, lead, particulate etc. released to the atmosphere during the process of combustion of petroleum fuels from motor vehicles.

The CPC has already identified a number of projects for implementation to achieve the above. The projects, it implemented, will enable CPC to introduce unleaded gasoline after 1996 to the market and reduce the sulphur present in auto diesel marketed in Sri Lanka from the present maximum of 1.1 per cent by weight to 0.5 per cent by the end of 1996.

(c)   Biomass

There is no apparent shortage of biomass in the country as a whole until the year 2000 [4]. However, there are regional deficits which makes firewood an expensive fuel in the urban areas.

With the impending fuelwood shortages at the turn of the century and with hardly any shift in demand for any other fuel (even in the year 2000 – 92 per cent of the households is estimated to be cooking using fuelwood) considerable effort has to be made in meeting the fuelwood demand from the year 2000.

The Forestry Master Plan (which is currently being reviewed) has proposed an extensive forest and fuelwood management programme which will enable a supply of 10 per cent higher than what is estimated. Hence the availability of fuelwood to meet the demand is expected to be extended to the year 2020.

The National Fuelwood Conservation Programme (NFCP) [6] which was handled by the Ministry of Power and Energy and the Ceylon Electricity Board is of importance in reducing the demand for fuelwood especially in the domestic sector. The urban and rural programmes are distinctly different in approach.

The most recent estimates indicate that approximately 700,000 improved efficient stoves are being used both in the urban and rural sectors. This is approximately about 20 per cent penetration of the total households in Sri Lanka. The recent surveys carried out indicated that in more than 85 per cent of households in the project, 25-30 per cent of fuelwood is saved.

The NFCP in now at a stage where it needs to be reviewed and its future role in the overall national energy plan has to be decided.

The average annual deforestation rate has been high. Consumption of firewood.

1. Development of agricultural residues and other wastes as substitutes for fuel wood.

2. Introducing more efficient fuel wood conservation technologies.

3. Development of fuel wood plantations.

4.0 National Energy Policy Guidelines

As energy is a vital input for economic development and social well-being of the population, it has to be expected that decisions taken in national development planning will have ramifications in the energy sector. For example, a plan pursuing an industrial development path based on less energy intensive industries will lead to a sectoral energy scenario that is totally different from one that is based on energy intensive industries. In this context, the need for close coordination between macro economic planning and energy planning cannot be over-emphasised. An energy plan developed within an integrated planning framework will also be resilient enough to cope with the uncertainties which are inherent in long term development planning.

The following policy guidelines [9] are proposed for consideration within an integrated energy planning framework.

1) Providing the basic human energy needs.

2) Choosing the optimum mix of energy resources to meet the requirements at the minimum cost to the national economy and the environment.

3) Optimisation of available energy resources to promote socio-economic development.

4) Conserving energy resources and eliminating wasteful consumption in the production and use of energy.

5) Developing and managing of forest and non-forest wood fuel resources.

6) Reducing dependence on foreign energy resources and diversifying the sources of energy imports.

7) Adopting a pricing policy which enables the financing of energy sector development.

8) Ensuring continuity of energy supply and price stability.

9) Establishing the capability to develop and manage the energy sector.

For Further Reading and References:

[1] Central Bank of Sri Lanka Annual Report 1992.

[2] Public Investment 1992-1996 Department of National Planning October 1992.

[3] Sri Lanka Peat Study, Ekono, Finnida, October 1995.

[4] K.K.Y.W. Perera, Energy Status of Sri Lanka Issues Policy Suggestions Policy Studies, March 1992.

[5] Sri Lanka National Report Ministry of Environment Parliamentary Affairs September 1991.

[6] R.R. Mel, National Fuel wood Conservation Project: Objectives, activities, evaluation and suggestions. Alternative Energy Development Branch, Ceylon Electricity Board, Sri Lanka. July 1993 (internal document).

[7] Sri Lanka Energy Balance and Energy Data, 1991 Alternative Energy Development Branch, Ceylon Electricity Board, Sri Lanka.

[8] Report on long term generation expansion planning studies 1994-2008, August 1993, Generation Planning Branch, CEB.

[9] Prof. Mohan Munasinghe et. al. – National Energy Strategy, Ministry of Power & Energy.

[10] P. Meier and M. Munasinghe, Incorporating Environmental Concerns into Power Sector Decision – Making: A Case Study of Sri Lanka. Environmental Policy and Research Division, The World Bank, Washington DC, USA. June 1992.

[11] National Environmental Act No. 47 of 1980, Government of Sri Lanka.

[12] National Conservation Strategy-Action Plan, Central Environmental Authorities, Ministry of Environment and Parliamentary Affairs, November 1990.

5. ENERGY SITUATION IN THAILAND 1994*

In 1994, the final energy consumption increase 11.5 per cent from the previous year. Modern energy consumption which comprised of petroleum products, natural gas, condensate, coal and lignite, hydro power and othersgrew 11.9 per cent while renewable energy (fuel wood, charcoal, paddy husk and bagasse) grew 10.3 per cent. Details of energy situation are as follows:

1. Primary Energy Supply

In 1994, Thailand's total primary energy supply amounted to 65.0 Mtoe, an increase of 11 per cent over the previous year, of which 58.4 per cent came from indigenous sources and 41.6 per cent from imported sources.

1.1 Indigenous Sources

Domestic primary energy production in 1994 was 37.6 Mtoe, with an increase of 10.1 per cent over the previous year. Details on domestic energy production by types are as follows:

Crude Oil

The average production of crude oil in 1994 was 26,553 bpd, an increase of 6.3 per cent from the previous year. The total production of crude oil was 1.3 Mtoe, shared 3.5 per cent of the total indigenous energy production.

Natural Gas

Natural Gas was a major domestic energy source. The average production of natural gas in 1994 was 1,038 MMscfd, an increase of 10.8 per cent from the previous year. The total production was 9.3 Mtoe or 24.8 per cent of the total indigenous energy production.

Condensate

The average production of condensate in 1994 was 30,615 bpd, an increase of 6.4 per cent from 1993. The total production was 1.4 Mtoe, shared 3.7 per cent of the total indigenous energy production.

Lignite and Anthracite

Lignite is another major domestic energy source used for power generation and industry. In 1994, the average production of lignite was 46,803 ton per day, an increase of 11.8 per cent over the previous year. The total production was 5.2 Mtoe, or 13.7 per cent of the total indigenous energy production.

* Prepared by Sawad HemKaman, Director, Office of Energy Cooperation, Department of Energy Development and Presention, Bangkok. This report is reproduced in the form in which it was received.

Moreover, anthracite has been produced for industry consumption. In 1994, the total production of anthracite was 0.009 Mtoe or 33 ton per day in average.

Hydro Power and others

Hydro Power has been developed for power generation since 1964. In 1994, electricity generated from hydro power totalled to 1 Mtoe, an increase of 22 per cent over the previous year and accounted for 2.7 per cent of the total indigenous energy production.

Moreover, other energy sources have been used for power generation such as geothermal, solar cell and wind. In 1994, electricity generated from these energy sources totalled to 0.001 Mtoe.

Renewable Energy

The total production of renewable energy (fuel wood, paddy husk and bagasse) in 1994 were 19.4 Mtoe, an increase of 9.3 per cent over the previous year, accounted for 51.6 per cent of the total indigenous energy production.

1.2 Import

Total energy imported in 1994 reached 28.3 Mtoe, with an increasing rate of 9.1 per cent over the previous year. The total value of energy import was 95,488.7 millions Baht with an increase of 7.1 per cent over the previous year.

Details on energy import by types are as follows:

Petroleum

Comprising with crude oil and petroleum products, the total petroleum imported was 27.2 Mtoe, an increase of 8.1 per cent from the previous year, accounted for 96.3 per cent of the total energy imported. The total value of petroleum import was 84,439.3 millions Baht, with a decrease of 1.4 per cent.

Coal

Coal imported in 1994, including anthracite, bituminous, coke and other coal, tolalled to 1 Mtoe, an increase of 45.2 per cent from the previous year, accounted for 3.3 per cent of the total energy imported. Total imported value was 1,728 millions Baht, an increase of 40.5 per cent.

Electricity

In 1994, electricity imported was 884 GWh or 0.08 Mtoe, an increase of 36.4 per cent from the previous year, accounted for 0.3 per cent of the total energy imported.

Total imported value was about 759.2 millions Baht, an increase of 29.6 per cent.

Renewable Energy

Renewable energy imported was charcoal. In 1994 imported charcoal reached 0.01 Mtoe, an increase of 27.3 per cent over the previous year, shared 0.1 per cent of the total energy imported. Total imported value was 38.9 millions Baht, an increase of 15.1 per cent.

1.3 Export

Total energy exported for 1994 was 1.2 Mtoe, an increase of 19.8 per cent over the previous year. Condensate was a major item shared 70.3 per cent of total energy exported. The rest were petroleum products, natural gasoline, renewable energy and electricity which shared 24.4 per cent, 4.3 per cent, 0.6 per cent and 0.4 per cent of total energy exported respectively.

2. Final Energy Consumption

The total final energy consumption for 1994 was 43.8 Mtoe, an increase of 11.5 per cent over the previous year. Details are as follows:

2.1 By Types of Energy

Petroleum Products

Petroleum Products still showed the greatest proportion of final energy consumption in 1994. Petroleum product consumption totalled to 23.4 Mtoe, up 10.6 per cent over the previous year and accounted for 53.2 per cent of the total energy consumption.

Natural Gas

Natural gas consumption in 1994 totalled to 0.6 Mtoe, or 66.5 MMscfd, with an increase rate of 19.5 per cent from the previous year, accounted for 1.3 per cent of the final energy consumption.

Coal and Lignite

Coal and lignite consumption in 1994 was 3.1 Mtoe, an increase of 23.1 per cent over the previous year and accounted for 7.1 per cent of the final energy consumption.

Electricity

Total electricity consumption in 1994 was 5.3 Mtoe, increased 11.1 per cent over the previous year and shared 12.2 per cent of the final energy consumption.

Renewable Energy

Total renewable energy consumption in 1994 was 11.5 Mtoe, an increase of 10.3 per cent over the previous

year and accounted for 26.2 per cent of the final energy consumption.

2.2 By Economic Sectors

Agricultural Sector

In 1994 the agricultural sector consumed energy 1.6 Mtoe, a decrease of 2.6 per cent over the previous year and accounted for 3.6 per cent of total energy consumption. The major energy consumed in this sector were petroleum products and electricity which shared 99.5 per cent and 0.5 per cent of its total energy consumption respectively.

Mining Sector

Energy consumption in mining sector was 0.04 Mtoe, a decrease of 16.7 per cent from previous year and accounted for 0.1 per cent of the final energy consumption. All energy consumed in this sector was petroleum products.

Manufacturing Sector

Energy consumption in manufacturing sector was 13.9 Mtoe, increased 18.9 per cent over the previous year and accounted for 31.7 per cent of the final energy consumption. The major energy consumed was renewable energy shared 28 per cent of the energy consumption of this sector, followed by petroleum products, coal & lignite, electricity and natural gas which shared 27.9 per cent, 22.3 per cent, 17.6 per cent and 4.2 per cent of the sector's final energy demand respectively.

Construction Sector

In 1994, the construction sector consumed energy 0.3 Mtoe, increased 83 per cent over the previous year, accounted for 0.7 per cent of the final energy consumption. All energy consumed in this sector was petroleum products.

Residential and Commercial Sector (including services and governmental institutes)

In 1994, the residential and commercial sector consumed energy 11.7 Mtoe increased 4.0 per cent over the previous year, accounted for 26.6 per cent of the final energy consumption. Energy consumed in this sector comprised of renewable energy 65 per cent, electricity 24.7 per cent and petroleum products 10.3 per cent.

Transportation Sector

Energy consumption in transportation sector was 16.3 Mtoe, increased 12.1 per cent over the previous year and accounted for 37.3 per cent of the final energy consumption. All energy consumed in this sector was petroleum products, comprising of 1.1 per cent LPG, 24.9 per cent gasoline, 53.8 per cent diesel oil, 15.6 per cent jet fuel and 4.6 per cent fuel oil.

6. ELECTRICITY MARKET REFORMING IN VIET NAM*

1. Viet Nam Electriciy Market is and will be strongly developing

Thanks to the new "reform and open door" policy, the economy of Viet Nam has been gradually stabilized and engaged into the development with quite high growth rate. During the last 3 years, the electricity demand has been growing with the rate of 13.1 per cent in 1993, 18.4 per cent in 1994 and expected to be of 21.5 per cent with the estimated power generation of Kwh 14.55 billions in 1995.

With series of industrial zones, to be put into operation, the demand of power electricity for services, trade and public consumption will continue to increase up to Kwh 30 billion (low plan) or Kwh 33 billions (high plan) by the year of 2000 with the average increase rate of 16-17.8 per cent for the whole 1996-2000 period. This is far higher than the previous estimation of the Master Plan, being approved by the Government (as with the high plan, the demand is of Kwh 27 billions and the annual average increase rate is of 13.8 per cent).

The highest possibility of exploiting the existing power sources is of Kwh 15.8 billions per annum. So, to meet the above mentioned demand in the year of 2000, we must, during the period 1996-2000 build and put into operation every year new generation sources with the capacity of about 500-700 MW. In addition, for the period after the year for 2000, we still have to invest into certain transitional power sources.

In line with developing new sources, we have, in the coming 5 years, to implement a huge volume of construction work for the transmission and distribution network including: about 6,500 km of transmission lines; series of substations of 110-220 Kv with the total capacity of 16,000 MVA; 58,000 km of medium and low voltage transmission lines. The investment into the power system will concentrate mainly on solving the overloading problem; rehabilitating and upgrading as well as modernising the electricity network in large cities such as Hanoi, HoChiMinh, Haiphong, Namdinh, Hue, Nhatrang, Danang, Quynhon, Vungtau, Cantho etc., sufficiently supplying electricity to the newly developing industrial zones in HoChiMinh City, Bienhoa, SongBe, Baria-Vungtau, Xuanmai, Hanoi, NoiBai, Haiphong, Quangninh, Danang, Dungquat.

We are considering a large programme with the aim to supply electricity power to the rural and mountainous areas. The target is 100 per cent of our provinces to be electrified by the National Electricity network in which 80 per cent of the villages and 60 per cent population can use the electricity power.

The drastic development of the Vietnamese Electricity market required large reforms in terms of organising production and sales, in financing and terms of investment, in improving the construction procedures as well as series of econo-technical matters.

2. New organisational restructuring in generation and selling of Electricity in Viet Nam

Previously, all the works, related to administration as well as generating and selling electricity were the responsibility of the Ministry of Energy. By the end of 1994, according to the Government Decree, the Viet Nam Electricity Corporation (EVN) was established. EVN is a large state-owned business with the task to implement all the functions, related to generating and selling electricity in the whole territory of Viet Nam such as: research, planification, investigation, designing, installation, generation, transmission, distribution of electricity power; production of electrical equipment and accessories, conduct Export import activities and services in the power sector aiming at meeting the nation's demand in line with the socio-economic development strategy of the country and the detailed plan drafted by the Government for each specific period.

In terms of organisation, the Viet Nam Electricity Corporation is composed of: a 5-member Board of Management, a 5-member Board of Directors including 1 General Director and 4 Deputy General Directors responsible for Development, Investment, Construction and Erection, Operation Management and Financial-Marketing.

EVN presently manages 34 member units, comprising of 12 power plants (with output capacity ranging from 33 to 1920 MW), 4 Power Transmission companies, 5 power distribution companies, 2 Power Investigation and Design companies, 1 Power Equipment Manufacturing company, 1 Power Telecommunication company, Financial Company, National Operation Centre, Energy Institute, Power Information Centre and Computer, Environment Technology and Scientific Centre. EVN has started its full operations since April 1995 and at present all operations have been going on smoothly as planed.

* Prepared by Prof. Dr. Tran Dinh Long, Vice Chairman, EVN's Board of Management. This report is reproduced in the form in which it was received.